Dad's Guide to Baby's First Year

for dummies®

A Wiley Brand

Dad's Guide to Baby's First Year

for dummies®
A Wiley Brand

by Sharon Perkins, RN,
Stefan Korn,
Scott Lancaster, and
Eric Mooij

for dummies®
A Wiley Brand

Dad's Guide to Baby's First Year **For Dummies®**

Published by: **John Wiley & Sons, Inc.**, 111 River Street, Hoboken, NJ 07030-5774, www.wiley.com

Copyright © 2016 by John Wiley & Sons, Inc., Hoboken, New Jersey

Published simultaneously in Canada

For general information on our other products and services, please contact our Customer Care Department within the U.S. at 877-762-2974, outside the U.S. at 317-572-3993, or fax 317-572-4002. For technical support, please visit https://hub.wiley.com/community/support/dummies.

Wiley publishes in a variety of print and electronic formats and by print-on-demand. Some material included with standard print versions of this book may not be included in e-books or in print-on-demand. If this book refers to media such as a CD or DVD that is not included in the version you purchased, you may download this material at http://booksupport.wiley.com. For more information about Wiley products, visit www.wiley.com.

Library of Congress Control Number: 2016944020

ISBN 978-1-119-27579-4 (pbk); ISBN 978-1-119-27581-7 (ebk); ISBN 978-1-119-27580-0 (ebk)

Manufactured in the United States of America

10 9 8 7 6 5 4 3 2 1

Contents at a Glance

Table of Contents

Introduction

Welcome to the wonderful, wacky, and yes, sometimes scary, world of dadhood! Being a dad starts before you ever see your baby's face and doesn't end until . . . well, it never actually ends.

This book starts at the very beginning and assumes you want to know what's going to happen for the next few years, at least. After all, once you've been a dad for a few years, what more is there to learn? Plenty, of course, but we don't want to overwhelm you, so we concentrate on the first 7 or 8 years.

We wrote this book because we either love being a dad (three of us) or we love the dads in our own lives (the other one of us). We want to see dads succeed, because a good dad can have a huge impact on a little one's life. We also want you to have fun being a dad, because there's more to being a dad than worrying about potty training, good schools, and whether or not your kiddo is good at sports.

Being a dad is an adventure, and we're happy to accompany you through the first few years.

About This Book

One of the best things about a *For Dummies* book is that we assume you're interested in knowing what you really need to know, without a lot of extra stuff thrown in. But because some guys really do want more detail, we include some extra info in the sidebars, which are shaded boxes. Feel free to read these if you want to dig a little deeper or to skip them if you want just the facts for now.

Keep in mind that this book is a reference book, so you don't have to read this book in order (unless you want to!); just use the table of contents and the index to help you find what you're looking for. You can dip into and out of chapters as you like.

Within this book, you may note that some web addresses break across two lines of text. If you're reading this book in print and want to visit one of these web pages, simply key in the web address exactly as it's noted in the text, pretending as though the line break doesn't exist. If you're reading this as an e-book, you've got it easy — just click the web address to be taken directly to the web page.

Foolish Assumptions

If you're reading this book, we assume you're either a dad, going to be a dad, or want to be a dad in the future. That doesn't mean that moms can't read this book — you can, because there's lots of information here that applies to both parents. If you're a grand-parent, this book may help you keep up with what's new in the world of parenting (stop rolling your eyes, we can see you!). If you want more detail about the pregnancy months, pick up a copy of *Dad's Guide to Pregnancy For Dummies,* by Matthew M.F. Miller and Sharon Perkins, RN (Wiley).

Icons Used in This Book

Icons point you to certain types of information. In this book, we use the following icons:

Tips include information that may help you be a better dad or partner.

TIP

This icon points out information we consider absolutely necessary for good dads to know.

REMEMBER

This icon gives you information that can keep you from making a really big mistake in the dad game.

WARNING

Beyond the Book

No book can cover everything there is to know on a topic. For that reason — and because you may not want to carry this book with you everywhere — we've created an online source you can turn to for some quick bites of essential information. To get this Cheat Sheet, simply go to www.dummies.com and search for "Dad's Guide to Baby's First Year For Dummies Cheat Sheet" in the Search box.

The Cheat Sheet for this book includes such valuable information as a step-by-step guide to changing a diaper — dads aren't born knowing this stuff, after all — some suggestions on soothing a crying baby, and best of all, ideas on how to have fun with your baby and toddler.

Where to Go from Here

While being a dad starts at the beginning and moves forward year by year, you don't have to approach this book that way. You might be in the throes of choosing a school right now and have very little interest in reading about potty training. That's fine — start with whichever chapter interests you at the moment. If you're a straight-through type of guy, feel free to start with page 1 and keep going. But for everyone else, skipping ahead to the sections that address your immediate concerns is just fine.

1

From Here to Paternity: Conception to Birth

IN THIS PART . . .

Discover how to adjust to the news — you're going to be a dad!

Get tips on living with your pregnant partner.

Find out all about your unborn baby.

Figure out what you need to buy for your newborn.

Get through the birth day without breaking too much of a sweat.

Chapter 1

Fatherhood

R ight now, somewhere across the globe, someone is becoming a father. He may be suited up in scrubs as his child is delivered by cesarean in a high-tech delivery suite, or holding his partner's hand as she gives birth in a pool at home. He may be pacing at the neighbors' hut in a village somewhere in the third world as his wife gives birth surrounded only by women, or heading through rush-hour traffic to get to the hospital on time. Wherever these dads-to-be are, they all have one thing in common. When they lay eyes on their new little baby, they know life will never be the same.

There's something about becoming a father that's universal. For ages, you've been just yourself: Building a career, buying a house, perhaps traveling and seeing the world. You've concentrated on becoming a person in your own right — an individual. You've had wild days and adventures; you've been places. Those are all great things to do with your life. But when you have a child, you begin a whole new adventure — one that doesn't end when your visa runs out or the bar closes. Your new adventure is lifelong. Being a father makes you think of your own father and all the fathers who came before him, and you realize you're something bigger than just a stamped passport and some good stories around the campfire — you're a bona fide member of the human race, a piece in a puzzle that has been put together over many generations. And there's a part of you that will go on into the next generation, and then hopefully the next and the next.

In this chapter, we explore what it means to be a father and talk about the reality of being a dad. The role of fathers has changed a lot in just the generation between our fathers and us. Dads are more involved, but they also have a lot more stress — work commitments, financial pressure, separation from partners, and information overload. But fear not — in this chapter and in the rest of this book, we keep fatherhood real with practical information, useful explanations, and a bit of humor. After all, children are lots and lots of fun, so why make the journey to fatherhood more serious than it needs to be?

Dispelling Common Myths about Fatherhood

Toward the end of the 20th century, we experienced a revival of fatherhood and the dawn of a new generation of dads — a generation of dads who are no longer content playing a supporting role in the upbringing of their children. Dads want to experience parenting fully, warts and all. Some brave dads are even taking over and sending mom back to the workforce. The number of stay-at-home dads is increasing year by year in most Western societies, a clear sign that something fundamental is changing about how we bring up our children and organize our lives. (If you're thinking about becoming a stay-at-home dad, we have lots of advice and practical tips for taking on your new role in Chapter 16.)

However, despite the generation of new dads, many dads are still faced with a few persistent stereotypes:

>> **Fathers are completely useless when it comes to looking after babies and children.** That's nonsense. Yes, dads parent differently from moms, but male ways of doing things are just

as valid and important. Research shows that fathers are just as good as mothers at caring for babies, responding to their needs and temperaments, and learning how to read babies' cues. Research also shows that children with involved dads do better in school and are more confident and independent later in life. Unfortunately, fathers have effectively been cut off from getting involved through preconceived ideas about parenting, peer pressure, or the demands of the modern workplace. The good news is most dads in the 21st century now have the option to do it differently and show the world that dads make fantastic caregivers.

>> **Fathers don't have to do any of the day-to-day care that babies and children require.** This may be true if you want to remain in the dark ages of fatherhood. Twenty-first century dads do caregiving because there's an important reason for it: The best way to bond with your newborn child is by taking part in all that day-to-day stuff. Changing a diaper, trimming his nails, and tucking him into bed each night aren't just jobs that need to be done; they're a way for your baby and children to spend a bit of time with you and get to know you. Your child will learn that when he needs something, you're there to take care of him, make him feel better, and comfort him when he's ill or teething, or just because he needs a hug. He'll learn words from you as you chat to him while he's in the bath, learn how to put clothes on from the way you dress him each morning, and learn all sorts of other good qualities simply from the way you are. You also brighten up his world no end with all the silly things you do.

>> **Moms laugh at dads when they're out with babies by themselves.** Maybe — but mostly because they probably find you really cute with your little one strapped to your chest! In most cases, women will flock from all corners of the room when you walk into that playgroup with baby on your shoulder. If you get the occasional overly "helpful" mom in the supermarket who doesn't think you quite know how to handle a crying baby, be confident that you can demonstrate who's daddy by settling your little one in one minute flat.

>> **Fathers don't have a social life.** Wrong — fathers (and all parents) have a different social life. You may have to invest a bit of time and thought into how you'll manage going out or

taking part in sports. But these things can all be organized. After all, dads are fantastic at organizing. It takes a while getting used to having an extra person in your life, but that doesn't mean you'll never be able to go out again. Chapter 8 provides hints and tips for getting out and about, with and without your little one.

>> **As a dad you don't have a sex life anymore.** Actually that one is kind of true, but only temporarily. The birthing experience, sheer exhaustion, and practicalities of looking after a newborn can make it somewhat tricky to get back to your pre-baby sex life with your partner. The word here is patience. Your sex life will return (check out Chapters 6 and 8 for more on this subject). But you may just have to be a bit more creative now that your little one is in the house.

The pros and cons of fatherhood

As with every life decision or change, there are good things and challenges. If you want to take a rational approach to fatherhood, consider the following.

On the plus side:

>> Fathers report their lives are more meaningful than before they had a child.

>> Fatherhood can make you a more compassionate, mature, and confident person.

>> You get to be a child all over again (yes, you get to play with cool toys and teach your child lots of silly tricks).

>> Being a father is a chance for you to hand down skills and values from your family. This will feel very good when you're nearing your final days.

>> You'll probably for the first time in your life truly understand your own father.

>> You get a real kick out of raising a child well and seeing her achieve lots of things.

The challenges:

>> Until around three months of age, newborn babies are a real handful. They cry, sometimes for no apparent reason at all, and you feel like the sound is piercing your brain. There's a reason recordings of crying babies are used as torture. Chapter 6 provides helpful hints about settling a newborn and coping with crying.

>> Sleep deprivation is also a well-known torture technique. Fathers of babies under a year old typically get 42 minutes less sleep a night than other men. Doesn't sound like much, but it adds up. For ways to deal with sleep deprivation, see Chapter 8.

>> You'll have less time for yourself and making plans really does mean making plans — spontaneity goes out the window a bit at the beginning. Check out Chapter 8 for ways to get out and about.

We think the upsides of fatherhood far outweigh the downsides, especially because most of the really annoying aspects (like sleep deprivation) get much easier the older your children get.

WARNING

A sad reality for a small percentage of fathers in the United States is that they may not get the chance to experience all the joys that fatherhood has to offer. Though we don't often talk about it in our society, miscarriage, stillbirth, premature birth, and death in infancy are terrible losses for some fathers to bear. Others have to deal with the fact that their child, so full of promise and hope, has a serious illness or disability that forces them to shift expectations of what being a father is all about. We talk more about these issues in Chapters 17 and 18 with lots of information and support for parents.

Knowing what to expect

Asking someone to tell you what being a father is like is a bit like asking how long a piece of string is. Answering that question is impossible. Like the uniqueness of your child's DNA, every father's experience is different. A good way to get an idea of what fatherhood is like is to spend some time with friends who have recently had a baby. Talk to your own parents too.

Here are some common factors that most fathers face:

» Sharing your partner's body with your child before and after birth can feel a bit weird. Sex during pregnancy can be brilliant or a bit challenging, depending on your partner's experience. (See Chapter 3 for more about sex during pregnancy.) In addition, after giving birth some women aren't into sharing their boobs with you and baby too.

» Sleep becomes a big issue. Babies don't understand that day is for being awake and night is for being asleep. Over time, your baby will adjust and eventually sleep through the night — the holy grail for most parents. But a baby who does this before six months of age is rare. Babies also need nutrition every few hours to grow, so if your baby is waking up in the night for feedings, consider it a good thing that he's thriving and growing. Chapters 6, 7, and 8 discuss feeding your baby and getting him to sleep.

» Expect to feel frightened, scared, overwhelmed, and sometimes lost as you navigate fatherhood. Just changing a diaper for the first time or getting clothes on a newborn feels awkward and wrong when you're new at it. So what — moms and all other dads who get involved have the same experience.

» You'll do things that you never thought you'd do, you'll laugh at things that seem completely ridiculous to you right now, and you may cry at times that you least expect. You'll also learn lots about yourself and experience things that you cannot experience any other way. Fatherhood is truly an adventure.

REMEMBER

Being a father is a lot about acceptance and going with the flow. A useful mantra to remember is "this too will pass," as every illness, teething episode, period of sleep deprivation, or colic *will* pass. Looking after a baby teaches you a lot about life, and you may find that you're more relaxed, confident, and happy as a result of having a child.

Parenting, for both fathers and mothers, requires a certain amount of letting go. When a baby is born, we want things for our child: The best of everything, and every opportunity and good thing in life that may come her way. You naturally want her to avoid the mistakes you made in your own life. But it doesn't work that way.

Your child is not an extension of you; your baby is her own person. She'll grow up to have her own ideas, her own interests, and her own strengths, and they may be vastly different from yours. You may want her to be a lawyer so she has money to pay for things you could only dream of, but what really makes her happy is working with animals or in a charity. Sometimes you just have to admit that father *doesn't* know best. You may be disappointed, but it's her life, and only she can live it. Support her — that's what great dads are for.

Trading in your lifestyle (but not the sports car)

Well, actually, we hate to say it, but you *may have to* trade in the sports car too. Becoming a father is about changing your state of mind and changing the idea of what's important to you. As a dad, the car's less about the ultimate drive and more about keeping your child safe and fitting the stroller in the back. Chapter 4 helps you negotiate safe transport for your baby, as well as what sort of stroller to get.

If you want a baby but don't want to change the way you live your life, you're probably better off waiting for a while to have children. Some things will inevitably change:

>> **Your work:** If you want to spend time with your family, you may consider working fewer hours or changing to a flexible working arrangement that you can negotiate with your employer. See Chapter 6 for more about finding a work–life balance.

You may even decide to give up work and be the primary caregiver to your child, making you a stay-at-home dad (SAHD). If this sounds like you, see Chapter 16 for more information. This book is written with the philosophy that dads, just as much as moms, take part in the day-to-day care of a child, so we've left out nothing about how to look after your little one.

>> **Your freedom:** Doing things when and where you want doesn't work when you've got a baby. If the swell is perfect and you just feel like going out for a surf, you may have to wait until baby is asleep or take him and mom along with you. It's the same with spending time out and about with your partner. Going out to dinner and a movie is no longer a spontaneous activity; it requires planning. Finding time for yourself alongside work and family commitments is one of the biggest challenges fathers face. Chapter 8 gives you ideas for getting out and about after your baby arrives.

>> **Your finances:** If you both had an income before your child came along, you'll be down to one income for a while. If you lived in a one-bedroom apartment, it's time to find somewhere bigger and a way to pay for it. We offer some tips on how to reduce the cost of caring for your child in Chapter 12.

>> **Your friends and family:** Your relationship with friends and family will change. If you live away from your parents, you'll probably find yourself having to spend a lot more time traveling to visit them more often. Some of your childless friends will really embrace you having a child and will become the fun aunt or uncle your child gets excited about seeing. Others will not be so keen on kids — even yours! — and you'll see them less as a result.

>> **Your vacations:** Going on vacation takes on a whole new meaning. You'll definitely have to postpone that backpacking trip around South America for a few years, at least until your kids are big enough to trudge alongside you. Family vacations are different — great fun, but unlike any vacation you've had since you were a child. Chapter 9 gives you some great ideas for how to manage a trip with baby in tow.

>> **Your lifestyle:** Risky lifestyle or sport activities like base jumping and free climbing are no longer just about risking your own life. You now have to consider the future of your child and family.

>> **Your health and behavior:** A child is one of the ultimate reasons to change some unhealthy habits like smoking, heavy drinking, eating junk food, and being a slob. Children need a smoke-free environment to breathe in, good healthy food, clean clothes and diapers, and good hygiene to prevent

illness. And who needs to grow up hearing language that might make a sailor blush? If you're a little lost when it comes to health and nutrition, we give you the goods in Chapter 14, where you'll find out about everything from what your child should be eating to exercising together.

Only Fools Rush In

Sometimes you can plan when you have a child; sometimes nature has her own ideas. Either way, fatherhood is a big deal — fatherhood's not like buying a new pair of shoes or getting a plant. Your child, if you decide to have one, has only one shot at life, and he deserves the best start you can give him. A committed, involved, and reliable father is a big part of that. If you're being pushed into having a child by your partner, talk it through with her; don't just go along with it because you're afraid of the discussion. Becoming a dad is an important step in life, so take some time to figure out how you feel about it and share your thoughts with your partner.

Hey, I'm not ready for this

How often in your life can you say you're really ready for something? Not often. Fatherhood, of all things, is probably the most difficult to feel truly ready for. Even if you've been planning to have a child, spent months going through IVF (see Chapter 2 for more about this), and been dreaming of the day you hold your child in your arms, the sledgehammer of reality will probably whack you over the head the day you find out you're really going to be a dad.

If your partner is already pregnant but you don't feel ready for fatherhood, you've got time on your side. In the coming months, as your baby grows and gets ready for birth, spend some time with other people's children, talk to other fathers, and let yourself ease into the idea of fatherhood. Think about the kind of father your dad is and what you've learned from him. Think of all the things you would do differently.

If you're really, truly not ready for fatherhood as the birth approaches, it may help if you talk to someone about your fears. Your healthcare provider can put you in touch with a counselor.

TIP

You can find a counselor yourself by looking on the Internet, but asking other people for recommendations, if you're comfortable doing it, is a better way to find someone who is on your same wavelength. A pastor or other spiritual advisor, if you have one, can also help you find the right person — or, in some cases, could actually be the right person to talk to.

REMEMBER

Don't forget to talk to your partner about what you're feeling. After all, you are in this together, so it helps to share your feelings and thoughts with her.

WARNING

Although having children can be the most amazing and joyous adventure, the strains of work, family, and other commitments can put a lot of pressure on a relationship. Unfortunately, many relationships don't survive this extra pressure. In Chapter 19, we talk about how fathers can cope with divorce and separation and still continue to be great dads.

My partner wants a baby

You're faced with a sticky situation — your partner is ready to have a baby, her biological clock is ticking, all her friends have babies, and she's eager to join the club. But you're not.

Here's our advice: Rather than fight the idea of becoming a parent — moan, whine, or try to ignore it until it goes away — give the idea of fatherhood some serious thought. Talk about it together with your partner, explain why you're not ready, but equally, listen to her point of view. Imagine yourself as a dad — how does that feel?

Mull it over. Where do you want to be in ten years? Dad to a child (or four) with the rewards that brings? Or still living a childless life with the freedom that brings? When you look back on your life in your old age, do you want children and family to be part of it?

You may feel like there's never a good time to have children or you just don't feel ready. Perhaps you're quite clear that you definitely don't want children. Cool, but then you also owe it to your partner to let her know.

Timing isn't always everything

Sometimes, despite thinking that you'll wait to have a family until after a big project is completed, or you've found a bigger house, or until you've been on that trekking trip to Nepal, nature jumps the gun. Your partner sits you down and says she's pregnant. Wow — you're going to be a dad. The key is to not panic. Freak out maybe, but don't panic (mostly because it takes a while for the baby to arrive). Okay, so you haven't painted the roof or skydived yet. Well, you never wanted to be one of those "boring older people" anyway, so there are still plenty of opportunities to do whatever you want to do, perhaps even with your children. Fatherhood doesn't mean you suddenly have to stay home every night whittling on the front porch; it just means the pace of life you live ticks along to a different clock.

Introducing the New-Generation Dad

Fathers today are a quantum leap from the previous generation of fathers. Twenty-first-century dads push strollers, get up for night feedings, change diapers, and have tried and tested burping techniques. We do it all — except for being pregnant, giving birth, and breastfeeding. As for the rest of it, there's nothing we can't tackle. If we dare say so, we can even do some things better than moms.

Dadhood: A good time to man up

All your life you've had just one person to take care of — yourself. You've made choices, taken risks, and shouldered the consequences. But becoming a father is "the big stuff." You have a vulnerable, dependent, helpless child on your hands who needs you for the most basic aspects of her survival, such as food, warmth, and love.

Becoming a dad can add a profound sense of meaning to your life. Your views on life, priorities in the world, and aspirations for your own future are forever altered. This is a good thing. By becoming a dad you become part of the circle of life that has been going for eons. You're passing on the baton to your child, packed with all your wisdom and skills, to send him off on his own journey. You've got so much you can share with your offspring.

Children need dads. A Canadian study showed that having a father in a child's life helps her develop empathy. Another long-term study showed that a father's involvement with his child from birth to adolescence helps build emotional stability, curiosity, and self-esteem.

REMEMBER

If you're going to have a child, be involved, committed, and passionate about your new role. Your child deserves nothing less.

Joining the movement

By becoming a father, you join the ranks of men for thousands of generations before you. You've come from a long line of fathers! So you're in good company. In the United States, the average age of first-time dads is 32.

So as a soon-to-be-dad, we'd like to encourage and inspire you to join the movement of involved and active fathers. Our children need involved fathers in their lives, and you also owe it to yourself. If you're going to be a dad, be a 100 percent dad and experience it all. You wouldn't do other things in your life halfheartedly, so get with it and give it your best shot. Make an effort, learn what you need to know, and spend as much time as possible with your child.

Exploring care routine strategies

The question of how best to raise a baby is one of the most hotly contested subjects today. The rows of parenting psychology books on bookstore shelves attest to that. We've become disengaged over the last few centuries from listening to our instincts. We've let medical science overrule our hearts and minds, and slavishly followed rigid routines and overbearing doctor's orders that have demanded that mother's convenience come first and baby's needs come second. We've joined the rat race and let work dictate our daily and weekly schedules.

Families are also smaller than they used to be, so children can grow up never having to help mom wash the diapers or settle a baby like they did back in our grandparents' day, when there were as many children in a family as you could find names for.

In recent years, there's been a swing back to letting the child's needs lead the way as well as research that backs up this method of parenting. Parents caught in the middle of grandparents' ways, their own instincts, and the swing back to gentler parenting methods can find deciding on a parenting method confusing. Media reports shower us with research that says everything under the sun is bad for our kids, and we're stuck between experts who promote their particular technique and the latest trend from celebrity parents. Chapter 10 has lots of great tips for raising your child in a warm, loving relationship, as well as making discipline work.

REMEMBER

Keep in mind that the way you want to run things in your family is up to you. Whether you adhere to a strict routine or are a bit more laid back about it, your little one will be okay as long as he is clean, fed, and thriving; is happy and cheerful; gets enough sleep; and is shown love and affection. Don't get caught in a trap of constantly comparing your baby to other babies; it generally leads nowhere and just adds to your frustration. Have confidence in the way you bring up your children and trust in your child developing in his own unique way.

These are some of the care routine strategies you may have heard of as you contemplate fatherhood and how you'll cope with a newborn:

>> **Strict routine:** In our moms' day, a strict routine with feedings and sleeping by the clock was promoted as being the best way to bring up a baby. Today, advocates of this method claim that having a strict routine or schedule establishes good habits early so you can detour sleepless nights and excessive crying. For some parents, this routine works just fine, and their baby easily slips into line. For others, their baby resists and parents end up even more stressed out that their little one won't play by the book.

>> **A routine, but not by the clock:** Babies need to feed and sleep at regular intervals, but rather than let the clock determine when that might be, reading your child's cues is the key to making the routine work. There's a pattern or routine of waking for a feeding, having a diaper change, spending some play or awake time, and then going back down for a sleep that continues throughout the day, but at night there's no play or awake time. Chapter 6 has more about establishing a routine.

>> **Attachment parenting:** This form of parenting mimics parenting styles found in developing countries, where cribs, bassinets, and strollers are rare. Your child is in contact with you at all times of the day, is carried around in a sling or baby carrier, and sleeps with you at night, so that she builds a strong bond and attachment with you.

REMEMBER

Many other strategies for raising a newborn exist. Do you leave him to cry when you put him down in order to teach him to fall asleep on his own, or rock him to sleep in your arms for every nap? Do you have the baby sleep in your bed, or put him in a bassinet in his own room? These are questions that you and your partner have to ponder and come up with your own answers to. You have to live with whichever strategy you come up with, so the strategy has to work for *you*. Chapter 6 gives you lots of ideas for raising a newborn.

REMEMBER

Another minefield you're going to have to get your head around is your child's education. Private, public, parochial, Montessori — these are all terms you're going to hear bandied about as your child gets older. Luckily for you, we've done some of the legwork in Chapter 15 so you can figure out the educational maze for yourself.

TIP

As your baby turns into a toddler, you'll have to start thinking about discipline. People often think of discipline as the way you punish your child for being naughty. But in our books, that's not what discipline is about. Discipline is about creating an environment where your child can learn to adjust her behavior and understand what's okay and what's not. Discipline is about clear boundaries, consistency, and consequences. We talk about discipline in more depth in Part 3.

The Seven Habits of Highly Successful Dads

Here's a collection of seven habits we observe in amazing dads — a collection of traits that each and every guy can develop on his journey to becoming a father:

>> **Confidence:** It takes time to feel truly confident about handling a newborn, but you gain confidence by doing things and getting your hands dirty (literally in some cases), even if at first things don't go right. Looking after a newborn, baby, or toddler can seem daunting at times but isn't actually that hard. It just comes down to being attentive to the needs of your little one, making an effort, and learning a few tricks.

No matter how hard things get — you're stressed out at work and the baby's waking up every three hours at night, your partner's sick, and you're doing all the housework — you'll get through it and you'll be a more confident dad (and person) as a result. So don't be afraid to wade in because it will give you a great sense of achievement, lift your spirits, and build your self-esteem when you don't have to rely on mom for anything to do with the baby (other than breastfeeding).

>> **Creativity:** Sometimes you truly have to think outside the box when you're looking after babies or spending time with children. Children have no trouble with pretend play and let their fantasies run wild, so just go with it. Sometimes you'll also have to find creative solutions to some basic problems, such as when you've run out of diapers. An old dish towel may have to do while you take baby to the store to get disposables.

>> **Endurance:** Sometimes the only way to cope with a situation is to endure it. When your baby is colicky and wakes every few hours at night, or is teething and cries constantly, you may be at the end of your rope trying to work out how to put a stop to that noise. Often there's no solution; there's nothing you can fix or do to make a difference. It's just the way it is, and you're going to have to suck it up. But understanding that everything in parenting comes and goes — that one day,

your little one will sleep through the night, one day, your child will have all his teeth, and one day, he will grow out of colic — will help you endure the bad times while they last.

Like patience, endurance can be hard to muster when you're tired, you've had little sleep, and you see no end in sight. The early weeks of a baby's life are a little like an endurance sport — just surviving the sleep deprivation, the crying that grips your brain and shakes it about, and the never-ending rounds of feeding, burping, changing, and settling can seem impossible. But even marathons end sooner or later, so take every day as it comes and before you know it you'll be celebrating your little one's first birthday.

REMEMBER

If you're having a hard time coping with a crying child and feel like lashing out — stop right now. Put your baby in a safe place, such as her crib, and take a breather. Count to ten. Even better, go outside for a minute or two, take some deep breaths, and calm down. When you go back, comfort your baby and call your healthcare provider or someone who can come and take over for a while, while you take a break.

>> **Optimism:** Your life as a dad will be much easier if you try to see the funny side of things and take the "glass is half full" position. At times you may be overwhelmed, stressed, or totally exhausted, and then it's easy to slip into thinking nature's way of organizing procreation totally sucks. When you get annoyed and you're feeling negative, your child is likely to pick up on it, and he might actively participate in making the situation even more difficult to handle. So shake yourself up and snap out of negativity. Try a different approach or do something to get in a better frame of mind. Chances are you'll get a more positive response from your child if you're more positive.

>> **Passion:** Immerse yourself in all the tasks that need doing around your baby, toddler, or child. By doing that, you'll develop a passion for being a dad, and you'll love being a dad with all your heart. Your child picks up on your passion and will be inspired to learn, develop, and grow with you at an amazing pace. In Chapter 7 you find more information about your baby's amazing brain, how babies develop, and how you can help their development as a dad.

>> **Patience:** Patience is a virtue — especially for dads! Patience is your friend and makes things a lot easier when you've got kids around. Without patience, you would just pop with anger and there'd be tears all around, even for you. Most of the learning in the early years (and perhaps even throughout life) is achieved through constant and frequent repetition. As a father, you're in the business of facilitating that learning, which means repeating yourself a lot, such as reading *Where the Wild Things Are* for the 53rd time, or telling your toddler not to pour his milk in the fish tank for the 17th time. As adults we're often not great at dealing with constant repetition because it's deemed boring or frustrating. By fostering your own patience, you'll be able to elegantly deal with constant repetition and keep your calm. As a result your child will get the support and encouragement he needs to learn. By being patient you avoid putting unnecessary pressure on your child to achieve something, which helps reduce frustration or feelings of inadequacy on his part.

>> **Presence:** Taking time to be with your child and partner in a family is important. How you spend that time with your family is also important. Children have a finely tuned awareness of your attention. They can tell right away whether you're actually engaging with them or merely present physically, with your mind miles away. Being present means you devote 100 percent of your attention to your child and you focus on what he's doing. You don't watch TV, read the newspaper, or get a bit of work done at the same time as playing with your child. If you're hanging out with your child, be fully present and in the moment. For those dads who don't live with their children anymore, hanging out with your kids isn't as easy as it used to be, so we've included some info in Chapter 19 about spending as much time with your kids as possible. Also check out Chapter 9 for ideas on playing with your child.

Help, I'm a Dad!

We wrote this book because we were once new dads like you, starting out with mysterious new babies, wondering which way the diaper went on. Being a dad is a scary, wonderful, adrenalin ride of a trip and one many of you will judge your lives on. But at first it's hard to know where to turn and who to ask along the way.

Asking for directions

Okay, we know, men don't like asking for directions. That said, it helps to have a map or some cool navigation gadget. In some cases you may need specialist information, which is impossible to cover in a general book or website, so we've compiled a list of resources (see Appendix A) and general tips for finding information.

Finding trusted organizations and sources of information

The people who know your baby best are you and your partner. You know what he likes and dislikes, what his little quirks are, and when something doesn't seem right with him.

It can be tempting to want to "fix" a particular problem a child has. Perhaps your baby is a bad sleeper during the day, or is colicky, or just won't take a bottle no matter how much you try. As adults we're used to having quick fixes and instant solutions for many problems in our day-to-day lives. For better or worse, with babies and children it's different. Many aspects of babyhood and childhood can't just be fixed. Things take time, perseverance, and a laid-back attitude. To overcome a particular issue, you may have to try lots of different approaches until you find one that fits.

So where do you find these different approaches? Your first stop should be your healthcare provider. She has experience with all kinds of children and can spend some time with your little one getting to know him and finding out what's going on. Another good place for information is the booklet that you may have been given by the hospital or your baby's pediatrician when your baby was born. These booklets often have good strategies for things like starting to feed your baby solid food, coping with crying, and dealing with diaper rash, along with local services you can call in times of need. This book too has invaluable information on these topics.

See Appendix A for more organizations you can get in touch with should the need arise.

Internet research

The Internet's a pretty handy thing. With just a few keystrokes, you can search for anything your heart desires. But beware — anyone can build a web page, run a blog, or comment in a forum, but that person may not have the expertise you're looking for. Gauge the quality of the information provided on websites by checking the organization or individual who's responsible for it, their credentials, their affiliation with recognized authorities, and any ulterior motives they may have, such as financial, political, or religious reasons.

On the other hand, checking out forums where other dads are sharing their problems and offering solutions can be handy. Just don't take as gospel that everything they say is authoritative. Remember that what works for one baby may not work for yours and vice versa.

As a starting point you can always check the site of the American Academy of Pediatrics (www.aap.org) for useful and trustworthy information. This national organization of pediatricians has articles and information on every aspect of parenting.

If your baby or child is sick, avoid diagnosing her by searching the Internet. A real healthcare provider is your first port of call should you be concerned about your baby's health. For more about common health problems, check out Chapter 14.

Turning to friends, colleagues, and family

When you're a new father, everyone in the world is excited for you and gets a bit nostalgic for when their own children were little. They'll want to share with you their hard-won pieces of advice and have an opinion on just about every aspect of looking after junior. Some of it will make sense to you; other gems will seem bizarre. Just add each pearl of wisdom to your pile of approaches to try should you need to. Ultimately you'll find out yourself whether or not something makes sense for your situation.

Turning to people who are close to you is an invaluable way to stay sane. If you're struggling, go hang out with a dad who's been through the wars himself. Looking at dads who've been through the crazy first weeks and months and then come out on the other side and want to have more kids is a great way to get inspired and motivated for your own journey. You may at first think they've lost their minds, but really, these dads are no different from you. They've survived, and as many dads say, "Every day just gets better." And no, they haven't joined some terrible cult and become brainwashed — they've just had children, and one way or another, that tends to have a big impact on everyone.

Not long from now it will be you sitting down with a new dad, hearing tips and advice flow forth from your own mouth!

Starting your own group

We all know a new dad or someone who's about to enter into the realm of fatherhood. Lots of dads meet at prenatal classes and keep in touch after that. Getting together to talk and share your experiences doesn't need to be a formal affair, with chairs in a circle and "feelings." It can be a beer while baby snoozes in his stroller or a coffee at a cafe with the little ones clamoring over each other on the floor. Getting together can be just a gathering at the park or watching a football game. Finding new dads to join you should be easy, but if you're feeling a bit isolated, peruse local bulletin boards or the Internet for local dad groups. See Chapter 16 for great networking ideas.

Another easy way to get together with other dads is to use the mom networks. Ask your partner about speaking to other moms about a dad get-together. Before you know it, a barbecue, picnic, or stroller walk will have been magically arranged, and you can take it from there.

Chapter 2

Getting Pregnant

D eciding to start a family with your partner is one of the biggest decisions you'll make in your life (yes, even bigger than buying a house or determining which football team deserves your undying support). Of course, getting pregnant isn't always a conscious decision — sometimes it just happens. Other times, just getting to the starting line of fatherhood is a journey through the not-so-magical world of fertility treatments and embarrassing conversations about sperm counts.

No matter how you get to the pregnancy starting line, there are still nine months to get through before you earn your dad wings. How you get there isn't as important as making a decision to approach the journey to parenthood together. Starting a family goes beyond just getting pregnant.

In this chapter you find out all about the adventurous and treacherous journey your sperm has to make before reaching his lady-in-waiting, the egg, and the equally risky mission the fertilized egg undergoes to get into its safe haven, the uterus. You find out tips and tricks to getting pregnant, and what options are out there if things just aren't coming together. And finally, once things are underway, we guide you through the process of getting ready for the coming months.

Here Comes the Fun Part

You've probably worked out where babies come from by now. Making babies is fun — we admit it — and so it should be! There aren't many projects in life that start with a little time in the sack with your best girl. The rest of the journey may be exhausting, challenging, or even frustrating at times, but at least this one first step can be all about a good time.

So go on, have sex, and lots of it. There aren't many manuals that tell you to do that, are there?

Conceiving naturally

Of course, in an ideal world, just making the decision to "start trying" would result in an instant pregnancy. But nature didn't make it that easy. No sirree. There are lots of barriers between your sperm and her egg; in fact, it's a miracle any of us were born at all.

Of the millions of sperm a man ejaculates during sex, only about 100,000 make it past his partner's cervix at the entrance to the uterus, having run the gauntlet of acidic vaginal secretions (Figure 2-1 shows the female reproductive system). Of the 100,000 sperm that get past the cervix, only a measly 200 make it into one of the two *fallopian tubes* where a ready-to-be fertilized egg is waiting for a date — *if* your timing is right and your partner is *ovulating* (producing an egg). Luckily, there are many sperm to start with because such a small percentage of them survive the journey. In the end it's a merciless race to see which one of your sperm emerges as the champion and fertilizes the egg by breaking into it.

Once the egg is fertilized, it moves down the fallopian tube and into the *uterus* or womb. Cell division starts, and before you know it (literally), the tiny cluster of cells begins nestling into the lining of the uterus wall, also known as the *endometrium* (see Figure 2-2). The cluster of cells then starts another long journey transforming into an *embryo,* and after eight weeks *gestation,* into a *fetus.* Bingo — your baby is on his way.

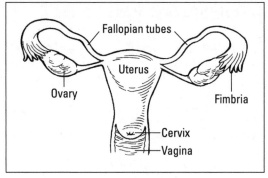

Illustration by Kathryn Born, MA

FIGURE 2-1: The female reproductive system.

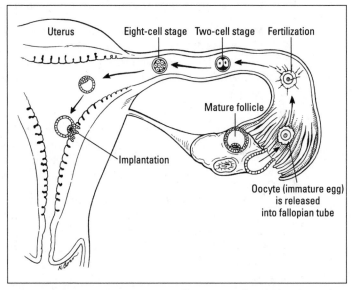

Illustration by Kathryn Born, MA

FIGURE 2-2: The journey of the fertilized egg from the fallopian tubes to implantation in the lining of the uterus wall.

Tipping the odds in your favor

Like a lot of things, getting pregnant is a matter of having quality equipment and good timing. Nail those, and your chances of getting pregnant are pretty good.

But you can help things along by

>> **Being fighting fit:** It goes for prospective fathers as well as mothers that the healthier you are, the better for conception. Now's a good time to stop smoking, lay off the booze and other recreational drugs, get into an exercise routine, and eat well. It can't hurt to do those things anyway.

>> **Letting gravity help:** Try to keep your partner lying down — propping her hips up with a pillow to help gravity even more — rather than getting up and heading for the bathroom right after sex. Help those precious sperm get to their destination by keeping your partner horizontal with her pelvis tilted upward. So cuddle up or do whatever it takes to keep her in the bed! Remember — every little bit helps.

>> **Making a date:** *Ovulation* is when an egg is produced ready for fertilization. It occurs on approximately day 14 of a 28-day menstrual cycle, with day one being the first day of your partner's period. So plan for that time to be your "business time." If your partner's cycle is irregular or you just need more reassurance, try an ovulation test kit to tell you whether the time is right for romance. Ovulation test kits — sold over the counter at pharmacies and large chain stores — are urine tests that detect hormones, like pregnancy test kits. Look for them near the pregnancy test kits in the family planning section.

>> **Making sure your little fellows are in tiptop shape:** Have a health check. Your doctor can check for any signs of sexually transmitted disease, any anatomical problems such as an undescended testicle, and any other issues you may not be aware of.

>> **Checking the safety of any medication you take:** Prescribed medication as well as over-the-counter drugs can have a negative effect on you as well as mom or baby, so check with your doctor before taking anything during the baby-making process — and beyond.

>> **Practicing:** Have sex at least once a day when your partner is ovulating. If you feel a little put off by scheduled sexy time, just have sex at least every other day — even in the off

season. You never know what might happen. Being "in the mood" for sex has also been shown to help conception! Finally, do some research on positions that aid conception and try them out — now that's an assignment you will enjoy!

REMEMBER

Stress can affect your partner's ovulation, so try not to get too worked up about not getting pregnant right away. Good things take time, and worrying about it won't make things happen any faster! Wanting to get pregnant is a great excuse for having lots of sex, so just enjoy it for a while. If your partner is age 35 or younger, the average time until conception after you begin trying is six months. Yes, that seems like an eternity when making a baby is foremost in your minds!

REMEMBER

Your healthcare provider will probably advise your partner to take *folic acid* if you tell him you are trying for a baby. Taking folic acid won't improve your chances of getting pregnant, but it will improve your chances of conceiving a healthy baby. See Chapter 3 for more information about the effects of taking folic acid on your unborn baby.

Conception's not happening

You've been trying for months. And trying. And trying. But conception's just not happening. You're getting sick of sex — as if you ever thought that would be a problem. But yep, you may be feeling exactly like sex is the last thing you'd like to do. As they say, too much of a good thing. . . . So don't beat yourself up over feeling sex-tired. Guess what — your partner may be having the same feelings.

WARNING

Couples under 35 years of age who have been having regular unprotected sex for a year and haven't become pregnant are said to be infertile, and those over 35 years old are deemed infertile after six months. If this is you, it may be time to talk to your doctor about getting some help.

Understanding What Can Go Wrong

Approximately one in six couples has an issue with getting pregnant. There are a lot of factors in both partners that can cause infertility, but let's just look at what factors could be affecting you for the moment. Problems on the male front — yes, it's possible that your boys *can't* swim — can account for 40 percent of "infertile" couples not being able to get pregnant. Low sperm counts, blockages to the sperm being ejaculated, poor sperm motility (which means the direction they move — going around in circles doesn't help make a baby), and sperm with an abnormal shape account for most fertility problems among guys.

Working out why conception hasn't happened

The following factors can contribute to infertility in men:

>> **Anatomical problems** such as erectile dysfunction or blockage caused by a varicose vein, called a *varicocele,* that connects to the testicle

>> **Exposure to harmful substances** and heavy metals

>> **Lifestyle,** such as smoking and drug taking, which can slow sperm

>> **Overheated sperm** caused by taking frequent hot baths or wearing tight-fitting underwear or tight trousers (even jeans have been blamed for this)

>> **Sexually transmitted diseases** like gonorrhea and chlamydia

REMEMBER

In 40 percent of cases of male infertility, the cause may not be known. Either way, going for a checkup is a good thing to do. So be a man and own up to this task — if there's a problem, at least you'll know, and chances are you can do something about it. This reduces stress overall, and your partner will definitely love you even more for having a checkup.

If the issue is not with you, but your partner, try to be aware that this can be a rather rough time for her and she's probably feeling like a bit of a failure. A lot of women believe that being able to carry and nurture a child is an essential part of being a woman, and not being able to do this may leave her feeling inadequate. As her partner you're in the best position to help her feel just as whole a woman no matter what.

Exploring other ways to get pregnant

If your partner is having trouble getting pregnant, the first step is to talk to your doctor. In some cases, lifestyle factors may be holding you back, and if the problem is a blockage, surgery could help. But in other cases, it may be time to consider assisted reproductive technologies and working with a fertility specialist.

These are some of the treatments you may want to talk about with your doctor or specialist:

>> **Intrauterine insemination (IUI):** Semen is collected, given a bit of a cleanup, and then inserted into your partner's vagina, uterus, or fallopian tubes. And yes, there may be a plastic cup and some dirty magazines involved — but hey, it's all for a good cause! For example, this treatment is available for sperm with poor motility, meaning they can't get to the egg on their own and need a little help.

>> **In vitro fertilization (IVF):** Also known as making a "test tube" baby. Your partner is given hormone treatments to kick-start her ovulation. When she is ovulating, your partner goes through a procedure where her eggs are harvested. The collected eggs are then mixed with your sperm and given a chance to be fertilized. The fertilized eggs are then put into your partner's uterus; then you wait to see whether they implant into the uterine wall.

>> **Intracytoplasmic sperm injection (ICSI):** Sounds sexy, doesn't it? Rather than mix sperm and egg and wait to see which eggs are fertilized, sperm is injected straight into the egg. As with IVF, the fertilized eggs are placed into your partner's uterus, where hopefully one implants.

REMEMBER

About two-thirds of couples dealing with infertility do have a baby through medical intervention, so medical intervention is definitely worth finding out about. Ask questions, even if it can feel a bit embarrassing at the start. By the way, this is good training for going through birth — many more embarrassing moments to come!

OMG, You're Going to Be a Dad

Partner's boobs sore? Check. Period missed? Check. Thrown up for no reason? Check. That could mean you're going to be a dad (either that or your partner just had a really stressful week). Either way — don't panic. If your partner is really pregnant, you've got around nine months to sort out your new life. Say goodbye to the way you currently live — farewell to the days of tidy living rooms, sleeping in, and endless hours of self-indulgence — and say hello to fatherhood! So with that in mind, it's really a good thing a baby takes around 40 weeks to grow from a tiny cluster of cells into a living, breathing, crying baby so you can get a few things in order, like confirming the pregnancy and figuring out the next steps.

Getting confirmation

Your partner has no doubt raced off to the nearest pharmacy on the first suspicion of being pregnant. Over-the-counter pregnancy tests can sometimes give inaccurate results, although they're more likely to give a false negative result than a false positive result. Testing the first morning urine can improve accuracy. Even if you have a positive result from a test, the first thing you want to do is make sure the pregnancy thing is actually happening.

Make an appointment with a family doctor or obstetrician, who will test your partner's urine for the hormone human chorionic gonadotropin (HCG) — that's the hormone responsible for the morning sickness and bone-crunching tiredness your other half has to look forward to. If the test shows increased levels of HCG (that is, a positive result), your doctor may perform a gynecological examination on your partner to check the physical signs of pregnancy more closely. In some cases, her doctor may draw a blood sample to determine the exact amount of HCG in the blood.

But even your healthcare provider is only able to provide a definite answer when the pregnancy symptoms are clear, which is around four weeks after fertilization. So it might be a good idea to hold off telling the world — in fact, you may want to wait until the first ultrasound scan anyway. Find out more about ultrasound scans and breaking the news to others in Chapter 3.

REMEMBER

Once you have confirmation of your pregnancy, a quiet (or loud) celebration with your partner is in order. However, it will have to be a celebration unlike most you've had in the past because alcohol, cigarettes, and other drugs are definitely off the menu. But hey — you'll find plenty of other ways to have a good time!

Knowing what to do next

Welcome to the exciting new world of *prenatal*, or pre-birth, care. This was once strictly the domain of the pregnant woman and her doctor (usually male for some reason), but things have changed. For starters you as the dad are going to be much more involved (say yes!). But you also have more choices about who you team up with for the journey to parenthood. Your partner's healthcare provider can refer her to pregnancy healthcare providers in your area.

The role of your healthcare provider of choice is to guide you through the pregnancy, birth, and early weeks of your baby's life. She monitors the baby's growth and well-being, and checks for conditions such as preeclampsia and *gestational diabetes* (see Appendix B for help with terms used in pregnancy). She also works with you to come up with a birth plan, if you want to create one (see Chapter 3 for more details on birth plans), delivers your beautiful new baby, and helps you in the first few days after birth. This may include getting your partner started with breastfeeding or helping with basic baby care tasks such as bathing or changing a diaper. In general, your lead maternity provider is your go-to person if you have any questions regarding health issues, or just need someone to talk to during the pregnancy. So check with her first before contacting other services or professionals.

REMEMBER

Yes, a lot of attention during this time will be on the mom-to-be. But that doesn't mean you can't ask questions and have a say in the kind of care your partner and unborn child receive. You, as dad, have a very important role in the making of your family, so don't feel embarrassed or afraid to ask about anything you're not sure of.

Choosing a healthcare provider

You'll find a maze out there of midwives, birthing centers, obstetricians, and hospitals. Knowing who does what can help you decide where you would like your baby to be born and what kind of care you would like to receive during and immediately after birth.

>> **Family healthcare providers** include medical doctors as well as physician assistants and nurse-practitioners. Medical doctors may specialize in family medicine or general medical care, called *internal medicine*. They aren't specialists in prenatal care or childbirth, but in rural settings, they may provide maternity care. Both nurse-practitioners who specialize in family medicine and physician assistants are often employed by and work with family medical doctors.

>> **Certified nurse-midwives** are trained health professionals who give prenatal care, deliver babies, help establish breastfeeding, and follow up for about four to six weeks after the birth to help when you're unsure about your baby's health and well-being. Lay midwives may have experience

but no formal training in childbirth. Midwives take a holistic approach to pregnancy and birth, and often counsel you as a family, acknowledging not just the physical challenges of becoming new parents, but also your mental and social well-being. They see pregnancy and birth as a natural process, not a medical one.

While they are trained in their field, they are not doctors and do not perform *cesarean sections.* If you choose to go with a midwife and complications arise during the pregnancy or birth, she will most likely arrange for you to see an obstetrician. Certified nurse-midwives generally assist with hospital or birthing center births, while lay midwives or licensed midwives may do home births. Lay midwives are not legally allowed to assist with home birth in many states. In some states, it's illegal to plan a home birth.

>> **Obstetricians** are doctors who specialize in *obstetrics,* or the health of women and babies during pregnancy, birth, and after the birth, called the *postpartum* or *postnatal* period. They generally work in hospitals; few medical doctors in the United States participate in home births.

During the birth, midwives or hospital nurses are on hand throughout labor to monitor your baby's progress. Obstetricians see their patients during labor as often as needed — more if your partner is high risk — and are present throughout the delivery itself. Obstetricians are primarily concerned with the physical health of the baby and mother, and generally don't assist with any nonmedical baby-care issues after birth, such as teaching you how to give your baby a bath. They won't come to your house to show you how to best change your little one's diaper, either. For help with general baby care, friends and family or a good prenatal class can be the biggest help. Lactation consultants offer excellent support for breastfeeding issues. Your doctor can recommend sources in your area.

Talk with whoever you choose as your maternity healthcare provider about the options for where your baby can be born: at home, in a hospital, or in a birthing center. The availability of birthing options depends on where you live and the provider you have.

Take time to find the right maternity healthcare provider for you. Your family doctor may make recommendations; friends and family may have suggestions based on their own experiences as well. Make sure you're really happy with your healthcare provider and that you have "good chemistry." Things can get pretty hectic during pregnancy or birth, so make sure you're in good hands and you're comfortable with your provider's personal and professional style. If you're not happy, consider changing. Both of you should be 100 percent comfortable with your choice of healthcare provider, but in reality, what's most important is that your partner likes her; she'll be seeing way more of her (and vice versa) than you probably will.

Things to do before morning sickness starts

Your life is about to change forever, so there's no time like the present to do some of those things you may have to trade in when your child is born.

Here are a few things we suggest for celebrating your impending fatherhood while you still have the time:

- >> Get in loads of unprotected sex (with your partner!).

- >> Take the vacation of your lifetime. Vacationing won't be the same for the next 18 years or so — make the most of it now.

- >> Ponder your own experience growing up and the things you would like your child to experience.

- >> Sleep in late, cook a leisurely brunch for you and your partner, or go for picnics.

- >> Splurge on something indulgent, like going to a fancy restaurant or a day spa.

- >> Start a journal, scrapbook, or blog to document the months leading up to your child's birth and make it a memento to give your child when she's older (yes — plenty of good material for an embarrassing 21st birthday slideshow).

- >> Read up on massage and practice on your partner. Invest in a few good quality aromatherapy oils and some sweet almond oil. (Hopefully, she'll return the favor!)

ADOPTING

You've been having sex on schedule for years now and had the tests to make sure your little guys are not only plentiful but frisky as well. Your partner has been through multiple cycles of IVF but it just hasn't worked out, and all the trauma of not getting pregnant is way past its use-by date. Perhaps you have decided to give up on having a biological child of your own.

Being unable to conceive a child doesn't have to mean you can't be a father. Adoption is another option you can look at.

Adopting a child means you take on the parental rights and responsibilities of looking after that child as you would if you were his biological father. That's a lifetime's responsibility. It can be easy to love your own child unconditionally, and you have to decide whether you're able to do that for a child who's not biologically yours. Many adoptions these days are open adoptions, which means the child and his birth parents stay in touch with each other. Lawyers who specialize in adoption, private agencies, and the child welfare system are all potential sources to assist with adoption and matching parents with a child.

The number of babies who are put up for adoption in the United States and other first-world countries is much lower than it was a generation ago. Some couples look at adopting a child from overseas. Americans adopt more children from China than from any other country, but many children are also adopted from Eastern European nations such as Ukraine, as well as from countries such as Haiti.

Whether you go the home-grown route or travel overseas, the adoption process is a lengthy and often expensive one — there are police and background checks, information evenings to attend, and visits to your home from social workers. Once you have jumped through all the official hoops, your profile may be put into a pool waiting to be selected by birth parents. This can take up to a year or more.

Chapter 3

Pregnancy: A Drama in Three Acts

Pregnancy is a bit like *The Lord of the Rings* trilogy: It has a beginning where the scene is set and there's a bit of chaos, a middle where things calm down a bit, and an end where everything comes to a head. The three distinct parts are called *trimesters,* and each has its scary and great bits (just like in the films), such as the first time you hear your baby's heartbeat at a checkup, feel your baby kick inside mom's belly, or see your baby's body twisting and turning on an ultrasound screen.

The easiest part of becoming a dad is the pregnancy bit. Fortunately, dudes don't get the morning sickness and leg cramps, and aren't the ones who can't get out of bed without a crane. By the end of the pregnancy, you're probably going to be a bit over hearing about what aches this week or what ridiculous food your partner has to have right now. But that's not to say there's nothing for dads to do during pregnancy. Apart from all the preparations (which we talk about in Chapter 4), there's all the stuff you can do with your partner to help her out a bit and to get to know your offspring (yes — before he's even born!). Your partner definitely needs a strong man for the finale, the birth of your baby (which we cover in detail in Chapter 5).

In this chapter we take you through the three trimesters and show you what your baby is up to on the inside. We also take the mystery out of morning sickness and explain why your partner can't sleep even though she's exhausted.

Act One: The First Trimester

After the initial excitement that you're going to be a dad, the hard work of supporting your partner through pregnancy begins. Of course, supporting your partner's not actually *that* hard, until you have to demonstrate your commitment to your new role when the initial ultrasound scan clashes with an all-important meeting you had arranged for that day.

Eating for two — or how to gain 30 pounds in 40 weeks

During pregnancy your partner is literally "making the baby" (in an assembly line kind of way), so good ingredients are essential for a quality end product, meaning that your unborn baby needs good food. Mom's healthy diet during pregnancy has a profound impact on the well-being of your little one even later in life, so encourage your partner to eat well. For you, this may mean laying off unhealthy options as well — there's nothing worse than tempting a pregnant woman with food she can't or shouldn't have.

Your partner also needs good food to help her deal with the physical, mental, and emotional changes and challenges she faces until your baby is born. The female body requires 10–12 percent more energy when pregnant.

So, what is "good food"? Your partner needs:

>> **Six servings of fruit and vegetables:** An apple or tomato is a serving; so is half a cup of salad. Leafy green vegetables are particularly good as they contain folic acid, which helps prevent birth defects such as spina bifida (see Chapter 18 for more about birth defects).

>> **Six servings of grains:** A cup of cooked pasta or rice, or a slice of wholegrain bread or a bread roll makes a serving. Whole grains are particularly useful because — you guessed it — they contain folic acid.

>> **Three servings of dairy:** A large glass of milk, a tub of yogurt, or two slices of cheese are each a serving. Low-fat milk helps control weight gain.

>> **Two servings of protein:** An egg, two slices of lean red meat, or two chicken drumsticks are one serving. Vegetarians can also get protein from nuts and seeds, legumes, and tofu.

REMEMBER

Folic acid, also called folate, is a B vitamin that is important to help prevent birth defects like spina bifida. Eating folate-rich foods such as whole grains, chickpeas, and leafy green vegetables helps your partner reach the recommended daily allowance of 400 micrograms. Most pregnancy healthcare providers recommend upping your partner's folic acid intake by using vitamin supplements, even before she gets pregnant. Check the recommended amount of folic acid, as some women in a high-risk category need more, and follow your health provider's instructions.

WARNING

Pregnant women shouldn't eat certain foods because of the risk of bacteria, such as listeria, to which pregnant women and unborn babies are extremely vulnerable. So don't go treating your sweetie to the following:

>> Any cooked food that has been in the fridge for more than 12 hours

>> Cold deli meats or pâté

>> Ready-made salads

>> Soft cheeses like brie, ricotta, and blue vein

>> Sprouted seeds

>> Sushi

>> Unpasteurized milk

Ask your primary care provider, obstetrician, or midwife for a comprehensive list of foods to avoid.

TIP

By the end of her pregnancy your partner may be really itching to eat a good bit of brie or sushi again, so a great way to celebrate the baby's birth may be to put together a platter of the things your partner's been missing out on for nine months. Start a "foods to remember after birth" list.

Understanding the medical stuff

During the next nine months you're going to learn a whole new vocabulary and get to know your partner's insides more than you may want to. Appendix B lists terms to help you decipher what your care provider of choice is talking about.

If you're unsure of where the various parts of the female reproductive system are located, see Chapter 2.

Dealing with common side effects in the first trimester

For some unfortunate moms, the first three months of pregnancy are a downright drag and can feel like an illness rather than the beautiful, natural process of creating life. There's no glow, and there's no bump to show off. Instead, as your baby makes itself comfy in your partner's uterus, he's making his presence known in other ways. Symptoms vary wildly from woman to woman, so there's no way of knowing exactly what's going to hit your partner. Here's a list of common complaints.

Morning sickness

Morning sickness typically involves feeling nauseous and, in some cases, vomiting. It's a common condition usually experienced during the first three months of pregnancy. Morning sickness doesn't pose a risk to the baby unless it's very severe. Morning sickness is caused by those crazy pregnancy hormones and usually subsides after 12 weeks. It can come on anytime but is usually worse in the morning because your partner's stomach is empty. At its worst, morning sickness is like having a hangover and being seasick at the same time, so no wonder your partner is off to the bathroom once again. Get used to it — bathrooms also become a prominent feature in the last trimester, albeit for different reasons (your partner needs to pee every ten minutes because the baby puts pressure on her bladder).

TIP

One thing that makes morning sickness worse is getting up on an empty stomach, so try having a plate of dry crackers or toast with a little jelly or peanut butter ready for your partner to nibble when she first wakes up. Other tips include eating smaller portions more often during the day, increasing intake of carbohydrates and reducing intake of fats, and stimulating pressure points on the inner arm just above the wrist crease, which supposedly reduces nausea.

WARNING

Morning sickness can get so bad that your partner may become dehydrated. The symptoms aren't always easy to spot, so double-check with your midwife, obstetrician, or primary care provider if your partner is having a really rough time with morning sickness. She may prescribe medications to help reduce nausea, in severe cases.

Exhaustion

Your baby's growing rapidly and taking a lot of your partner's energy. Getting through a day at work may be more than your partner's up to, so you can score lots of points if you take on more of the household chores, prepare meals, and do the things your partner's not up to doing.

Sensitivity to smells

Pregnancy does strange things to a woman, not least of all her ability to smell everything. Your partner can walk into a room you left three hours ago and smell your aftershave. She's sensitive to most smells, especially things like perfume, food, and gasoline fumes — they may even make her vomit — so if you're heating up your favorite garlic bread (the one with extra garlic and blue cheese), open a window or put on the exhaust fan.

Tender breasts

You've probably heard of the following concept: "You can look, but you can't touch." For many expectant dads, the same concept now applies to their partner's breasts. Pregnancy hormones cause your partner's breasts to become a bit bigger, but they'll be sore and tender. So while you may be admiring your partner's new shapely form, it may pay to wait until she invites you to party before gate-crashing her bra.

Moodiness

Blame it on the hormones, because your partner hasn't turned into a grumpy, unpredictable monster; she's just at the mercy of her body. Go easy on her if she's a little off kilter right now. Talk to your partner and figure out a way to communicate when she's in one of her moods, because *progesterone*, the hormone responsible for all this, isn't going to go away for a long time yet.

ACTIVITIES TO AVOID

Some activities are not recommended for moms-to-be, such as:

- Going on rides in theme parks (because of the acceleration the body experiences during the ride)

- Extreme sports and adventure sports (such as bungee jumping, parachuting, and wild water rafting)

- Dyeing her hair (because of the chemicals used in dyes)

- Traveling on a plane (in case the baby decides to arrive early, although this is mostly relevant toward the end of the pregnancy)

For a comprehensive list of things to avoid, ask your healthcare provider.

REMEMBER

Though your partner's feeling yucky, this is your chance to shine. You can treat your partner and make her feel special in lots of simple ways at this difficult stage. Come home with a little gift (baby socks are great), give her a pregnancy massage (along with some nice oils to battle stretch marks), or get a good DVD for the night. If your partner bites your head off for trying, don't take it personally. Try again next week.

What's your baby up to?

Between 6 and 12 weeks, your baby grows from around one-quarter of an inch long to around 2 inches in length (see Figure 3-1). In other words, your baby has grown about 800 percent in six weeks. No wonder your partner is so tired.

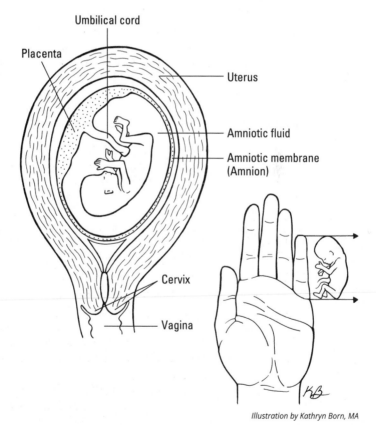

Illustration by Kathryn Born, MA

FIGURE 3-1: At 12 weeks, your baby is about the size of your little finger.

TWO (OR MORE) FOR THE PRICE OF ONE

You've just found out, through the magic of an ultrasound scan, that you're going to be a father of not one, but two babies at once. You're freaking out. Being dad to two at the same time is hard work, but of course not unmanageable. Being dad to two at the same time is a great opportunity to be twice the man (at least) that you are today!

Having twins, triplets, or more babies at once is called a *multiple birth*. Multiple births happen in two ways. Identical or *monozygotic* twins are formed when the fertilized egg divides into two very early on, and two separate embryos develop. Non-identical twins, also known as fraternal or *dizygotic* twins, occur when two eggs are fertilized at once in the fallopian tubes. Triplets can sometimes be a combination with two identical twins and a fraternal twin, but not always.

In pregnancy, twins are more at risk of arriving prematurely (38 weeks for twins is considered full term) and having a low birth weight. Your healthcare provider will guide you through the intricacies of multiple birth and will probably monitor your partner's well-being throughout the pregnancy more carefully.

Unfortunately, it often means that the side effects of being pregnant are more pronounced, so morning sickness may be more intense; weight gain faster and earlier in the pregnancy; and things like varicose veins, heartburn, and shortness of breath more pronounced. Find out more about common side effects for the last two trimesters later in this chapter. Also see Chapter 2 for more info about IVF and multiple births.

During this time, your baby's organs take shape, with the heart beating from about six weeks. Though neither you nor your partner can feel it yet, your little tadpole (they look like that at the beginning) is moving around in there. She's floating in amniotic fluid in her amniotic sac. The placenta is developing to act as life support for your baby.

Between 6 and 12 weeks, your healthcare provider may do an initial ultrasound scan. The first ultrasound is a pretty big deal for most parents-to-be. You get to see your baby for the first time — granted, you may not initially be able to determine what's what until your health provider points it out — but it's something you'll never forget. Unfortunately, early ultrasounds can also pinpoint problems with the pregnancy. This happens in about one in six cases; if something's wrong, your partner may have a spontaneous miscarriage or need to terminate the pregnancy for medical reasons. Your healthcare provider typically mentions this before the scan, but talking about this scenario with your partner before you have your first scan is a good idea.

Act Two: The Second Trimester

The morning sickness is waning, your partner is feeling a little less exhausted, and she's beginning to show a bit of a baby bump — welcome to the second trimester. Weeks 13–28 are usually the best period of pregnancy. You start to see your partner's body change as the baby grows and feel the baby's first kicks by putting your hand on her belly — a pretty amazing feeling.

Because 80 percent of miscarriages happen in the first 12 weeks, many parents don't announce they're pregnant until the second trimester.

Now is also the time to ask about a *nuchal fold* test to check for potential birth defects, especially if your partner is age 35 or older. A nuchal fold test aims to determine the likelihood of your baby being born with *Down Syndrome.*

Enjoying the golden trimester

Most pregnant women feel a lot better throughout the second trimester. As your partner's belly is getting bigger, the reality that you're going to have a child really sets in. Exciting times! Sometime in the second trimester, your partner probably also starts feeling those first kicks and bumps. Typically this happens around 18–20 weeks. They may be hard to spot at first, as that little foot tries to get in touch with you through all those abdominal muscles, but feeling those kicks for the first time is a pretty magical moment.

You see your partner transform as the baby grows, and she may start planning what to buy (not more clothes!) and how to decorate the baby's room. This is called "the nesting instinct," and you pretty much have to go with it. When it comes to purchasing things for the baby, however, dads are hugely important as they tend to "keep it real." Many household budgets are under a lot of pressure when the baby arrives, and with your partner being high on hormones, you should go shopping together to avoid a local financial crisis. See Chapter 4 for an overview of what you actually need to buy.

Around 20 weeks, your midwife, obstetrician, or family doctor may send you for an ultrasound scan to make sure that the baby's development is on track and that things are progressing smoothly. If you can't wait another 20 weeks to find out your baby's flavor, you can usually find out at this scan, unless junior has his legs crossed!

REMEMBER

Sex during pregnancy is absolutely okay in most cases (ask your doctor) and apparently is even good for the baby as well. Bonus! The second trimester may be the best time to share a bit of passion, although it depends greatly on how your partner is feeling throughout pregnancy. By the way, it's not out of the question to have sex almost up until labor, depending on how your partner feels. Couples have been known to use sex to bring on labor (see Chapter 5 for more about bringing on labor).

Understanding more medical stuff

Your caregiver will start to feel for the baby at each checkup by asking your partner to lie down. He also uses a *Doppler* or a fetal heartbeat monitor to listen for the baby's heartbeat, which at a remarkable 120–160 beats per minute, sounds like a dance party's going on in there. Your caregiver also checks the *fundal height*, or the length of the uterus as it progresses into the abdomen.

Your midwife, obstetrician, or primary care provider also routinely asks your partner for a urine sample to check for protein in her urine. Blood pressure gets the once-over too, as high blood pressure and protein in the urine are both indicators of preeclampsia.

Dealing with common side effects in the second trimester

Most changes during this trimester are a result of the growing size of your baby. They include

>> **Back pain:** This is perhaps one of the most common complaints of pregnant women and is caused by the growing weight of the baby, additional strain on the spine, and a change in the center of gravity that the body needs to adjust for.

>> **Constipation:** This is a common problem during pregnancy. The main reason for constipation in the second trimester is an increase in the hormone progesterone, which slows the movement of food through the digestive tract. Later in pregnancy the problem of constipation is likely to be made worse by the pressure of the growing uterus on the intestines. Taking iron supplements, which many pregnant women take, can also make constipation worse.

>> **Heartburn:** This burning sensation in the middle chest is caused by the hormone progesterone, which softens the uterus so it can stretch, but also softens the esophagus, allowing acid to come back out. So if your partner complains about heartburn, don't be offended — your cooking isn't the cause.

>> **Leg cramps:** These seem to plague pregnant women more at night, but no one's sure what causes them. Blame the hormones, we reckon.

>> **Softening ligaments:** The ligaments in the pelvis stretch, which widens the pelvis to prepare for birth. It can give your partner a floating sensation in the joints and cause sharp stabbing pains when she stands up too quickly or rolls over in bed. This is called *round ligament pain* and is nothing to be worried about, although knowing about this pain is good.

You can't do much about these things, other than continue to be a superstar with your support, love, and encouragement.

What's your baby up to now?

At 24 weeks, your baby is nearly 12 inches long (see Figure 3-2). She also has her calendar full doing these amazing things:

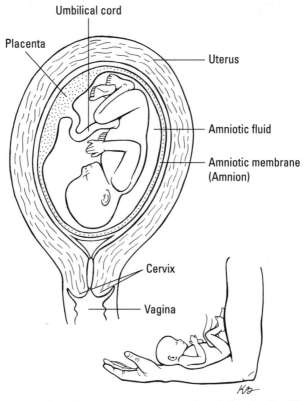

Umbilical cord

Placenta

Uterus

Amniotic fluid

Amniotic membrane (Amnion)

Cervix

Vagina

Illustration by Kathryn Born, MA

FIGURE 3-2: At 24 weeks, your baby is about the length from your elbow to your wrist.

>> **Getting her eyes done:** Pigmentation in the iris (the colored portion of the eye) develops. If your baby is of European descent, she'll be born with blue eyes that may change color in the months after birth. African American, Native American, and Asian babies can be born with brown or blue eyes, and eye color can also change with time.

- **>> Having a facial:** Your baby's using the world's best moisturizer, *vernix,* a waxy coating that keeps her skin from getting wrinkled as she floats around in fluid all day. She's also growing fingernails, hair, and eyebrows.

- **>> Listening to music and your voice:** Your baby can hear now, but won't know what she's hearing for a long time yet, though research suggests that babies know their parents' voices when they're born from what they hear in the womb. Amazing, isn't it?

- **>> Preparing to rock and roll:** At the end of the second trimester, your baby is almost done growing and developing all external and internal organs.

Act Three: The Third Trimester

You're on the final lap now. Don't get too excited though; you still have some hoops to jump through. Start thinking about childbirth education classes, which your care provider can refer you to. These classes can be extremely valuable in terms of educating you about the process of birth, can answer any burning questions you might have, and can allow you to meet other prospective dads who are just as excited — or terrified — as you are. Lots of people go on to keep in touch with their classmates as their babies grow. Your hospital probably offers these classes for expectant parents. If you're interested in a certain birthing method, such as the Bradley method or Lamaze, you may find classes that discuss these birthing types.

TIP

Checking with someone who has already attended a prenatal class you are interested in is definitely a good idea. Some classes are more dad-inclusive than others. For example, some providers split the group into moms and dads to talk about specific issues or situations. Having a guys-only session as part of a prenatal class is great, as it provides the ideal opportunity for some "man talk" about pregnancy, babies, and fatherhood.

Making choices about the birth

The time's come to start looking forward to The Birth. That baby is going to have to come out. In ye olden days, birth was a straightforward thing — woman goes into labor, sheets are torn into strips, water is boiled, there's a lot of yelling, and then baby comes out. These days, with technology and greater awareness of the anatomy of birth, you're faced with a lot of choices concerning how junior enters the world. Home birth or hospital birth? No drugs, or all the drugs you can get? With lots of family, a video camera, and updates on Twitter? Or just your partner, the person delivering the baby, and you?

First up to think about — and possibly foremost in your partner's mind right now — are pain relief options. There's a swing toward having as little intervention or being as natural and drug-free as possible during labor and birth. But ultimately the pain relief options really depend on your partner's preferences. Toward the end of pregnancy, she's probably grappling with the idea of what labor is going to be like and the pressure to be as stoic about it as possible. Supporting your partner and standing by whatever decisions she makes regarding her body and the birth of your baby goes a long way toward making it easier on her.

Here's a look at what's on the menu:

>> **Drug-free:** Heat packs, massage, breathing exercises, and being in water may help relieve the pain of labor. Keeping active during the birth and avoiding lying on her back can also help your partner manage the pain.

>> **Epidural:** An epidural is a local anesthetic injected into the spinal column. It blocks out all pain and is often used during cesareans so the mother can be awake when her child is born. Around 60 percent of American women have epidural anesthesia in labor.

>> **Narcotics:** Intravenous pain relievers, including narcotics and sedatives, can cause drowsiness in both mother and baby, though usually without any long-term effects. Most healthcare providers won't give them if they think your partner is close to delivery, because they can depress the baby's breathing. They can also cause nausea.

Another big decision is where and how to have the baby. No doubt your partner has researched all options by now. Unfortunately the "I just want to wake up in the morning and my baby will be here" option doesn't exist. She's probably let you know what her next best option is — or you may ask her about it. The most common scenarios are

>> **Birth centers or free-standing birth centers:** Having your baby in a special birth center run by midwives may provide you with additional options to try particular birthing techniques or varying positions during labor. However, birth centers generally take a non-interventionist approach and don't provide epidurals. And if you need a cesarean section or your baby requires special care, you'll need to be transferred to a hospital.

>> **Home birth:** This option has become more popular but is still the exception in the United States. Less than 2 percent of American women give birth at home. For a home birth, you need the support of a midwife, usually a certified or lay midwife, if your state regulations allow, because most nurse-midwives deliver in hospitals or birthing centers. If your partner wants a water birth, you can rent special equipment to facilitate the birth at home.

>> **Hospital birth:** Most women in the United States opt for a hospital birth. Some hospitals provide extra facilities for water births or natural (as in no pain relief) births.

REMEMBER

Talk with your care provider about your options and discuss the pros and cons of each one. Don't be afraid to ask questions and be sure you know everything you need to be confident about the upcoming birth. As your partner's number-one support person, you need to know what's going on just as much as she does.

REMEMBER

Your health insurance may dictate your choice of healthcare providers or even which hospital you use. Check out your policy at the beginning of pregnancy to avoid unwelcome surprises later.

Understanding even more medical stuff

As you head into the home stretch of pregnancy, you have more checkups with your midwife or obstetrician, and you and your partner work out a *birth plan.* This sounds like an oxymoron, as birth is one process that you just have to surrender to — you have very little control over what happens. Lots of pain relief options and delivery methods are available, so be clear with your midwife or obstetrician about which of these you're interested in and which you're not. That's what a birth plan is — a clear understanding of how you would like things to go so that the person delivering your baby knows your wishes.

REMEMBER

Keep an open mind about how the birth will go. If you've planned for a nice water birth at home, be prepared that if things don't go as smoothly as you would like, you may have to be transferred to the hospital. Or if you've said there's absolutely no way your woman needs pain relief, she may be yelling for an epidural in the first five minutes. The ultimate aim is delivering your baby safely into the world with the least amount of anxiety and trauma on your beloved so you set off on your parenting path on the healthiest and safest foot.

Your healthcare provider checks the baby's position and makes sure she's in the right place. During this trimester your baby makes her way down headfirst toward the cervix, ready for birth, a process called *engaging.* If she has her feet pointed down toward the cervix, she's in a *breech* position. If she stays breech until the birth, chances are your care provider will recommend a cesarean birth.

Your caregiver may also take swabs from your partner's vagina to test for *group B strep,* which is a bacteria that can infect your baby as she's being born. This is often done during the second half of pregnancy. If traces of it are discovered, your partner will probably need to be on an antibiotic drip during labor.

Dealing with common side effects in the third trimester

By now the golden glow of the second trimester is getting a bit tarnished. As your partner nears her due date, your baby is starting to take over her body — literally. Her internal organs are getting pushed and shoved all over the place and her abdominal muscles have split in the middle to make way for that wide load she's carrying. Your partner may even waddle already, as her relaxed ligaments widen her pelvis.

Some common complaints during this time include the following:

>> **"I've got baby brain."** Pregnant women often feel like they're losing their marbles. They tend to forget stuff, don't remember simple or frequent activities, and appear to be running around like headless chickens. These symptoms are believed to be caused by hormones, lack of sleep, and the general toll pregnancy takes on the body.

>> **"I can't sleep but I'm so tired all the time."** Insomnia is one thing most mothers-to-be in the third trimester agree on. Her joints may be sore, back aching, with a baby that kicks all night and heartburn to boot. Your partner may also need to get up to hit the john every five minutes. Lying on her back to sleep can put pressure on the *vena cava,* an important artery feeding the heart, so she has to lie on her side at night, and turning over in bed can be a little trying. You can suggest she try a pillow under her right side, where the vena cava is, which tilts the weight of her body off the artery.

>> **"I've got varicose veins, and worse — hemorrhoids."** The third trimester can be hard on a girl. She's getting rounder by the day and may waddle; she's tired, and not getting enough sleep is making her grumpy. And then hemorrhoids turn up and make her feel downright miserable. She's not feeling like a radiant mother-to-be anymore; she's feeling like a veiny, fat frump. Varicose veins and piles can be caused or made worse by the weight of the baby on her body, so get her to take it easy and rest a lot.

>> **"My ankles are swollen and I'm big as a house."** As well as carrying a rapidly growing baby around, your partner's retaining fluid and has more blood flowing through her body. In hot weather or after standing for long periods, this blood collects in her ankles. Your partner should put her feet up whenever she can and avoid salty foods. A few foot rubs from dad wouldn't be out of line either. Calling her "fatso" or "chubby" does not go down well, even if you think she looks hilarious.

>> **"Why doesn't anything I eat taste right?"** Blame that pesky progesterone — along with everything else, it causes food cravings. Finding anything that tastes just how she wants it to be may be very hard for your partner, and predicting what she needs is almost impossible. We suggest that you roll with it and keep up your partner's spirits by suggesting lots of different options.

TIP

Taking slow walks together, reading or singing to the baby in bed at night, making lists of potential names together, and taking photos of that burgeoning belly make for a good time and help you support each other as the big day approaches. These are some of the last days that your family numbers just the two of you, so take time to be with your partner right now.

Preparing for Project Push — are we there yet?

Yes, almost! Your baby's just putting on the finishing touches before making his glorious entry into the world. He's been keeping busy by

>> **Beefing up:** At the start of the third trimester, your baby weighed around 2 pounds, but by the end, he has reached his birth weight — between 7.5 and 8 pounds, on average. The most rapid weight gain — half a pound per week — happens in the final few weeks.

>> Getting in position for take-off: In most cases your baby is head down with his feet under your partner's rib cage (see Figures 3-3 and 3-4). No wonder she's uncomfortable. If your baby is butt down, he's breech, which could necessitate a cesarean section. But babies can and do turn into the *vertex,* or head-down position, any time in pregnancy. After 36 weeks, it becomes less likely, due to the cramped space.

>> Practicing for life on the outside: Your baby is taking practice breaths and — somewhat less endearing — urinating into the amniotic fluid. His eyes are open, and you may see him holding the umbilical cord or sucking his thumb on ultrasound.

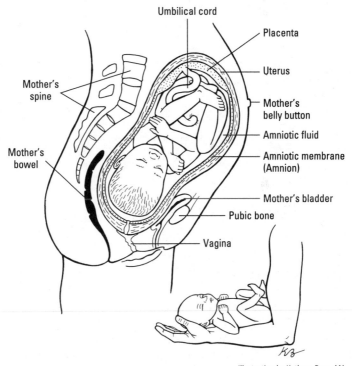

Illustration by Kathryn Born, MA

FIGURE 3-3: At 32 weeks your baby is about 16–17 inches long.

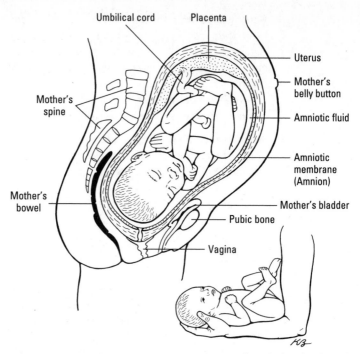

Umbilical cord   Placenta

Uterus

Mother's
belly button

Amniotic fluid

Amniotic
membrane
(Amnion)

Mother's
spine

Mother's
bowel

Mother's bladder

Pubic bone

Vagina

Illustration by Kathryn Born, MA

FIGURE 3-4: At 40 weeks your baby is about 20 inches long, and, in
97–99 percent of cases, in the vertex, or head-down position.

Chapter 4

Preparing for a Baby in the House

F ew things change the way you live as much as welcoming a baby into your life. Having a baby is like having a house guest who never cleans up after himself, cries a lot, and has more needs than the two of you put together. Adding a baby to the family is not as simple as clearing out the spare room for him to sleep in. He needs stuff: clothes, bedding, diapers, all sorts of things you need to think about that become part of your daily life as a father.

As you count down to your baby's birth, you need to get things done to avoid hassles down the line — get those bags packed and ready for the hospital, get the bassinet and a car seat sorted, and be ready to go at a moment's notice. When he arrives, chances are you won't have a lot of time for decorating the baby's room or shopping for socks, so it's best to get those things out of the way now.

In this chapter you discover the ins and outs of what to look for when buying things like nursery furniture, strollers, diapers, clothes, and toys. You find out what diaper rash is and how to prevent it, and how to help your baby when he's teething. We give you lots of checklists for everything you need to do before the birth and what you need to take with you to the hospital or have prepared for a home birth.

Getting the Right Gear

Who would have thought a baby would need so much stuff? Getting set up for a new person in your house takes a bit of thought — and a mountain of cash if you're not careful. Rather than expecting you to go out and buy every bit of gear the baby shops say you must have, we tell you what you really need.

TIP

To keep costs down, send the word around among your co-workers and friends that you're having a baby. They may have cribs, bassinets, car seats, and strollers they're no longer using. You can completely outfit a nursery for very little or even for free if you have generous friends and relatives.

Baby needs new shoes . . . and a whole lot more

Baby clothes come in more shapes and styles than you would have thought possible. Babies don't dress like miniature adults. They hate itchy materials, fussy buttons, and other things you might put up with to be fashionable. However, because adults and not babies buy clothes, you'll find a whole spectrum of adorable stuff specifically designed to appeal to adults, covered with duckies and little toy cars.

Distinguishing types of baby clothes

Be forewarned: It's hard to resist this stuff, especially for moms-to-be. But check out what works for you before you break the bank on Prince George–inspired smocked rompers or other outfits that really don't fit your lifestyle.

» **Bodysuits** are long- or short-sleeved T-shirts t⸍
the baby's diaper area and snap at the bottor
changing. They are handy for keeping everyt⸍
so that baby's tummy doesn't get chilly, and
him looking pulled together. They're great ᴜᴜ.
summer months when a short-sleeved bodysuit can ᴠᴇ .
by itself without pants or as pajamas.

» **Footies** are all-in-one outfits that either snap or zip up the
legs and front. They're like bodysuits with leg coverings and
socks. Some snap up the back, which is really inconvenient,
and we recommend steering clear of them. Most have feet,
but you can get some without feet (called "nonfooties" or
"coveralls") for summer. Most also have long sleeves.

» **Sleeping bags** (also called gowns) are like footies with
sleeves but no legs, just a sack covering your baby's legs and
feet. The American Academy of Pediatrics advises parents
not to use blankets in cribs for infants up to one year, so
having her wear a sleeping bag means she can't get cold.
Gowns that have elastic around the bottom are also good for
late-night diaper changes, because if her legs are bare under
the sack, you can get to her diaper more easily and disturb
her less.

Listing the clothes that your baby needs from the get-go

The following list is a guide to what you should have ready to
go for your newborn baby. You can customize your list as you
find your dad–legs and figure out which items work well for you.
You can also tweak the list to suit the seasons. As a general rule,
baby clothes should be loose–fitting, made with breathable and
soft fabric, not too tight at the neck, and easy to open and close.
Remember, you can go through three to four sets of clothes in a
day because of diaper leaks and baby spit–up. You need

» **Lots of bodysuits.** Count on at least six, but the more, the
better.

» **Four footies.** As with bodysuits, the more, the better. These
are popular baby shower gifts.

>> **Four pairs of pants of some sort.** Overalls are pretty cute, but make sure they have snaps in the legs so you don't have to take the whole lot off to change her diaper. Elastic waists on pants are easier than fumbling around with zippers and snaps.

>> **Four sleeping bags for nighttime.** Look for cotton material rather than polar fleece or microfleece, as those fabrics aren't breathable, and she may get overheated.

>> **Two jackets for going out.** Look for jackets that are easy to zip or snap; buttons take too long to do up.

>> **Two sweaters or wraparound jerseys.** Choose the kinds that don't need to go over her head. Most babies hate things put over their head.

>> **Lots of pairs of socks.** Make them all the same if possible — one is always getting lost.

>> **Four hats.** These are preferably made of a Lycra-cotton mix so they stretch, or lovely soft wool if they're handmade. Some babies hate hats and pull them off; look for something that snaps or ties under the chin if your baby is one of them.

>> **Lots of bibs with either snaps or Velcro.** Bibs with ties can be a pain to put on. Velcro stops sticking after a number of washings. Some large bibs go over the baby's head.

>> **Two pairs of soft shoes.** In our experience, shoes that have elastic around the heel stay on better than other slip-ons. Babies don't need real shoes until they're walking outside.

>> **Two pairs of gloves or mittens.** Get some that clip to your baby's outerwear because babies tend to lose them (intentionally and unintentionally).

Trying tips for choosing baby clothes

Here are some tips for selecting clothes and getting your baby all dressed up:

>> Most babies get grumpy at having clothes pulled over their heads. Avoid anything that doesn't have a few snaps

opening at the shoulder or an envelope-style neckband (two overlapping pieces of fabric that stretch easily when put over her head) to make pulling the clothing over her face painless.

>> When putting on a sweater or any other top that doesn't go over your baby's head, it's a good idea to lay it on the surface you're dressing your baby on before you lay her down. Then all you have to do is slide her arms into the sleeves and snap her up, and you're good to go.

>> Avoid anything that has a back opening. Your baby spends a lot of time lying on her back in the early months, and it can't be comfortable having snaps under you. They're also tricky to get on when you're getting her dressed.

>> Avoid anything that looks like it's going to be a pain to put on. Some babies really dislike getting dressed, and trying to tie silly little ribbons when she's having a meltdown isn't our idea of a good time.

>> If your baby arrives in winter, look for clothes that have folds sewn into the ends of sleeves — they're actually mittens. These are great to keep your baby from scratching herself with those needlelike newborn nails.

>> If in doubt about sizing, buy clothes that are too big. At least you know junior will grow into them. Avoid the newborn or 0–3 month sizes, unless your baby is tiny or a preemie. (The nearby sidebar has more information on sizing.)

>> If you've been given a lot of hand-me-downs, be aware that the fire retardant in some clothing may be worn and will not be as effective as it is in new clothes.

>> You will be given a ton of new clothing as presents, so if you find you have too much, don't be afraid to take it back to the shop and swap it for something you can use in the future, like the next size up.

>> Dark colors show baby spit-up much more than light colors, but light colors show baby poop much more! Just go with the colors you like.

SIZING THINGS UP

Until he's school age, figuring out what size your little one wears can be challenging, because babies grow and gain weight at different rates and, like adults, have different body types. Many 6-month-olds wear 12-month clothing; this doesn't mean your daughter is going to grow up to be an NFL linebacker. Here are the basic categories:

- **0–3 months:** Birth to three months, or newborns under 8 pounds. Full-term babies outgrow this size very quickly.

- **3–6 months:** Manufacturers vary, so look at their weight charts. Some manufacturers also cut their clothing to be narrower than others. When in doubt, try it on (the baby, not you).

- **6–9 months, 9–12 months, 12–18 months, 18–24 months:** These sizes often have little relation to your child's actual age. Go by the weights listed on the clothing label.

After two years, things get even more confusing. Some manufacturers continue to list ages in months, while others switch to years. Sizes listed in months are sometimes, but not always, more fully cut to accommodate diapers than clothing with sizes listed in years.

If your baby is premature, look for clothing made especially for preemies. Some manufacturers also make clothing in newborn, or NB, sizes.

REMEMBER

Handling a baby during the first few months can feel a bit tricky because she can appear really fragile. So think about what steps you need to go through to put on a particular item of clothing. If the clothes seem complicated to close or open, don't buy them. Don't be afraid to try out the garment in the shop with a baby doll. Borrow someone's small child to take with you if you feel silly carrying a doll into the store, or better yet, borrow someone's real baby if he'll let you.

Shopping for shoes

Your baby won't need shoes for a while yet. A good time to start looking for shoes is when your little champ starts crawling. Studies show that going barefoot is best — but that's not always practical. For a baby who isn't walking yet, soft-soled shoes with elasticized heels work well and protect toes from being scraped on the floor or ground.

Here are some tips and tricks for buying your toddler's first pair of shoes:

>> Let your baby walk around in the shoe just like you would if you were trying on new shoes for yourself.

>> Choose shoes with half a finger's width of wiggle room at the front and end, but no more than that — he'll trip over his own feet.

>> Look for shoes that are as similar to bare-feet conditions as possible. He doesn't need arch support at this stage!

>> Babies' feet get hotter and sweat more than adults' feet do, so choose natural breathable materials rather than synthetics.

>> Many cheap children's shoes give out in the toes — toddlers are always crawling on the ground, and then they're up on their feet, using their toes to leverage themselves. Make sure the shoes have extra-sturdy stitching in the toes for long wear.

>> Soles that grip are important too, as junior needs all the help he can get to not slip when he's learning to walk.

Filling the toy box

When your baby is born, all he does for a while is poop, pee, eat, cry, sleep, and gaze — often with an unfocused stare — at things. So he doesn't need electronic gear, a racing car set, or a mini piano. What he needs are things that give him a real sense of the world he's just come into — simple objects that provide new sights, shapes, textures, smells, sounds, and sensations.

These can easily be provided by spending time with your baby, singing to him, and touching his skin and fingers with textures like an old comb, fabric, your hair, leaves, the cat's fur — you get the idea. As he begins to grasp and brings his hands together, things like a rattle or a chain of plastic rings can keep him fascinated for ages.

When your baby starts teething, he looks for things to put in his mouth to push against his gums to relieve the discomfort. Many toys double as teething rings, even if they weren't originally designed to be.

Some good ideas for baby toys include

>> **Cloth or hard cardboard books.** Look for ones with flaps or things to touch sewn into them, so your baby can experience different textures. Reading to your child daily is one of the most important gifts you can give him.

>> **Plastic keys.** For some reason babies love your car keys, so give them their own set. These are great for teething too. However, nearly every baby will still prefer your keys to his, so keep yours out of his reach.

>> **Play gyms.** Play gyms are mats with arms curved over the top where you can attach colorful objects like soft toys or musical objects for your baby to look at as he lies on the mat. Just make sure he can't pull down anything that he shouldn't be chewing on. Nothing is safe from his gummy mouth once he's got the hang of his hands.

>> **Rattles.** You can buy rattles or make your own from old plastic containers filled with noisy objects. Ensure the lid is on securely and never leave your baby alone with an object that could come apart.

>> **Soft toy animals.** One of these will probably become your baby's most treasured friend, and it will never be the one you favor, so buy only stuffed animals you won't mind seeing for the next six years. Avoid button eyes and other removable parts that baby could choke on.

REMEMBER

Less is more when it comes to toys — no matter what the toy manufacturers tell you, nothing beats spending time playing and exploring with your baby. Brain development is assisted by appropriate stimulation and human contact.

To make sure toys are safe for your little one, check for any parts that may come off and become a choking hazard, as well as toxins, such as toxic paints. Inevitably your little guy will try to put all toys (and most other things) into his mouth, so make sure they're safe to put in his mouth. The following website provides guidelines on purchasing safe toys for your littler one: www.cpsc.gov/en/Safety-Education/Safety-Guides/Toys/.

Strollering in style

Strollers have evolved into high-tech, fold-at-the-touch-of-a-button contraptions that can double as shopping carts, hold water bottles, be taken off-road, and cook you lunch (just kidding). Many strollers integrate with your baby's first car seat, so you can transfer the whole seat into the stroller without removing him when he's tiny.

Baby stores are packed with different models of strollers. A stroller is often one of the bigger purchases you make in this fatherhood game, so shop around.

TIP

Some research suggests that babies in strollers that face toward you rather than out into the world are better as your tyke is less stressed. Facing each other encourages more talking, laughing, and social interaction.

These are some of the things you need to look out for:

>> Can you put a car seat or bassinet attachment on it in the early months, making it easier to transfer junior from bed or car seat?

>> Does the stroller come with a fitted sunshade and fitted weather cover?

>> Does the stroller fit through the door of your favorite stores? Can it be easily maneuvered through a packed supermarket? If you're looking at three-wheeled strollers, make sure the front wheel isn't fixed so you can maneuver it easily.

>> How easy is it to adjust the back of the seat? Can your baby lie down flat in it for sleeping? Can the back be raised up high for a growing child to see more of the world around him?

>> How easily will the stroller fit in your car trunk — or in your house? Some models can be bulky.

>> How easily does the stroller fold down? The last thing you want is to be pulling levers all over the place when you've got a fussy baby to deal with. If you're traveling by bus, strollers that can be folded down with only one hand are ideal so you don't have to hand your baby to a total stranger while you wrestle with getting the stroller onto the bus.

>> How well does the stroller support your child's growing spine and neck?

>> How well will the stroller survive if you want to take it on unpaved walkways or paths?

TIP

The following website provides valuable safety information on strollers and buggies: www.cpsc.gov/en/Newsroom/News-Releases/2014/CPSC-Approves-New-Federal-Safety-Standard-for-Carriages-and-Strollers/.

Choosing the right car seat

Getting a cute mobile for your baby's crib is optional, buying a stroller that you can take mountain running is optional — but using a car seat for your most precious cargo is not. Yeah, sure, you free-ranged in your parents' car when you were little and lived to tell the tale, but sadly some children haven't. So take advantage of the fact that things have evolved somewhat since those days and use a car seat for every journey you take in the car with your baby.

As with strollers (see the preceding section), so many models of car seats are out there that it pays to shop around. Luckily you've got a few months to do this! There are different sizes according to the age and weight of your child, generally falling into these categories:

>> **Infant car seat:** This is a car seat specifically used for newborns up to approximately 20 pounds. The car seat fits into a base that stays in the car, which is strapped in using the car's existing seatbelts. Infant car seats should only be used in a rear-facing position — the best position for children in a car for as long as you can keep them that way.

An infant car seat can be taken out with your baby in it — leave the base in the car or you'll look pretty silly — and attached to some strollers. They're not meant to fit over a shopping cart, no matter how many people you see using them that way. Baby car seats also have a movable handle so you can carry your baby around in it like Red Riding Hood's basket of goodies. However, the seat will constantly bump your legs, jarring the baby and bruising you. Putting it into a stroller is easier for both of you.

>> **Child car seat:** Some car seats are convertible, meaning you can use them all the way up from newborn to your child's 21st birthday — or almost. An insert holds your baby in place when he's tiny and is removed when he's older. Car seats usually have straps that attach to bolts in the back of the back passenger seat or to the floor when in the rear-facing position. If your car doesn't have bolts, they can be purchased and put into the car by a mechanic for very little money.

>> **Booster seat:** Every state has its own laws about when your child can sit in a booster and how long he needs to use one. Check the Governors Highway Safety Association website at `http://ghsa.org/html/stateinfo/laws/childsafety_laws.html` for a current list.

REMEMBER

Infants should stay in rear-facing car seats until they are at least two years old. Rear-facing positioning reduces the risk of death or serious injury by up to 75 percent, according to a 2007 study. Kids with long legs are still better off riding rear facing.

WARNING

Think twice about buying a secondhand seat. Seats sold in the United States have expiration dates printed somewhere on the seat. After this date, the plastic may start to weaken, providing less protection in an accident. Car seats that have been in an accident may also be damaged in places you can't easily see and should not be used.

WARNING

Add-ons like custom car-seat covers can be cute, but they're not always safe. Don't use anything aftermarket on the car seat, not even if the manufacturer says it's designed to fit. Check this website for more information: `www.safercar.gov/parents/CarSeats/Car-Seat-Safety.htm`.

Feeding, bathing, and entertaining

You thought you were done shopping in the baby aisle? Oh no — there's much more to fill up your house with. You find most of these things lurking in homes where kids live:

>> **Baby bath or tummy tub:** You need something to wash your baby in. While the kitchen sink will work for a while — as long as you clean out the carrot peels first — he'll eventually need something a bit larger, but not as large as the regular bathtub.

Changing tables that converted to infant baths used to be common, but many parents don't have the room for them. If you do have one, it will save some wear and tear on your back. Otherwise, you'll need something to set in the big bathtub, at least until your baby can sit up by himself. A bath support is a ramp that baby can lie back on that holds her at a 45-degree angle so her head is safely kept out of the water. There are many different styles and you — and your baby — may prefer one type to another, so shop around.

>> **Bouncy chair or infant seat:** Most kids have spent time in a bouncy chair or infant seat, which is a baby chair that your baby can lie in to watch you go about your day from a better angle than lying on the floor. These seats are portable and easy to clean, and she can even sit outside in one while you're gardening. Some have built-in vibrating mechanisms that calm a fussy baby, while others have activity trays that keep baby busy. These seats come with safety straps that should be used *every* time you put the baby in it.

>> **High chair:** When your baby starts solids, you're going to need somewhere she can sit to be fed. A wide range of high-chair models is available, from chairs with an ergonomic design made of wood that hasn't been treated with chemicals to chairs with more levers and straps than a space shuttle. Having a detachable tray that you can take off and clean regularly (after every meal!) is essential, as are safety straps so you can be sure she isn't going to wriggle her way out of it and get hurt. As an alternative to a high chair, you may want to use a model that attaches to your table. Later on you can use a little booster seat that you strap to a normal chair.

>> **Swing:** No, this isn't the kind of swing you attach to the apple tree. This kind lives inside your house and takes up about half your living room. Baby swings can be lifesavers if you have a fussy baby because the constant movement soothes him, although watching it — and listening to it squeak and play the same horrific tune over and over — may drive you crazy.

Take a look at Chapter 8 for information about baby slings, front packs, and carriers.

Making Room for the Baby

When you were growing up, do you remember how important your bedroom was? It's more than the place where a child's bed is or where his clothes are stored. It's a child's sanctuary, his own special space that has all the things he loves close by. Although he won't know this for a while yet, you can start creating that individual, happy space for him before he's born. But first we cover what every nursery needs to have.

Finding functional furniture and gear

Crib, bassinet, dresser, changing table, rocking chair, book-shelves, toy boxes — the nursery is one place you can spend a whole bunch of money on all new stuff if you're not careful.

Here are some of the basic items you need to set up a nursery.

Somewhere to sleep

For the first few months, most babies like to sleep in an enclosed space like a bassinet or other small area. Many parents use play yards, which are small playpens that often have a bassinet area that fits on the top, for the first few months.

A bassinet is like a basket on legs. If the bassinet is on wheels, you can move it from room to room easily during the day for naps (babies can sleep anywhere when they're newborns) and wheel it into either your room or the nursery at night. When baby has outgrown the bassinet he can graduate to a crib, where he'll sleep until he's about two or has figured out how to climb out of it.

If you're getting a secondhand crib or bassinet, check it thoroughly to make sure nothing could fall apart and injure your baby. Older cribs may not satisfy current safety regulations, which state that crib rails must be no more than 2⅜ inches apart. You should not be able to fit more than two fingers between the mattress and crib side. Side rails that lower can also be dangerous for your baby.

To find out more about ensuring your baby's safety when sleeping and reducing the risk of SIDS (Sudden Infant Death Syndrome) or SUDI (Sudden Unexplained Death of Infants), check out Chapter 17. Also check out the Consumer Product Safety Commission's website, Safe to Sleep, at `www.cpsc.gov/en/Safety-Education/Safety-Education-Centers/cribs/`.

Somewhere to be changed and dressed

A lot of parents buy changing tables — tables at the right height so you don't have to lean a lot to change baby's diapers or get her dressed. Some experts advocate that babies should be changed on the floor to avoid having baby roll off a changing table, but others just stand by the rule that baby is never left on the table unsupervised — even for a second. Whichever you choose, having a changing mat or a load of cloth diapers to have under her to catch protein spills — pee, poop, or vomit — is essential.

Even if you're going the disposable diaper route, we believe a few packages of cloth diapers are an essential accessory. They can act as changing mats, can be put over your shoulder to catch any baby spit-up when you're burping her, can be used to protect the couch for a quick change, and are handy to clean up spills when you're out and about. They're inexpensive, washable, and very hardy, and every diaper bag should have one or more.

Somewhere to store clothes

You would think that a person so small wouldn't need much room for her clothes, but she grows so big so fast that she needs room to store not only the clothes she currently fits into, but also the ones she grows into. Hand-me-downs and presents from well-meaning friends and family mean clothes are rarely in short supply. Child-sized hangers for her wardrobe can be bought from a houseware or discount store.

TIP

If you're given too many hand-me-down clothes, having a system in place for sizing stops you from feeling overloaded. Have designated boxes for each size and store them in your baby's closet or dresser. As she grows out of one size, you've got another size ready to go. This is a great job for you when your partner goes through a period where she can't organize herself out of a paper bag because of all the hormones going crazy during pregnancy or after birth.

Odds and ends you can't live without

Other things that are handy to have include the following:

>> A diaper bucket with a tight-fitting lid for soaking soiled clothing, bedding, and cloth diapers.

>> A clothes hamper or basket.

>> A rocking chair or armchair where mom can breastfeed or you can give the last bottle of the day before bed. An armchair or rocking chair is also somewhere to share stories, songs, and cuddles as your baby gets bigger. Some moms find chairs without arms most comfortable, so try out a few options. Many come with an ottoman or recline.

>> A pedal trash can with a lid — the big size if you're using disposable diapers. Yes, the pedal is essential!

>> Something to house toys and books, such as a bookshelf or toy box.

>> Diaper cream or powder, wipes, and other toiletries in arm's reach of where you change your baby. (Find out more about these in the later section "Crème de la crèmes.")

>> A lockable medicine box where you store health items like pain-relief medications, a thermometer, and nail clippers (see "Stocking up on health essentials" later in this chapter).

Decorating the nursery

Decorating your baby's room is another way to clean out your wallet in a hurry, as there are thousands of things to put in a little person's room to add personality and style. Expectant moms have been known to get carried away, so you may have to display a bit of good old male shopping rationale. Babies spend a lot of time gazing into space when they're really small, as if they're tuning into a radio show you can't hear, and like looking at high-contrast objects around them, such as black and white shapes. Keep the decorating simple. As your baby develops his taste and his needs change, transforming the nursery into a little child's room won't take a complete overhaul.

Here are our tips for keeping it simple:

>> Keep the colors and designs neutral, so that the room can easily be redecorated as your baby grows. Teddy bear wallpaper may be cute when he's a few months old, but not when he's seven.

>> Use pictures of close friends and family on the walls so your baby can grow up knowing who the important people are.

>> You or your partner may want to make something special for the baby's room, like a painting or piece of embroidery.

>> Mobiles hanging from the ceiling don't need to be fancy. A string of shells hanging from driftwood can entertain a small baby, but make sure anything you hang is extremely durable, so it doesn't fall apart on the baby's head. Also make sure the mobile is well out of baby's reach because small pieces or hanging strings can be a choking or strangling hazard; remove the mobile when he's able to get it to it.

>> Use removable decals on the walls, so they can be easily taken off as baby grows up and out of the nursery themes. Choose things that won't damage the wallpaper or paint.

>> Involve your child in the decoration of his room as he gets older. After all, his room is his space.

Keeping pets and babies safe from one another

A lot of couples have a cat or a dog before baby comes along. The change a little person brings affects the pet's life as well as your own. Your pet will find itself a long way down the pecking order once your cherub is on the scene and will have to put up with pulled fur, loud noises, and being chased in the not-too-distant future.

Show your child how to be gentle with animals and people from the get-go, as well as how to approach dogs with caution. A child should always hold her hand out for a dog to smell and stay still when it comes near so the dog doesn't see her as a threat.

Teach your child not to touch strange animals (almost impossible until she's a bit older) and to wash her hands afterward as animals can carry all sorts of nasties in their fur.

Don't leave your child alone or out of sight with pets. Cats can react badly when your baby decides it's time to "ride the kitty" and may even give junior a scratch or two. If the mantra of being gentle to the cat doesn't warn your child that felines are not to be messed with, then a scratch on the nose most certainly will.

REMEMBER

Dogs and cats can feel neglected when a new baby joins the family, so spend time making them feel settled and happy. Don't move your pet's special sleeping areas or toys away to make room for baby. Try to keep your pet's routines as settled as possible so it doesn't feel left out.

TIP

A great way to keep cats out of your baby's crib is to fill it with balloons during the day. If your cat hasn't encountered balloons yet, chances are it'll go near them only until the first one bursts.

Filling the Changing Table

There's a reason you see a whole aisle of the supermarket dedicated to baby stuff — there's a lot of it, and there are a lot of things to choose from. Parents also make for really easy prey for marketing people. A few sleepless nights and sheer desperation do amazing things to your shopping habits. So taking a good look at all the stuff you can buy before the baby arrives makes the shopping-in-a-hurry experience easier on you later on. Don't worry about buying the wrong diaper cream, teething gel, or diapers. You go through lots of them and have plenty of opportunities to try out different options. But we can help you get a head start.

TIP

Check out Chapter 12 for some great money-saving tips for home-made versions of baby stuff.

The great diaper debate

As a guy, you probably don't think about diapers much. Until you become a dad, that is. Get used to diapers; they will become a major part of your life, because they stand between you and a whole lot of pee and poop.

You can select from three main options when choosing what to wrap your baby's bottom in: cloth diapers that can be washed and used over and over (a diaper service can provide these as well), disposable diapers that you throw away after each change, and hybrids where you throw away some parts and keep the main parts.

Of course, you can go diaper free and practice *elimination communication* if that's your thing (see Chapter 6). This takes more commitment than most dads have, but if you have a lot of free time, it can eliminate a lot of diapers!

Cloth diapers

Cloth diapers have come of age — again. No longer are cloth diapers those scratchy, leaky, bulky cloth things that require a degree in origami to fold into the right shape and hold together with safety pins. Now cloth diapers come already shaped like a baby's actual bottom, and Velcro covers make putting them on and getting them off as easy as a disposable diaper.

TIP

Cloth diapers do require a bit more money upfront plus the time and energy to wash them, but some comparisons show that cloth diapers come out cheaper than disposables. Modern cloth diapers can also be used on more than one child and can be bought in good condition secondhand. Eco-conscious dads can rest assured your child's diapers aren't clogging up landfills for years to come.

Disposable diapers

If you think just changing diapers is gross, having to clean them may be a step too far for you. Disposable diapers mean you never have to clean a diaper. They can be a better option if you're on vacation or for carrying in the day-to-day diaper bag so if your baby needs a change when you're out and about, you don't have to carry a dirty diaper around until you get home. Recently eco-friendly dye-free, latex-free, chemical-free disposables have entered the market. They're now available in most big box stores but may be pricier than the major brands. They're typically made from cornstarch and other sustainable resources, and often don't contain any of the chemicals that keep babies dry but which may cause diaper rash, as well as being bad for the environment.

TIP

Disposable diapers may be right for you if you live in an area where water is scarce. Cloth diapers use a lot of water in rinsing and washing.

Hybrid diapers

Hybrid diapers are made of a washable underpants part and a disposable pad. Hybrid diapers generally require an upfront investment in the pants but tend to work out cheaper in the long run. They come in some pretty cute patterns that may have your partner jonesing to buy some and can double as shorts in the summer.

Crème de la crèmes

Diaper rash is a big concern for most babies from time to time. Diaper rash occurs when the ammonia from baby's stool and urine irritates his skin, making it red and tender, and making him pretty unhappy with life. The easiest way to stop diaper rash in its tracks is to expose the bottom to air and sunlight for a good half an hour a day. Changing his diaper regularly and using a barrier cream or powder can protect his bottom from a nasty rash too.

Like all things baby, you can find an enormous range of diaper creams on the market, and your partner might have a few ideas of what to get. Don't feel overwhelmed by the vast choice of products available. At the end of the day, anything from the supermarket that has zinc oxide in it will do the trick. You can also try using petroleum jelly as a barrier cream.

Manufacturers want you to buy all sorts of other creams to make your little champ smell good, have nice skin, relax, fall asleep better, and so on. By all means, try them out, and if you find one that works really well, keep using it. In general we recommend keeping it simple and using natural oils, which are cheap and effective. Olive, coconut, and almond oil have been known to be particularly effective for most temporary skin irritations and even cradle cap (see Chapter 7 for more about oils and cradle cap).

Stocking up on health essentials

Having an arsenal of potions and lotions on hand in the early months and years is essential. Here's what we think every dad should have in his baby fix-it kit:

» **Almond or coconut oil:** Your baby doesn't need moisturizers or scented lotions. If she has dry skin, pure oil is best without all the toxins and fillers big companies use to preserve their products. Cold-pressed, unrefined vegetable oils made for baby use are best — health food stores may be your best source for these.

» **Antibacterial cream:** Stop infections in cuts and grazes by treating them with antibacterial cream. Ask your healthcare provider for recommendations.

» **Baby wipes and warmer:** This may seem silly to you, but imagine having your butt wiped with a cold, wet piece of paper, and it might make more sense. Wipes makes cleanup easier, and warmers that warm the wipes makes your baby's life more pleasant. Win-win.

» **Child's sunscreen and insect repellent:** These are essential if you live in warm climates and in the summer, but the best form of protection is clothing and keeping out of the sun. Babies' skin is a lot more sensitive than adults' skin, so junior can burn even when he is not exposed to direct sunlight.

>> **Digital thermometer:** If junior is sick with a cold or flu, you can help determine when it's time to whip him off to the doctor by using a digital thermometer to check his temperature. Take your baby's temperature by putting the thermometer under his arm, called the *axillary* temperature, or by using a digital thermometer that fits into the ear canal, if he's older than 6 months. Temporal thermometers that are swept across the forehead can also be used. Most parents break out in a cold sweat at the thought of using a rectal thermometer, but it does give an extremely accurate reading. A reading of 100.4 degrees Fahrenheit or greater is considered a fever, no matter which thermometer you're using.

>> **Nail clippers or baby nail scissors:** Babies can scratch themselves easily, so you need to keep their nails short and neat. This is easier said than done. Try clippers or special baby scissors to see what works best for you. A nail file may also be easier to use on your wiggling baby.

>> **Pain reliever:** Children's acetaminophen or ibuprofen for kids is used for pain and fever after immunizations, teething, and fever when your baby has a cold. Use a plastic syringe with measurements marked on the side to dispense the medication and check with your doctor for the correct dosage (which is worked out by baby's weight).

Aspirin is not suitable for young children and can be dangerous in some cases.

>> **Teething relief:** Teething gels can help soothe a teething baby's gums.

Check with your pediatrician before giving your baby any type of medication if he's younger than six months old. Always check the label on any medical product (or any product, in fact) to make sure it's suitable for your baby's age. If you're unsure whether it's suitable, check with your pediatrician.

Be prepared to keep adding to your household first-aid kit with bandages, scissors, and tweezers as your little one gets older and encounters more little accidents.

Being Prepared for What's Coming

There's so much to do and only nine months to do it in. Along with watching your partner's belly grow and preparing for the biggest change in your life yet, you can do a whole bunch of things to minimize the chaos in your world right now and save yourself a bunch of grief down the line. Here are some ideas.

Finding out about pregnancy and babies

If you thought your school days were over, think again. Parenting education is upon you, and your partner may send you to prenatal classes! While most childbirth education or prenatal classes focus on the birth of your baby, it's a good idea to pick up some tips and tricks about getting through the first few weeks and months. Fortunately there are now many courses available where, as a guy, you feel less awkward — some are designed just for dads.

You may wonder whether you *really* have to go to prenatal classes. The answer is yes — not necessarily because you learn amazing things, but because your partner appreciates it and you can network with other couples and dads who are in the same boat.

Prenatal classes can also help you decide whether to go for a home birth, a hospital birth, or an *elective cesarean,* where you choose to have a cesarean on a particular day.

TIP

Class content varies wildly, so try to shop around early if you can and check what's offered before you sign on the dotted line. Apart from the standard options we mention earlier, you can also find alternative classes or providers by asking your healthcare provider and checking with your friends who have had babies. Your local hospital will almost always provide some type of class, from labor prep to newborn care skills.

If you want to go beyond the basics of baby and child care, you can also check out courses that teach baby massage, baby sign language, and activities with babies.

Getting to the hospital (on time)

You've no doubt seen the movie where Mrs. Pregnant goes into labor and Mr. Pregnant drives like a crazy man to get to the hospital before the baby's born. If you're having a hospital birth rather than a home birth, then some variation of the movie scene could well happen to you. We don't advise driving fast or tearing around corners like a Formula One driver — after all, you want to all arrive in one piece at the hospital. Unlike the movies, a parking space will not magically appear right outside the delivery suite doors, so it pays to do a little investigative work about where you can park before the big day.

TIP

Have some cash in the hospital bag for parking, or check with the hospital when you do your hospital tour to see whether they have any special parking for families in the maternity ward.

You may also want to check some time in advance of the birth that you know how to get to the hospital. Some people do a test run to see how long it takes them. You don't want to be messing around with the GPS or maps on the way there. Your partner may not thank you for having to spend any more time squashed in the car while going through contractions than she has to.

You may also want to consider the following:

>> Does the car have all the necessary bits and pieces of paperwork, such as an up-to-date license, registration, and insurance card?

>> Is the car accessible night and day, or is it blocked in by other cars sometimes?

>> If your car is out of action, is there someone you can call as a back-up?

>> Is there enough gas in the tank to get you there?

>> Do you have a car seat to transport your baby home?

Assembling home birthing equipment

If you're having a hospital birth, you don't need to bring anything to the delivery suite other than your beloved and her hospital bag, which in some instances can be pretty big indeed. But if you're having the birth at home, you need some equipment to prepare for the big day. Your midwife will undoubtedly give you a comprehensive and somewhat daunting list that may include the following items:

>> **A birthing pool:** These can be rented or purchased from private companies; your midwife will probably know of a source. Some can even be used as a paddling pool for your child afterwards.

>> **A container for the placenta,** unless you're burying it in the backyard.

>> **Towels:** These are for cleaning up and wrapping the baby in after birth, and for mom and dad if you've both been in the pool.

>> **Waterproof mats to cover your carpet:** A tarp covered with newspaper and an old blanket or sheets should do it.

Packing the hospital bag(s)

The old conundrum of knowing what to take on vacation and what to leave behind is nothing compared to the quandary of what to take to the hospital when your baby is on her way. Packing the hospital bag is often broken down into three sections — things needed for mom during the birth, things needed for mom after the birth, and things needed for the baby. Things needed for dad often get a bit neglected, because fathers weren't welcome anywhere near the action for a long time. Fortunately times have changed, and chances are you are the best man for the job to get organized about Project Birth. Here are some suggestions for a mom-, baby-, and dad-friendly hospital bag:

What the parents need during the birth

You'll need some or all of the following items for the big event:

- **Camera and batteries:** Make sure you know how to use all the buttons.

- **Cellphone and charger:** Check with the hospital before making phone calls to announce your little one's arrival, because some hospitals don't allow cellphones to be used inside.

- **Music, pictures, and other personal items:** Take anything that you and your partner think will make the labor easier by setting a nice mood. Check with your healthcare providers first, because some hospitals may not allow some personal items in the delivery suite.

- **Snacks and drinks:** Some labors can take a long time (24 hours is not unusual), and it's hard work on mom doing all the pushing and dad doing all that supporting. Nuts, chocolate, energy drinks, power bars, crackers, or whatever you like can be packed in a lunchbox for you to nibble on during the labor. If she's in the hospital, your partner may not be allowed anything more than ice chips, so take your goodies out of her sight to munch or slurp on.

- **The appropriate clothing:** Mom's feet may get cold during a long labor, so pack a pair of nice, comfy, soft socks. If you're having a water birth, you may want to pack a pair of shorts so you can get in the pool too.

There may be a lot of waiting around, so pack a book or something to keep you occupied. However, remember what you're really there for — getting into a good book may not be the best way to spend your time when you're supposed to be supporting your partner.

What mom needs after the birth

In all likelihood, you'll be spending a few hours with your new baby, calling everyone you want to call and feeling a little giddy. You'll probably head home for a shower, something to eat, and some sleep. But mom needs at least these things to help her settle into her stay at the hospital:

» A change of clothes for coming home because it takes some time for a pregnant belly to shrink down enough to fit into pre-pregnancy clothes. Reminding mom of this before she ever leaves the hospital could depress her unnecessarily.

» Lanolin nipple cream that doesn't need to be washed off before breastfeeding.

» Maternity bras and nursing pads in case of leaking breast milk.

» Maternity pads, though these can be supplied by the hospital.

» A pen and notebook for recording a few things after the birth.

» Pajamas or a nightie that opens at the front for breastfeeding, a dressing gown, and slippers. Some women prefer to wear the hospital's gowns at first, so they don't ruin their own gowns with bodily fluids (which are often copious after delivery).

» Soft cotton undies. Pregnant tummies don't disappear immediately, so her maternity undies may be best.

» Usual toiletries your partner would take on vacation, such as a toothbrush, shampoo, cleanser, deodorant, moisturizer, lip balm, contact lens supplies, hair bands and brush, and any medications.

What baby needs after the birth

The little person you'll be taking home will need the following items:

» **Disposable diapers:** Even if you are going to use cloth diapers, *meconium,* the sticky, tarlike stool your baby expels in the first few days after birth, is best handled by disposable diapers as meconium can be hard to get out of cloth ones.

Many hospitals won't give away free diapers to take home anymore, so be prepared and take a few extra for the ride home.

>> **Pacifier:** While a pacifier is probably one of the most commonly known baby accessories, lactation consultants may not be that happy about you giving your little champ a pacifier if you're experiencing breastfeeding difficulties, because pacifiers are believed to cause "nipple confusion" in some cases.

>> **Supplies for bottle feeding:** Formula (newborn), bottles, nipples, and a bottle warmer if you're going to bottle feed.

>> **Blankets:** It's safer to put a blanket over the baby after he's in his car seat than to put a heavy coat on him. It's difficult to tighten the straps enough to keep him safe if he's wearing heavy outer clothing.

>> **Something to wear:** A couple of newborn-sized all-in-ones with feet and long sleeves, some hats, and some socks or booties. Newborns are used to being in a nice hot spa pool and have no way to control their temperature yet, so even in summer they need to be kept warm. You may also have a special "coming home" outfit picked out.

Check with a lactation consultant for any breastfeeding equipment, aids, or remedies your partner may need.

Surviving the baby shower

It's no longer strictly true that baby showers are all about mom, where a bunch of women sit around drinking tea and playing games like "guess what mess is in that diaper." Dads are getting in on the act too. No, not sitting around eating sandwiches and oohing over Aunt Vera's knitted booties, but getting together to mark your transition into fatherhood. It could be going out with friends or a joint occasion with both you and your partner's friends.

We definitely recommend having a "man shower" to celebrate the occasion (and no, your man shower's unlikely to be similar to your bachelor party. Or at least, it better not be).

Working with checklists

In all the excitement of becoming a father, it's really easy to forget stuff, so devise a comprehensive list of everything you think you'll need and put it somewhere you can't miss it. Don't leave it up to your memory — you're bound to forget something.

Your checklist should include:

>> **Car seat:** Do you have a car seat and know how to fit it into your car?

>> **Home birth list:** Mats to protect floors, home birth pool if you want it, towels for yourself and the baby, any other requirements your midwife needs.

>> **Nursery:** Baby has somewhere to sleep and bedding to sleep in, baby has clothes to wear, you have something to store clothes in, baby has diapers and bottom protection, you have something to change baby on.

>> **Pet care:** Who will look after any pets during the birth while you're not at home?

>> **Phone list:** Should include emergency numbers, your healthcare provider, friends, family, and work.

>> **Your hospital bags:** For during the birth, for the hospital stay, and for baby.

>> **Your transport:** Ensure your car has all its paperwork and gas, you know your way to the hospital, you have parking money, and you know where parking is.

REMEMBER

If you've decided on a hospital birth, check out your options (if you have several hospitals to choose from) because standards and facilities vary significantly. Most hospitals offer special tours for pregnant couples to see what the facilities are like and where you need to go on D-day. This tour is really useful because you can check out details and take lots of time to ask everything you ever wanted to know about giving birth in a hospital.

Chapter 5

It's Showtime! Birth

B eing born is, ironically, one of the most dangerous things you do in your life. In third-world countries, just being born or having a baby can be risky. That said, infant mortality rates are at the lowest in history and constantly dropping. In most first-world countries, problems during birth are rare and plenty of help is available if things start to go south during delivery.

But that doesn't mean you can take everything for granted. You need to know what's going on during birth. Knowledge is power, so we've put together this chapter to keep you in the loop. That said, no two births are the same and no one can tell you what's going to happen during the birth of your child. The process may seem a bit random and very drawn out, but usually that's just part of the journey to dadhood.

In this chapter you find out about the different phases and stages of labor, see how to recognize when real labor starts, and discover when to call your care provider. We discuss strategies for making labor less of a pain for your partner and how to keep both of you sane during this trying time. We also give you some advice on keeping your cool at the big moment when your child is born and guide you through the heady first minutes, hours, and days as a father.

The Final Countdown

The nursery is ready, the freezer is stocked with meals, the car seat is installed, and you may be pacing around the house waiting for it all to start happening. It's like sitting in a reception room, waiting for your name to be called so you can finally become a dad. Keep yourself occupied with some last-minute tasks and a bit of brushing up on what happens during and immediately after labor.

Discovering what you need to know about labor

You can't be too prepared for labor. And as you're number one in the pit crew, understanding what's going on is essential. To help you get your head around this momentous occasion, Appendix B outlines terms used in labor and birth to help you understand what's going on.

There's a lot to take in, so here's a quick guide to what generally happens during labor.

Like many good things in life, labor happens in three stages:

>> The **first stage** is when your partner's cervix softens, then widens, called *dilation,* making space for the baby to come through and out of the uterus. The uterus *contracts* at regular intervals, allowing the baby to come through. The contractions become increasingly painful. These are *those* contractions you've heard so much about on movies and TV. The cervix is fully dilated at ten centimeters. For a first birth,

the first stage takes an average of 6 to 14 hours (but can take a day or more), so you can see that your presence with a strong shoulder and heat packs galore will really help.

» The **second stage** is the pushing stage, and ends when the baby actually comes out. The second stage is also helped along by contractions that increase in length and intensity during this stage. Finally, your little one is born!

» The **third stage** is a little less glamorous (as if birth is at all glamorous) and involves the placenta, that lifeline to your baby, being delivered. The placenta is also called *afterbirth*. It takes from five minutes to an hour to appear after the baby does. Most women are too exhausted by this stage, or energized by finally meeting their baby, to notice much about expelling the placenta.

Think that's all there is to it? Nope! The first stage also has three phases, and your partner will probably be too caught up in the moment to recognize them as they happen to her:

» **Latent phase:** Contractions are 5 to 20 minutes apart and become more frequent as they progress. The cervix dilates to about 3 centimeters.

» **Active phase:** This phase is characterized by the cervix dilating from about 3 centimeters to fully dilated. Contractions increase in length and intensity, coming every three to five minutes and lasting around 60 seconds, so your partner doesn't have a lot of downtime to think about anything. It's up to you to recognize what's happening and get things organized. This is usually when getting to the hospital or opening the door for the midwife to deliver your baby at home is right up there on your to-do list.

» **Transition:** Okay, your partner's allowed to lose it now — and probably will. This is the point just before the pushing starts. Contractions are very intense, sometimes overwhelming, and your partner may say things like "I can't do it!" (plus a whole lot of swear words we don't need to list here, including some aimed directly at you. Don't worry — this too shall pass!).

One of the more obvious signs that things are about to kick off is when your partner's water breaks. This usually happens in the most inappropriate situation — but hey, it's all natural, so don't be too embarrassed when the big box store you're browsing through has to call for a "cleanup in aisle one." However, labor doesn't always follow immediately on the heels of membrane rupture. It may, but in some cases labor starts up to 24 hours after her water breaks. Either way, call your doctor or midwife to inform them that her water has broken; in some cases, your doctor may want her to come to the hospital to be checked. Read about more signs of the first stage of labor later in this chapter.

Understanding your role in labor

We've talked a lot about supporting and being there for your partner. So what does "being there" really mean? Ask a lot of dads who have been through the birth of their children and the first answer that may spring to mind is "stand around like an idiot and feel guilty and inadequate." It's easy to feel sidelined when the focus is on your partner and she's in kind of a crabby mood with you, which you would be too if you had seven pounds of person coming out of an orifice. She's focusing on what her body is doing; listening to the coaching and advice of her midwife, nurses, or obstetrician; and coping with pain, hormones, and emotions you can't even begin to imagine (and don't want to).

In general your partner relies on you to sort out a long list of support tasks that you can do with dignity and humility. So if your partner needs a shoulder to hang onto for leverage when she's pushing, give it to her. If she needs three ice chips and a back rub, get them for her. If your partner says she can't do it anymore, tell her with conviction that she can. Being there means taking care of your partner when she needs you to and, most importantly, taking charge when she needs you to. Labor can be totally overwhelming for your partner, and she's vulnerable to every emotion in the book. She's also vulnerable to being pushed around by the hospital system: an obstetrician who may be angling for a cesarean birth when your partner is dead set against it and wants to keep pushing for a bit longer, or an overly pushy lactation consultant who is stressing out your exhausted partner. If something doesn't feel right, you have to make a decision for the good of your partner and baby and advocate on their behalf. It's all about your family, so you get to be "the man who calls the shots" when push comes to shove.

Dads can really make their role count during labor by being

>> **A link to the outside world.** Let friends and family know what's going on, because they'll be eager to hear how the birth's going. You can also be the first to announce to the world that your new son or daughter has arrived — a very special thing to be able to do!

>> **Strong.** Help out where you can by making sure your partner is as comfortable as she can be, is well stocked with whatever makes her comfortable, and is warm or cool enough.

>> **The rational calm voice in the hustle and bustle.** Even when things get stressful or hectic, try to keep your cool on your partner's behalf and advocate for her if things are slipping out of control.

REMEMBER

Take your cues from your partner. Her needs are pretty specific, and she'll let you know about them. But don't try to tell your partner you know how she feels, because you don't. Any complaining (to her) of any sort from your end may not be received well.

THERE'S AN APP FOR THAT

If you have a smartphone, it probably won't surprise you to find out that there are apps specifically designed to monitor the duration and frequency of your partner's screaming (read contractions) during labor. Here are a few current, free apps for smartphones:

- Contraction Master Free (iPhone and Android)

- Contraction Timer (iPhone and Android)

- Easy Contraction Timer (Android)

- Full Term (iPhone and Android)

TIP

Have a standby support person in case labor goes on for a long time, or you desperately need some rest. Talk about who would be suitable with your partner. Perhaps her sister or mother could fill in for you while you have a meal or take a breather. You'll be of very little use if you pass out from exhaustion or starvation.

Getting ready with last-minute preparations

As you count down the days to your partner's due date, you can be feeling all sorts of things — excitement about meeting your baby for the first time, or absolute terror about the reality of your new responsibility. It's okay; we've been there. You may also be a bit worried about how you'll handle the labor, your role in it, and how well your partner will cope. Worrying is okay, and yes, lots of guys cry, pass out, or throw up during labor, which is all part of the journey. Basically just ride it out.

Before the fun starts, double-check (or triple-check) a few things, such as ensuring you've

>> Arranged for someone to look after your pets/plants and clear your mail (you may be gone some time)

>> Briefed people at work, or left handover notes or contact details in case you need to leave suddenly

>> Charged your camera batteries or packed charging cords

>> Got the hospital bags packed and ready to go, even if you're planning a home birth, in case you need to transfer to a hospital in a hurry

>> Made sure the car seat is ready to go and have practiced putting it in and taking it out of the car

>> Stored phone numbers of friends and family on your cellphone and packed your charger

The checklists in Chapter 4 will help you remember anything you may have forgotten.

BRING IT ON!

Though only five percent of babies are born on their due date, passing that magical day without a babe in her arms will probably weigh on your partner's mind. She may have been viewing the due date as the finish line and to go over it without a result may push her to the end of her rope. By now, the less desirable effects of pregnancy, like fluid retention, heartburn, insomnia, weight gain, shortness of breath, waddling, and having that baby kick her insides won't be such a novelty. Your partner wants her body back and your baby out.

There are techniques you can try to help bring on labor and some can even be fun, but none can guarantee results. No doubt everyone you meet who has asked you "Is the baby here yet?" will follow up with one of these ideas. Don't try any of them without discussing it with your partner's care provider first.

- **Drink castor oil.** Drinking castor oil to cause diarrhea is an old-fashioned way of bringing on labor. We don't recommend drinking castor oil because it tastes pretty nasty and may not accomplish anything outside of an uncomfortable case of diarrhea.

- **Have acupuncture or acupressure.** Some people swear by the results of having acupuncture needles or pressure applied to certain points of the body. Others think it's coincidental when labor naturally happens soon after the procedure's done.

- **Have sex.** The *prostaglandin* in your semen may help to *ripen* the cervix, making it ready to dilate.

- **Make your loved one a spicy meal.** The aim is to give your partner diarrhea, which can start contractions. It may just give her more heartburn or abdominal discomfort, though.

- **"Sweep the membranes" or "strip and stretch."** Sometimes called having a "sweep" done, during this rather uncomfortable procedure the midwife or doctor puts their fingers inside the cervix. Once inside, they stretch open the cervix and strip membranes away from it. This is not a do-it-yourself project — ever!

- **Take a walk together.** The rocking motion may help stimulate contractions.

(continued)

(continued)

Your partner isn't considered overdue until 42 weeks after conception. If labor hasn't happened, you can discuss with your care provider if and when to induce the baby. This involves using prostaglandin to ripen the cervix, rupturing the amniotic sac, and using *Pitocin,* a synthetic form of *oxytocin,* to start contractions.

Action! The Process of Labor

Your partner thinks something may be happening. Don't panic. It may be launch time, or it may be a false alarm.

When you think she's in labor

You will have signs that the birth of your baby is not far away, but it can be days or weeks before full-on labor really starts.

Here are some indicators that things are about to get interesting, but you shouldn't get too excited yet:

>> **A bloody show or mucus plug:** The mucus plug that blocks the cervix during pregnancy comes away, along with blood from broken capillaries in the cervix. This usually happens when the cervix begins to dilate slightly and can happen weeks before labor actually starts.

>> **Braxton-Hicks contractions:** These are mild contractions, like a strong period pain or cramps. They're not labor contractions, but may be confused with them.

>> **Intense or increasing back pain:** This pain can also be a sign that things are beginning to happen.

>> **Loose bowel movements:** A few days before labor, the body releases prostaglandins, which help soften the cervix in preparation for dilation. Prostaglandins also cause things to be a bit lax in the bowel department.

Don't worry if none of the things in the preceding list happens before the contractions start. Every labor, birth, and woman is different, so call your care provider if you're not sure about what's happening.

When the first stage of labor begins, it may feel like birth is really happening, but it isn't yet. The difference between the latent phase (also sometimes called early labor) and the active phase (sometimes called active labor) of the first stage of labor is the length and intensity of contractions. If you're still a bit confused about the various stages and phases of labor, check the definitions earlier in this chapter.

Call your midwife, obstetrician, or other caregiver for support. She can give you guidance on whether you need to grab the car keys, settle in for the evening, or stay on full alert with a stopwatch in your hand.

When your partner is really in labor

All aboard the roller coaster get buckled in, because you're in for a real treat. The birth of a child happens everywhere around the world thousands of times a day. And you can bet that every birth happening right now is unique. Lucky you — you get to be part of your baby's story right now. The high of seeing a child born is like nothing on Earth — and you're about to meet *your own* child. How cool is that?

First things first. You'll know your partner is in labor because

>> Contractions are regular, lasting 45–60 seconds, and increasing in frequency.

>> Contractions are getting stronger and your partner may not be able to speak during a contraction.

>> Progressive cervical dilation is occurring.

Time to call your care provider if you haven't already.

Helping your partner through childbirth

Many women spend the latent phase of labor at home, where they're more comfortable and have lots of room to move around. Even if you're planning a hospital birth, it may pay to stay at home for as long as is feasible. Some women who go to the hospital too early tense up because they're at the hospital and later on experience fatigue earlier than if they'd stayed at home longer. Contractions shouldn't be too unmanageable, and you can try these techniques to relieve whatever pain your partner is feeling:

>> Apply a hot water bottle to your partner's lower back where she feels the most pain.

>> Give your partner a gentle back rub with some almond or olive oil.

>> Help her sit up in place if she decides to have epidural anesthesia.

>> Keep your partner moving, if she's up to it. Movement can help labor progress, and gravity means the baby's weight puts pressure on the cervix, helping it to dilate.

>> Run a bath or turn on the shower for your partner. If her water has broken, her care provider may not want her to get in the tub, so ask first.

>> Turn down the lights.

As contractions get stronger and you move into the active phase, transition, and the second stage of labor, you can carry on with these pain-relief techniques. Let your partner guide you as to what she needs. At some points your partner won't have any energy in her body to do anything other than ride out a contraction, especially in the second stage when she's putting everything into pushing the baby out. Holding up your partner's body and letting her lean on you in whatever way she needs helps your partner a lot.

I'LL HAVE WHAT SHE'S HAVING

Meg Ryan may have been faking an orgasm in the hit movie *When Harry Met Sally*, but we doubt the handful of women starring in the documentary *Orgasmic Birth* were. Yes, you heard us. Natural birth advocates Ina May Gaskin and Sheila Kitzinger have long said that birth doesn't have to be about pain and can be so pain free as to be "ecstatic" or even orgasmic. Giving birth at home, in an intimate setting like one in which you'd make love, can be quite a different experience from giving birth in a hospital under bright lights knowing some stranger could walk in at any moment. Women who've had orgasmic births report feeling waves of pleasure with each contraction, which peak again and again. During labor, oxytocin and endorphins flood the body. These hormones are also released during sex.

Having an orgasmic birth shouldn't be the goal for women, advocates say, but it's worth recognizing that labor doesn't have to be a pain. If it happens to your partner — lucky you!

Keeping sane

Labor can take a long time. You may get a chance to have a breather between contractions, or you may not. Giving all your energy to your partner is exhausting, so try to take some time out for yourself as well if you can.

It may help to have some people on speed-dial that you can call if it all becomes too much. Check with your partner before the big day, because it would be terrible to have a person turn up during labor who your partner really doesn't want to see there.

Acceptable things for dads to do during labor include

>> Supporting your partner's decisions — to take pain medication or not, to have an epidural or not

>> Crying when the baby is here

>> Doing some stretching exercises to keep fresh and fend off sleep

- Drinking water

- Eating snacks (not in front of your partner, unless she's allowed to eat, too)

- Fainting (warn the nurses first, so they can move all equipment out of the way)

- Getting some fresh air — as long as it's brief

- Going to the toilet (as long as it's not too often and doesn't take too long)

- Leaving the room because you're about to be sick or faint

The following actions are really in stark contrast to the future super dad you're aiming to be:

- Bringing your best friends or work buddies into the delivery suite

- Doing work on your laptop

- Leaving the hospital to participate in your weekly poker game

- Playing video games on your cellphone

- Sneaking into the birthing suite next door to sip from your pocket flask

- Taking photos of other women in labor

- Telling your partner to keep it down because you're negotiating a business deal on the phone

- Watching your favorite show on TV (unless your partner wants to see it too while she is riding out the contractions)

- Peeing your pants because it's all too emotional

Giving nature a helping hand

Sometimes during labor nature needs help to get your baby out into the world. There are lots of reasons for this: The baby may be in distress, or your partner's health is in jeopardy, or she's exhausted and wants the baby out immediately! None of these interventions can really be anticipated. Keep in touch with your partner, and if she's adamant she doesn't want any intervention, be her advocate.

When the medical equipment comes out, try not to freak out. Some of it can look scarier than it really is. The equipment's going to help you meet your baby sooner rather than later.

Vacuum extraction

A *vacuum extractor* helps pull the baby out of the birth canal. It's used when the baby's head is low in the birth canal but needs an extra bit of oomph to help him along. The baby's heart rate may indicate he's in distress, or his position is making it tricky for him to be born naturally.

A suction cup is put onto the baby's head and your partner may have to have an *episiotomy*, which is a cut to the vaginal opening to make room for the cup to go in. A vacuum delivery can cause swelling to the top of the baby's head, but usually causes little or no trauma to the mother and baby.

Forceps

Forceps look like a scary pair of tongs. They are used to grip the baby's head on both sides and pull him out of the birth canal. Forceps aren't used as often as the vacuum these days because of the risk that the mother's insides can be damaged, not to mention the bruising and risk of damage to the baby's head. An episiotomy is routinely required as well.

Emergency caesarean

The big daddy of medical interventions during labor is the *emergency cesarean.* They're called "emergency" to distinguish them from elective cesareans where you opt for birth this way. All cesareans take place in an operating room, so you'll have to dress for the part by wearing a gown and covering your face and hair (or head, as the case may be.) Your partner is given an *epidural* or *spinal anesthetic* to numb pain (although in some cases the cesarean has to be performed under general anesthesia), and an incision is made in your partner's belly, usually near the pubic bone, known as a bikini cut. The abdominal muscles are parted and the *peritoneal cavity* is opened to make way for the uterus. The uterus is then opened, and the baby and placenta are brought out.

Having a cesarean isn't an "easy" way of having a baby; it's major surgery, and you may not want to look behind the sheet that stops your partner from seeing her insides come out. Having a cesarean also means your partner will take weeks to recover, and she won't be able to drive or lift anything heavy for up to six weeks. She will also be on pain medication and will have to rest a lot as she recovers, and she'll stay in the hospital for four days or so.

REMEMBER

If your partner had her heart set on a vaginal birth or a natural drug-free birth and it hasn't worked out that way, she'll be feeling disappointed and upset with herself. Add this to the hormones rampaging through her body and you have one sad new mom. Give her all the love and support you can muster right now; she needs you.

The Big Moment Has Arrived

The moment your child is born is a peak experience that's difficult to describe — totally unique, beautiful, and out of this world. Enjoy it. You may find yourself shedding a tear or two at this important moment. Don't hold back, being emotional is totally cool and you're definitely not a lesser man for it (quite the opposite in fact, we think). Cherish this snapshot in time because the moment you lay eyes on your child for the first time can't be rehearsed or repeated.

Cutting the cord

Dad — because that's what you are now — this is your chance to shine. You now have another important job to do, should you choose to accept it, and if your care provider offers. (Complications right after birth might make this unadvisable.) After the baby is born and she is coping on her own without help from mom, the umbilical cord is clamped and set up for you to cut. This small task can take on several significant meanings for your new family. For your partner, cutting the cord can represent the end of her pregnancy and the start of motherhood. For you it may symbolize your part in your new family. Most importantly for your little one, cutting the cord symbolizes a point in time where all life support systems from mom are cut off and his body has to sustain him. Cutting the cord is a big deal, so embrace the significance and enjoy the procedure.

TIP

The cord is really rather thick and gnarly, so apply some elbow grease and give it a good strong cut. You may want to ask your nurse, midwife, or other support person to take a photo.

When time stops: Meeting your baby

So you're looking at your child for the first time. It can be incredible, scary, bewildering, and amazing, all in the space of a few seconds. Time seems to stop as you feel all these emotions washing over you.

Take a moment now to have a good look at what's been cooking for nine months — little fingers, little toes — as mom may have her hands full being taken care of by medical staff right now.

Notice all his little features and enjoy the amazing sight of a newborn baby. Typically there is no rush anymore once your baby has been checked and is handed to you. So you can easily take some time out to make your first acquaintance with the little one. What a great start to a lifelong bond. As dads you often get to spend time with your little ones first! How cool is that?

Keeping your cool

It's been a long day or two. You've let your partner and your midwife or doctor guide you through the process, and you have to admit to yourself you've been a pretty damn awesome support crew. You've advocated for your partner, you've kept her well stocked with whatever she needed, and she's right now looking forward to some cuddle time with your baby and a good rest. But you may find the demands of the system — your healthcare provider needs to zip off to another appointment before you're ready, you can't be transferred from the delivery suite to the ward because of paperwork — will override you right now, so keep advocating for your partner and child if they need it.

Welcoming Your Baby to the Real World

It may be tempting once baby has finally arrived to think that the hard work is over. You may be gazing blissfully at your new baby, frantically calling family, or tempted to run to the shop for cigars. Cool it for a few minutes more, because there's more stuff to get through.

What happens immediately after birth

Making sure your new baby is in good health is top priority. Most likely, your baby has come out a rather scary shade of blue or gray, but within a few minutes of breathing actual air, she starts to take on a rosier complexion. She's covered in vernix, the waxy coating that protected her skin in the womb. Your baby may even have a pointy head, caused by her soft baby skull plates moving as she came down the birth canal. Yes, babies can be a bit of a sight when they first emerge into the world! Some babies howl when they're born. Others just like to take things a bit more quietly and have a look around first.

If your baby needs a bit of help breathing, your caregiver may massage her back with a warm cloth, or suction fluid from her mouth or nose. Don't worry; she'll be just fine and pinking up within a minute or so.

At one minute after birth and five minutes after birth, your care provider does an *Apgar test* on your little one, giving her an *Apgar score* on a scale of one to ten, one being lowest and ten being highest. There are five criteria for your little miss to jump through: color, pulse rate, reflexes, muscle tone, and breathing. This test alerts your care provider to any concerns about the baby's health. After her first test, your caregiver or nurse dries your baby and hopefully hands her over to mom for some skin-on-skin time before anything else. Hospital policies vary on this, but in the user-friendly environment hospitals are trying to create, asking will usually get you what you want, as long as it's safe for mom and baby.

Within a few minutes, your baby is breathing and surviving on her own. The umbilical cord stops pulsating, which means your caregiver will clamp it in two places and get it ready for cutting. This is your turn to shine, dad.

Your baby is then measured and weighed. Those details go into your child's personal health book. Most places take a footprint from baby, and often a thumbprint from mom as well. Check with your caregiver if you would like to do one to keep, either in your baby book or on a keepsake.

TIP

While baby is snuggling with mom (or dad if mom's too worn out), your caregiver puts a plastic band around her ankle or wrist — or both — with your names, date of birth, and weight. These can become mementos of your baby's birth when they come off a few days later. In most places, mom gets a matching bracelet.

The first few hours

Once all the commotion has died down, there are a few practical matters to attend to. Have you started calling friends and family yet? Mom and baby usually have a bit of skin-on-skin time and get to know each other a bit first, then have something to eat. Yep — feeding your baby is going to be mom's number-one priority for some time, so they may as well get right into it now. Your care provider helps mom and baby get comfy with a first breastfeed, or if you've decided to bottle feed, helps with the mechanics of getting your little one taking her bottle.

Once that's all taken care of, getting baby dressed and getting mom into clean, comfortable clothes and bed are next on the agenda. Mom will be pretty tired, so you may need to give her a hand standing up and getting about, especially if she's had an epidural during labor. Or it may be your turn to get to know your baby a bit better while your partner's occupied.

A bit of food and drink for mom is usually in order now, too. It's been a long time since either of you had a decent meal. Taking care of any food cravings your partner couldn't eat while being pregnant may also be high on the agenda. That said, all you may feel like is some well-deserved rest. If you are in a hospital, see to it that any formalities are dealt with quickly so you, your partner, and your little one can get some rest.

The first few days

Many parents have been lulled into thinking their baby is an angel in the first 24 hours. Babies can be very sleepy and settled for the first day, and you may be fooled! But it's also a very busy time getting feeding established and finding your feet in your new role as dad. Your baby should be having about six feedings in a 24-hour period to start off with, so supporting mom by taking care of diaper changes, burping, or anything else that needs attending to can help her out a lot. If mom is still in the hospital, you can be a real hero dad for spending as much time as possible with the baby so your partner can rest some more. Many hospitals have 24-hour rooming-in for dads.

Meconium

Your perfect, cute little bundle will produce the foulest, stickiest, goopiest poop imaginable in the first few days of life. This black tar is called *meconium,* and it's perfectly normal. Meconium is nature's way of flushing out all the various fluids and contents of your baby's intestines. The meconium is gone within a few days. After that your baby's poop should turn to a strange orangey-yellow color. The great news is a newborn's stool hardly smells, easing you gently into the changing soiled diapers routine.

Going home

If your baby was born in the hospital, your care provider and the hospital decide when your partner and baby can go home. For some new moms, going home can't come fast enough. Other moms may feel they need longer in the hospital for the support a 24-hour on-call care provider brings, or they may not feel physically up to leaving the hospital, depending on how the birth went.

Don't let the hospital push you out if you're not ready for it. Talk about your concerns with your caregiver, but keep in mind that you can't stay in the relative safety of the hospital forever!

Blues

About day three after birth, mom may be feeling a bit low. This is perfectly normal and will pass. Your partner may burst into tears for no reason (that she can tell you anyway) or just feel overwhelmed by responsibility. If your partner had a hard pregnancy and is looking forward to getting her body back, finding it isn't "back" yet may be very disappointing. Chances are your partner will also be sore in all sorts of places and performing simple personal hygiene tasks or even just going to the toilet can be really tricky. Do your dad thing and try to support your partner by helping out, telling her she's awesome, and enjoying your baby. By the way, these initial blues have nothing to do with postpartum depression, which is likely to come later if you or your partner ends up experiencing it. See Chapter 7 for more on postpartum depression.

The First Year

2

IN THIS PART . . .

Who's your baby? Now you know! Find out how to take care of your newborn.

Get tips on surviving the first three months of your baby's life.

Keep up with your baby's changes from months three to six.

Handle parenthood from months six to twelve.

Chapter 6

Being Dad to a Newborn

Your baby is finally here. Does being a dad feel "real" now? If not, don't worry. The first few days and weeks after birth can feel surreal. It does get better though. If you felt a bit left out during pregnancy and birth, now is your time to show your worth. Your baby is here and needs time with dad, as much time as possible. Realizing that your baby is an actual person and that you're responsible for her now can also be quite daunting.

Every baby is different and every family is different. While this book is designed to take some of the mystery out of your mysterious newborn, no one can tell you how to take care of your baby as well as you can. In the coming days, weeks, and months, you'll discover how to read your baby like no child-care professional, doctor, or midwife ever will. Yes, babies have similarities and outside help is there if you need it, but finding out how to read your baby is a skill you develop on your own. Every dad does.

In this chapter we give you some shortcuts on your journey to being a great dad with guides to the practical aspects of baby care, like changing diapers, dressing, and bathing your baby. You get the lowdown on feeding, sleeping, burping, and dealing with crying. We also talk about how having a baby shakes things up in your life like nothing else can and look at ways to cope with that change.

Dealing with the Aftershock

Starting out with your new baby — a vulnerable, unfathomable being — is a scary experience. Stepping through the door with your little bundle as you come home from the hospital, or waving goodbye to the midwife if your baby was born at home, are momentous steps on the path to becoming a family. You may feel overwhelmed flying solo with your partner and the new baby, but that's quite normal. Every parent in the world is probably feeling the same. Don't stress; simply take each day as it comes.

It's life but not as you know it

Remember when you slept in on the weekend, had a leisurely brunch with your partner, and then went for a walk, taking just the house keys and your wallet? You'll be able to do that again, but not for many years. Getting your head around how life works now can be a struggle, but that's where dads can shine once more. As dads, we're great at adapting quickly to new situations and making the best out of any challenge we face (say "yes!").

Looking after a newborn is literally a 24-hour, seven-day-a-week job, and it's exhausting. Expect your baby to sleep a lot in the first couple of days — it usually takes babies a few days to "come to life," so don't let her frequent sleep schedule in the hospital lull you into thinking you've got the perfect child. She may wake up with a vengeance the minute you walk through the front door!

But good baby or not so good, she needs a feeding every two to four hours, so even at night she'll be waking up. Even if your partner is breastfeeding, you don't get off night duty. You can help by doing any diaper changes and burping so your partner doesn't feel she's doing everything. If you're bottle feeding, you can take turns so at least one of you gets a decent stretch of rest. Of course, if you go right back to work — not recommended if you can get a few weeks off for paternity leave — you may need to sleep during the week most nights and maybe do more weekend duty.

You may already be tired from supporting your partner after a long labor and birth, and because your baby is waking every few hours, you're not getting a good eight hours of sleep like you used to. You can't catch up on the sleep you've missed, but you can minimize your own exhaustion by resting when the baby sleeps. This goes for both you and your partner in these heady first days. It may pay to get used to the idea of taking turns for everything. While one of you is busy, the other should rest or catch up on some much-needed sleep. Here's a perfect opportunity to shine as a dad by sharing the load with mom. Remember — apart from breastfeeding, dads can do everything a baby needs done, and there is no natural disadvantage or disposition. You are just as qualified at handling a newborn as mom. In other words, you both don't know much and are learning as you go.

Any information you've read about caring for babies tells you there are lots of chores to do in the first weeks. That's not necessarily true. On days where everything goes smoothly — baby wakes, has a feeding, is burped, gurgles cutely for a bit, and then goes down for a nap without a whimper — you may wonder what all the fuss was about and sit around twiddling your thumbs. But not every day goes smoothly. And not every cycle of feeding, burping, and sleeping goes smoothly in a day. At any point the following may happen:

>> Baby's diaper overflows or leaks, necessitating not just a bath and clothing change — for both of you — but also a rug shampooing.

>> Your baby shows symptoms you decide to have checked by your healthcare provider.

>> Your baby spits up or vomits — copiously — after a feeding. As with a diaper change, this can set off a complete cleaning job.

Whenever you suddenly have to deal with something unexpected, your plan for the day is disrupted. Get used to it, as it happens a lot with children. Life becomes a lot less predictable, and plans go awry. But we think unpredictability's a good thing, and you can enjoy it rather than choose to be a victim of it.

Expect to have to change your baby's clothes (and yours) frequently, clean the carpet or furniture, or visit the after-hours clinic. Your baby also may have days where she just refuses to sleep or cries incessantly — which is a special kind of torture — and you could end up spending an entire day or night rocking her, walking her in a stroller, or carrying her in a sling just to get some peace. If there's one thing you can count on with newborns, it's to expect the unexpected.

Take offers of help whenever you can. Grandmas are often chomping at the bit to come and help for a week or two, so let them, if you can do so without getting on each other's nerves too badly. Having a neighbor or friend close to you who you can call when things are trying and who understands you're running on empty is also very handy. You could ask your support people to drop off a meal for the two of you, take over pushing the stroller while you sit in the backyard away from the crying, or do a load of laundry. A few hours' break from the baby can make all the difference.

If you feel you're at the end of your rope, don't despair. Get someone to give you a break for a couple of hours and chances are you'll feel much better.

Meet the baby

It can be easy to fall into the trap of letting mom take care of everything to do with the baby. This is really easy to do as some new moms have a tendency to "take over" and secretly or unconsciously harbor the belief that dads are somewhat inadequate when it comes to dealing with babies. Of course this is not so. There's no reason to compete to see who is better at looking after a baby. In some cases, you may have to suggest that your partner go away — nicely, of course — and do something else while you look after the baby.

We highly recommend you take care of baby from the beginning so you become more and more confident at handling your baby. You can consider yourself "graduated" from dad school when you are perfectly happy to spend an entire day alone with your little one.

If you develop a mindset of seeing your baby as a developing person who needs your help every step of the way, rather than a source of work and chores, you're already a winner in becoming a future super dad. If you've decided to adhere to a strict routine or the baby is unsettled or unwell, seeing him as a problem that needs to be fixed or a timetable that needs to be met can be tempting. He may seem like a blob that just eats, poops, and sleeps, but a lot's going on inside that little baby right now. Although he can't show you quite yet, he's getting to know you, too.

Babies don't generally smile until six weeks, although they can appear to be smiling, which is nice even if it is uncontrolled. You'll know when the smile is intentional. He'll look you in the eye and his face will light up like you're the best thing he's ever seen, which of course you are. In the early weeks your newborn will stare at you, checking out your face, learning the sound of your voice, and snuggling into you for snoozes. These are important bonding times.

When your baby holds your gaze and checks you out in detail, a lot of developmental work is happening in his brain. Give him every opportunity to look at you without feeling like you have to do something else to entertain him, like jiggling him around or throwing him up in the air. Breastfeeding moms have the advantage that this happens naturally during feedings, so you need to carve out some extra time with baby to get your fair share of baby time.

TIP

Be a 100-percent dad. Do the full spectrum of care tasks — changing your daughter's diapers, bathing her, and wiping spit-up off your shoulder — in the first few days, because that's how your baby bonds with you. Performing these tasks tends to give you a different perspective on life, and after a while you may find that little dramas like baby poop on the carpet are really no big deal.

You've got the blues, too

Expect mom to shed some tears in the first week. Hormones are playing war games in her body right now, and she'll be up and down like a yo-yo. Sometimes the best you can do is to listen, remain calm even if she yells at you, and stay positive at all times. These are just clouds passing, and chances are her mood will change in a few hours. So don't sweat the small quarrels, emotional outbursts, or little annoyances.

YOUNG DADS

Being a father, no matter the age when you become one, is about commitment — commitment to being there for a new young life, guiding that new person toward adulthood and independence. For young men who find themselves becoming fathers, the commitment is no different, although without the advantages of age and maturity, fatherhood can be even more of a challenge.

In addition, your relationship with the mother may not be a stable one, your parents may think you're too young and therefore not prepared to be a father, and there may be tension between your family and the mother's. Some people may think it's better not to have the baby at all.

But the more you show you're committed, the more people will respect your determination, and the more your baby will feel the love and security having a father brings. You can show your commitment by being involved with your baby from the day you find out your partner is pregnant. Go to pregnancy checkups and prenatal classes, start making arrangements for how you'll financially support your partner and child, and show that you're man enough for this very important job. Enlist the support of both your and your partner's families.

To be legally recognized as the baby's father, you need to have your name on the child's birth certificate. Doing so makes it easier for you to have access to him if your relationship with his mother breaks down.

For online info about young dads, take a look at http://goodmen project.com/ethics-values/teen-fathers-typical-day-andrew-smiler-hesaid/.

What you may not know is that dads can get the blues after birth too. At these times communicating well with your partner about what you're going through is really important.

Sometimes the blues can morph into postpartum depression, a serious mental health issue for new parents. Have a look at Chapter 7 for more about postpartum depression.

Looking after a Newborn

So now that you've got the baby, what do you do with him? How do you look after him? Feeling responsible for a new person can be hugely overwhelming, but babies are pretty straightforward. All they really need is love, food, warmth, sleep, and a clean pair of pants.

In general, newborns exist in a 24-hour cycle of sleeping, feeding, being awake, and sleeping again. Your baby tires very easily and is awake for only about an hour or so at a time. A large chunk of that time he's being fed, burped, and changed if necessary, but there's time for a bit of interaction with dad, like story time (tell him anything you want — he loves to hear your voice), a few songs, or even a walk outside together before the next nap time.

REMEMBER

You'll usually see your baby's healthcare provider (usually a pediatrician) in the first few weeks after the birth to monitor your baby's growth and your partner's well-being, and to see how you're getting on in your new lives as a family. Your partner will also see her obstetrician or other healthcare provider around 6 weeks after birth. So if you ever feel you don't know where to turn or who to turn to, your healthcare providers should be your first port of call.

See the contact details in Appendix A for people to call in your area. Help isn't far away.

TIP

Get a fridge magnet (or make yourself one) with phone numbers of your healthcare provider, community health nurse, or breastfeeding organization. Phone numbers of national health organizations such as Le Leche League are listed in Appendix A.

Getting your hands dirty

In your role of dad you get to master a few practical jobs that are probably entirely new to you — until now.

Diaper changing 101

There's no magic to changing a diaper; they're actually really easy to change (see Figure 6-1). Being prepared before you start is the key, as is keeping cool when the diaper you're taking off is fuller than you thought it was. To change a diaper, you need

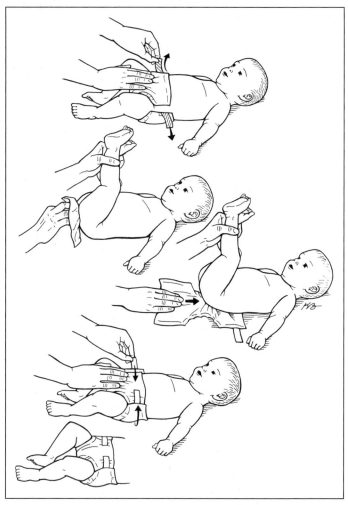

Illustration by Kathryn Born, MA

FIGURE 6-1: How to change a diaper.

>> A changing table or changing mat on the floor, bed, or sofa where you have lots of space around you and good access to your baby lying in front of you

>> A clean diaper and diaper cream or powder ready to go

>> A small plastic bag to put the soiled diaper in

>> Baby wipes or a bowl of warm water and some cotton wool or cloth standing by to wash baby's bottom

>> Towels or extra cloth diapers within reach just in case there's a last-minute explosion or leak while her diaper is off.

REMEMBER

To minimize the risk of your baby falling from the bed or changing table while you change him, either keep a hand on him at all times or change him on a mat on the floor.

TIP

If you're a gadget dad, you may want to check out baby wipe warmers. Often baby wipes can feel really cold to a baby, so these devices help to warm the wipes.

As we talk about in Chapter 5, your baby's first poop is called meconium and it's unforgettable — sticky, greenish-black, and tar-like. Your baby's stools gradually change color as her digestive system is cleaned out and she adjusts to her new food.

>> **Breastfed baby stools** are runnier than meconium and an orange-yellow color. Breastfed stool has a sweetish odor.

>> **Formula-fed baby stools** are firmer and a green-mustard color. Formula stools have a stronger, less agreeable odor.

If you're reading this before you've had your baby, it may seem very odd to be talking about the color and consistency of baby poop. However, you'll probably find stool discussions become part of your new social chitchat with your partner and other parents.

REMEMBER

To help prevent diaper rash, give your baby some pants-free time each day if you can. Leave the diaper off so the skin can be exposed to the air and light. Use a diaper cream when she has a diaper on to protect her skin. See the section about creams in Chapter 4 for more information.

ELIMINATION COMMUNICATION

The practice of elimination communication (EC), also known as infant potty training or natural infant hygiene, means dispensing with diapers and reading your baby's cues to tell you when he needs to relieve himself. You simply learn when junior needs to go and pop him on the potty. Using sounds like "ssss" and getting him used to specific places where he can "go potty" can also act as a cue that triggers your child to relieve himself.

Those who practice EC say it empowers children by letting them take charge of their own toilet training, encourages a stronger bond between parent and child as you learn to understand your child's needs and cues better, and makes your baby feel more secure because she knows you'll take care of her when she needs you to.

Practicing EC doesn't mean you have to go the whole hog and be diaper-free completely — many parents try EC only when they're outdoors, or only during the day. Others encourage potty use at set times of the day, such as right after waking up, or before or after a bath. If you're interested in giving EC a try, take your time and see what works for you. Being watchful and conscious of your child's cues is the first place you'll need to start. Be prepared with a potty and some old cloth nappies to take care of accidents.

Take a look at http://ecsimplified.com/ or www.diaperfree baby.org/ for more information.

Bathing

Babies don't need baths every day, but a cleaning of the face and neck where dribbled and regurgitated milk can collect is a good idea on the days you don't give a bath. Wash around her bottom with every diaper change to prevent diaper rash. Some babies don't like to be naked for long; others love being in the water.

REMEMBER

For babies who aren't fond of a bath yet, sponge baths are an option. Simply wipe him off with a soft, damp cloth, emphasizing his face, neck, hands, and bottom.

Holding your newborn securely at all times when you're bathing him is important — you'll both feel more secure that way. The best way is to hold him around the shoulders so that your forearm is supporting his head and your hand is holding the shoulder farthest away from you. Hold on tight — he can be a wriggly little monster even at this young age.

Here are some tips for bathing your little one:

>> Check the temperature of the bath with your elbow. The water should be lukewarm; that is, if the water feels hot, it's too hot, and if it feels cold, it's too cold. You can also check the temperature with a bath thermometer; aim for a temperature just above 100 degrees Fahrenheit. You can buy little plastic toys that hold thermometers to monitor the bath temperature.

>> Ensure the room temperature is quite warm. Your baby is naked and wet, so she can feel quite cold even when you feel perfectly fine in your clothes, especially when her head is wet for extended periods (try washing the head last).

>> Collect everything you need before you start — a washcloth; a towel; and soap, shampoo, or body wash made for babies.

>> Gunk can collect in all those rolls he's sporting on his legs and arms, so give them a wipe. The same goes for his hands, so uncurl his little fists to wipe his palms. Pay particular attention to the neck. Spilled milk rolls down the neck and can sneak into that chubby triple chin he's got at the moment.

>> Wash his face, hair, and neck where milk often collects with a soft cloth.

>> When cleaning baby girls' bottoms, wipe from front to back. You don't need to pull back your little boy's foreskin to wash underneath either, if he's not circumcised. If he's circumcised, the tip of the penis may look a little raw at first or turn yellowish as it heals. Call your healthcare provider if anything about it freaks you out.

>> When wiping junior's face, wipe his eyes from inner to outer corners using cooled boiled water and cotton wool. This helps prevent an eye infection. If he has a sticky eye, as is

common in the first weeks after birth, you can also use cooled boiled water and gently wipe his eyes from inner to outer. You may want to do this before giving him a full bath, while he's still got his clothes on. Don't expect him to like this or cooperate — a second pair of hands to hold his head still may be helpful.

Take a cordless phone or cellphone with you when you bathe your baby. You can never leave a baby unattended in the bath (he can drown in a few inches of water). Sometimes you may find you've forgotten something or need help. A phone is really handy if your partner or another person is elsewhere in the house — you can call her!

Your baby sports a little stump of umbilical cord for about five to ten days after birth. The stump is kind of shriveled and not that appealing to look at, but it needs to be kept dry and clean to prevent infection. All you have to do is wash it with cotton swabs or balls and warm water when bathing baby or changing her diaper, and pat it dry. Your healthcare provider should give you instructions on care. Fold down the front of her diaper to prevent the diaper from rubbing against the cord and irritating it. Some newborn diapers have a cutout area specifically for this purpose. If in doubt about the cord, call your midwife or doctor.

Dressing

Newborns aren't big fans of getting dressed and undressed, so keep clothing simple. Having a pile of sleep suits with snaps or a zipper down the front is perfect for these early days when baby is in and out of bed or having his diaper changed a lot during the day.

In general, your baby should be wearing one more layer than you. If you're not sure how hot or cold your baby is, put a finger down the back of his neck. He should feel warm rather than too hot or cold. Newborns often have cooler hands and feet, which is why sleepers with feet are nice to have.

If your newborn seems irritated by something, it can be as simple as a scratchy label rubbing her neck or a thread wrapping itself round her toe. It may be a good idea to cut off labels, especially if they feel rough or scratchy. Fortunately, many manufacturers now print information on the material itself, eliminating tags altogether.

Feeding . . . and feeding . . . and feeding

Feeding your baby to help her grow and be healthy is an absolute given. But how do you feed her and when?

Breast or formula?

The World Health Organization recommends breastfeeding as the best way to provide nutrition for a baby. Breast milk is the ideal food for your baby for the first six months of her life, providing targeted nutrition for her age and boosting her immunity. Breast milk is always at the right temperature and generally readily available. Breastfeeding encourages bonding between mother and baby, and last but not least, breast milk is free.

However, this isn't an ideal world, and sometimes the situation just doesn't allow breastfeeding to work. Breastfeeding may not work for your family for many reasons. That's okay — there's an alternative to breastfeeding. Formula is a milk substitute — babies under one year should never have actual cow's milk — with added vitamins and nutrients to support growth and development, and plenty of babies thrive on it.

Whatever you and your partner decide to feed your baby, there are pros to both breastfeeding and formula. In some cases, both breast milk and formula can be fed to your baby, which means dads get more time in the feeding seat. Breastfeeding moms can also express milk using a breast pump, which means you can help with the feeding even if there's not a can of formula to be seen.

As a dad, you can get out your advocating shoes again and support your partner in whichever method of feeding she prefers. If your partner has given breastfeeding her best shot but it hasn't worked out, it can be tough emotionally for her. Your partner may feel like a failure, or less like a "real" mother to her child. She may be sensitive to the opinions of others around her, family and health professionals included, who don't understand the decision. Don't worry about the opinions of others; you don't have to justify yourself to anyone. Be confident that you're doing the best for your family.

TIP

Before deciding what and how to feed your baby, get as much information as you can so you're fully informed of the choices and their implications.

Bottle feeding

If you're bottle feeding, you need the following gear:

>> **Bottles and nipples:** There are numerous baby feeding "systems," so check them all out before buying the first one you see.

>> **A way to clean the bottles and nipples:** A bottle brush works to get inside the bottle. You don't have to sterilize bottles anymore.

Formula should be made up right before a feeding according to the instructions on the can or container. Have a supply of bottles and nipples ready to go for when your baby's hungry, to save time — and your eardrums.

TIP

Even if your partner's breastfeeding, getting the bottle feeding equipment anyway is a good idea. Your partner may want to express breast milk, in which case you'll need the equipment listed for bottle feeding.

REMEMBER

Feeding your baby is about creating a nurturing relationship between you and your child, as well as food. Your baby is held close when being breastfed, and the same should go for bottle feeding too. You can hold your baby in the same loving way as if she were breastfed, sing to her, or have a little chat while she feeds. You'll find she gazes up at you adoringly and checks out every little nook of your face.

WARNING

Never, ever prop a baby bottle. Your baby could choke and aspirate formula, causing a potentially life-threatening situation.

How much and when?

Newborn babies love to eat. They grow rapidly and their stomachs are small, so they need regular feedings to keep them tanked up. Having regular feedings also encourages milk production. If your partner is breastfeeding, her milk supply adjusts to meet baby's demand.

Your baby tells you when she is hungry by

>> Opening her mouth and thrusting her head to the side, as if rooting around to find your partner's breast.

>> Sucking her fists or clothing.

>> Crying, which is a late sign of hunger and means feed me now or else! Try not to let your baby get to this state before feeding her.

A good sign that you're on the right track with feeding your baby is that he's putting on about the right amount of weight for his age. Babies usually lose weight in the first two weeks after birth. After the first few weeks, baby usually gains around ½ pound per week. Don't worry; this rate slows as they get older.

REMEMBER

Newborns usually need to be fed every two to three hours, or about eight to ten times in a 24-hour period. You'll know your baby is getting enough to eat because she'll have at least six to eight wet diapers a day; her urine will be light yellow, not dark; and her stools will be soft. If you're concerned, call your health-care provider.

Burping it up

Bringing up a good hearty belch may come naturally to you, but for baby, whose digestive system is still immature, a bit of air caught in her tummy or gut needs help to come out or it can be very painful. Usually a gentle pat on the back or a gentle rub counterclockwise does the trick. Your demure little princess will come out with a burp to make you proud.

You can use three good positions to burp your baby (see Figure 6-2):

>> On your lap with baby facing down

>> Sitting on your thigh facing out

>> Over the shoulder, with baby's head held upright on your shoulder

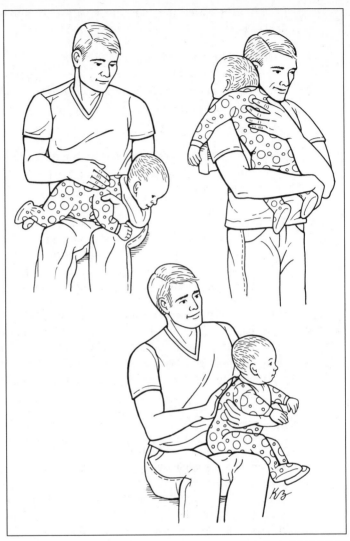

Illustration by Kathryn Born, MA

FIGURE 6-2: Three good positions for burping your baby.

Don't forget to support baby's wobbly head. To protect yourself against any spit-up, drape a flat cloth diaper or receiving blanket over your shoulder or lap.

TIP

Your healthcare provider may suggest trying drops that help reduce gas production and discomfort. Babies that cry more also suck down more air, which distends the abdomen and causes discomfort. A baby who spits up frequently or writhes and cries after a feeding may be suffering from reflux, a painful sensation caused by the regurgitation of gastric acid. See Chapter 7 for more information about reflux.

Sleeping — you and the baby

Newborns wake regularly in the night and day for food, so getting a good eight-hour stretch of sleep is unlikely at this stage. As he gets older, your baby will sleep for longer chunks at night and will stay awake longer during the day.

Your baby tells you he's tired by

>> Fussing or whining

>> Jerky, tense movements

>> Rubbing his eyes

>> Staring into space or turning away

>> Yawning

Crying is a late sign of tiredness and may mean your baby is overtired. When baby is overtired, he may be more difficult to settle as he's wound up about being tired.

IT'S ALL A MATTER OF STYLE

When you feed your baby can be just as controversial as *what* you feed your baby. Most healthcare providers today advocate *demand feeding,* which is letting the baby determine when she is fed rather than feeding her according to a schedule. If at all possible, demand feeding is best for your baby and gives her a sense of security that her needs will be met.

Teaching your baby about night and day

Babies don't have a sense of day and night when they're born, so part of your role as dad is to teach them the difference. Babies usually follow a cycle of sleeping, feeding, burping, changing, playing, and sleeping again during the day, but you can leave out the playing at night. Where you are animated and chatty in the day, you are all business at night, keeping baby's room dimly lit for feedings and diaper changes, and putting him straight back to bed when you're done. Changing your baby into day clothes during the day can help signal that night is over.

Having a bedtime routine can help signal that night is on the way and that's the time for sleeping (see Chapter 8).

Settling your baby

There are as many approaches to getting baby to sleep as there are children! How you get your baby to sleep is perhaps the most controversial topic. Strategies range from the cry-it-out approach where you put your baby down for a sleep in a bassinet or crib and let him cry until he falls asleep, to the attachment parenting philosophy of keeping baby in close contact with a parent in a sling or pouch to sleep and having him sleep in a bed attached to yours at night.

Other parents use a technique called *controlled crying*, where baby is left to cry for a short period of time, say a couple of minutes, before being soothed and comforted, then left for a slightly longer period. The length of time between visits is stretched out, and eventually baby goes to sleep.

Some parenting experts warn against rocking your baby to sleep or doing anything where she falls asleep as a result of parent intervention, as baby becomes dependent on that technique to sleep. Putting your baby down sleepy but awake and letting her fall asleep on her own teaches her good sleep habits.

The settling approach you and your partner use is up to you. Decide what approach works best for your family.

TIP

Reach an agreement with your partner before deciding which technique, method, or routine to follow. Using different approaches tends not to work.

REMEMBER

If you're having severe trouble settling your baby for days or weeks on end, calling your healthcare provider, breastfeeding group, or other moms may be helpful. Your own mom may also have a thing or two to teach you, but remember to take what you like and leave the rest! This is *your* baby.

Swaddling

One technique for helping babies to sleep is swaddling, which involves wrapping a light blanket around the baby to keep him snug (see Figure 6-3). Swaddling also helps control the Moro reflex, which is when your little one seems to startle or jump out of his skin for no reason at all!

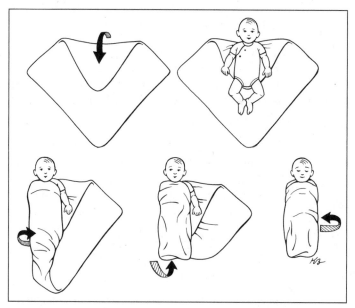

Illustration by Kathryn Born, MA

FIGURE 6-3: How to swaddle a baby.

Crying — you, your partner, and the baby

At some stage crying is bound to take place in your household. A healthy baby may cry for several hours a day (or more). Crying is your baby's way of telling you he's hungry, lonely, tired, gassy, too hot, or in need of a diaper change. Sometimes he cries for no apparent reason at all.

Trying to figure out what the problem is while your baby howls can be stressful. Sometimes you may find yourself wanting to stop the noise whatever way you can. Crying can make you feel angry and frustrated, and you may want to lash out physically.

TIP

If you feel the crying is getting to be too much for you, put your baby in a safe place like her bassinet or crib, and then take a few minutes to calm yourself outside. A very short but demanding exercise can help get rid of some excess adrenalin as well, so "get down and give me 20" to work things out.

Whenever your baby starts crying, get into the habit of checking three things: Is he hungry, does he have a dirty diaper, and is he comfortable and well (does he have a high temperature, are there any signs of vomit, and are there any other obvious signs of a health problem)?

After you've checked your baby, do one (or all) of the following to try to calm and comfort your baby:

>> Burp him to help him get rid of gas (if he's just had a feeding).

>> Cuddle and sing to him in a calm, soothing voice or put on a CD of gentle lullabies.

>> Give him a warm bath.

>> Put him down for a nap; he may just be tired (no kidding).

>> Put your baby in the car and go for a drive around the block (not the most environmentally friendly alternative, but sometimes driving's the one thing that works).

- **»** Switch on a household appliance that makes a monotonous sound, such as a hairdryer, vacuum cleaner, or washing machine. Or download some "white noise" sounds from the Internet and play the noise to your baby.

- **»** Take him for a walk in the stroller or baby carrier (at any time of the day or night).

- **»** Try a gentle, soothing massage (see Chapter 7 for tips on baby massage).

Daddy time

Spending time with your baby doesn't have to be all work and no play. Every diaper change is an opportunity to have some fun with your little one.

Besides the usual chores and jobs you do with your baby, you can hang out together in other ways that are just good old-fashioned fun. Try these out for size:

- **»** **Bathe or shower together.** Bathing can be a little nerve-wracking at first. Make sure mom is standing by with a towel when you're ready to get out. Hold the soap — you don't want things to get slippery!

- **»** **Enjoy some tummy time.** Tummy time is where your baby lies on the floor on her stomach and tries to lift her head, which helps develop junior's core strength. Read more about tummy time in Chapter 8.

- **»** **Have a chat.** Babies coo from a few weeks old and delight in having their sounds repeated back to them.

- **»** **Read to your baby.** It's never too early to turn him on to reading. He'll delight in the experience of being near you and seeing magical shapes and colors in the pictures.

- **»** **Sing to your baby.** You can sing a ton of good songs with your baby, but you can always make up your own. And baby doesn't care if you can't hold a tune. He'll just adore you more for it.

>> **Take a trip to the park.** Your champ's a little too young for slides and jungle gyms, but he'll love sitting on your lap with you on the swing for a gentle swing back and forth. He'll also love being outside and around other children.

Juggling Your Other Priorities

Before your baby came along, you were a partner, a son, a brother, a friend, an employee or boss, and a member of your extended family. Now that baby has arrived and your priorities have changed, fitting in all those aspects of your life can be a struggle. Not only can you jeopardize the relationships you have with people in your life by letting fatherhood take over everything, but you can also lose your relationship with yourself and find your own well-being at risk.

Making time for yourself

You don't stop being the person you were before baby came along. You still need to take care of yourself so you can be the best father — and partner and so on — you can be for a long time. Just as moms need time to themselves, dads deserve some time off too. Having a chat with your partner about continuing to fit in activities you enjoy or time with friends is important.

REMEMBER

Making time for yourself may make you feel a little guilty and can be tricky to manage, but you need to take care of yourself before you can take care of anyone else.

Looking after your partner

There is a tendency for childcare organizations to hammer the message "baby comes first," which is of course important. However, taking care of the baby can't be at the constant expense of your relationship. After all, if your relationship goes down the drain, there's a lot more trouble ahead.

If you're the primary caregiver, you know what it means to look after a baby all day and sort out the household at the same time. Being the primary caregiver is a lot of hard work, so get your partner to help out when she gets home. If you're the main provider, make sure you chip in and do whatever needs to be done when you get home. Yes, working all day and then helping out at home with looking after the baby is tough, but you'll get through it. Looking after a baby and child does get easier over time — promise!

Above all, you and your partner need to have "us" time and spend quality time together. You can do this by getting friends or family to look after the baby for a few hours while you go out, or even making a big deal out of a special occasion and celebrating at home when baby is asleep.

Here are some more ideas to keep your relationship alive and kicking:

» Invite some friends (especially those you are both friends with) over to cook dinner for you. Yes, inviting people to cook you a meal is pretty gutsy, but most people are only too willing to help out. This way you two get to see your friends, have a classy meal, and don't have to do any work!

» Surprise each other with little gestures like leaving messages, buying a little treat or present, or getting out a DVD.

» Take a walk together with baby asleep in the stroller. That way the two of you can get some gentle exercise and spend time together.

Connecting with family

Your newborn isn't just your pride and joy, but the pride and joy of your entire extended family. There is nothing like having a child to help you realize what your own parents went through when you were a kid. They will undoubtedly want to be part of your new child's life. So share the love!

Having a lot of interaction with his grandparents, cousins, and other close relatives is invaluable for your baby — the more love coming at him, the better. Having your baby feel comfortable and safe with family members also means having a lot of babysitters on hand and extra pairs of hands when you or your partner are finding things tough. It also helps your baby develop his social skills and builds confidence.

DEALING WITH VISITORS

They say it takes a village to bring up a child. When your baby has arrived, you may realize that at least half of that village wants to drop in to check out the new addition to your family. Apart from your immediate family, expect to see neighbors you didn't know you had, uncles and aunts you haven't seen since you were a kid, old colleagues, acquaintances, and of course all your and your partner's friends. Although you may want to show off your greatest creation, the demands of looking after a newborn (the sleep deprivation, the unfolded washing, the plates that are piling up everywhere) and your own anxiety about parenting don't make a great mix for entertaining. But you can turn a horde of visitors into an army of helpers:

- Don't serve tea or coffee when visitors come over. Point them to the kettle, or the vacuum cleaner, or the washing machine.

- If someone calls and says she's coming over, get her to pick up any supplies you're too busy or exhausted to get from the supermarket yourself.

- People love to help and contribute in any way they can, so make the most of offers.

- Put up a sign on your front door with something like "Parents and baby sleeping, please call to let us know when you're coming over." Screen calls — that's what answering machines and voicemail are for.

- Don't be afraid to say no when you just don't feel like having people over. People are generally quite understanding, especially if they have children themselves.

Managing the work–life balance

Managing your commitments at work and your life outside paid employment is often a tricky one in this fast-paced society. Technology that allows you to work and be contactable 24 hours a day doesn't help you separate work from leisure time. Even before becoming a father, finding time to do the things you love may have been a stretch. Now that you have the extra demands of a family, it may be time to readdress your work–life balance and take some steps so you don't burn out.

Flextime, or working more flexible hours, is becoming more accepted, especially for men. In some workplaces, you may be able to design your own hours, bank up hours worked to take days off in lieu, or add a no-overtime clause to your contract. While not all companies in the United States are mandated to provide it, your company may offer time off through either paternity leave or through the Family Medical Leave Act, or FMLA. Ask your HR person about your company's benefits.

Re-entering the wonderful world of sex

Having a little nooky is probably the last thing on mom's mind for a few weeks after birth, and this can be rough on a new dad. The lack of lovin' isn't because you smell bad or have suddenly become repulsive. Blame it on the hormones, lack of sleep, leaky breasts, and the time it takes to recover from birth.

Women who've had a rough labor and some kind of intervention like a cesarean birth or vacuum or forceps delivery should wait longer and may not want to resume intimate activities any earlier than 8 to 12 weeks. A tear or an episiotomy (see Chapter 5) can take six weeks or more to heal. On top of that, your partner may not feel very sexy, having been through the birth and seen the look on your face as baby's head emerged. Your partner may feel self-conscious about her postpartum body.

There's also the mental attitude required for having sex. The memory of what birth felt like may last longer than the stitches, making the idea of sex unappealing.

You need to be a bit patient. Take cold showers and do plenty of exercise if need be. Most doctors recommend waiting at least six weeks after birth before having sex. That's the length of time it takes for the uterus to get back to pre-baby size after a vaginal birth.

But things get better. Your partner is really just taking time to heal, get her head around things, and regain some of her mojo. It may take a few months, but her appetite for sex will return. In the meantime, continue to support and love her, and show intimate affection for her in other ways with massages, foot rubs, and cuddles.

REMEMBER

When you're both ready to resume sex again, take it slowly. Let your partner control the pace and position, so things are comfortable for her. And don't forget contraception. It's a myth that breastfeeding stops another pregnancy — are you really ready for #2 yet?

Chapter 7

The First Three Months

You've made it through the birth, know which end of your baby the diaper goes on, and have an idea or two about how things are shaping up in your new family. Now you're really into the business end of fathering.

The first three months are possibly the most challenging in your new role as dad, as you come to grips with a vulnerable new life who is slowly learning more about her world and learning that you are there for her all the way.

In this chapter we deal with chores that need to be done to maintain your baby's health and hygiene, and tackle some problems that you may be facing, such as colic and reflux. We explore your baby's rapid development and how you can make the most of these important early learning stages. We also revisit postpartum depression and who you can turn to for help, and show you how to make your home a safe environment for your soon-to-be-curious, mobile baby.

Getting to Know Your Baby

There's no substitute for spending time with your baby and getting up close and personal. Babies are funny creatures and grow faster than you expect. They are kind of blobby one day, and all cute and big-eyed the next. You'll be stunned at how much they change in the first three months.

Your baby is unique in hundreds of ways, such as the way he yawns, the way he coos at the radio, and the way his hair sticks up like an orangutan's. These are all special things that will probably disappear as he grows up, so make time to absorb them while you can.

REMEMBER

Everything in your baby's life is new, and she doesn't have the experience to interpret situations or sensations. Watching your baby feel sand under her feet or see a dog for the first time can be hilarious. Things that we take for granted are totally new and bizarre to your little one. Spending time with your baby is a great way to rediscover the world and sometimes can lift your spirits when you've had a rough day.

When your baby was born, you probably didn't know which way to hold him up. Now you know which way he likes being burped, his favorite toys, the best times of day to go out and about, what songs he responds to, and the best methods for settling him at night. If you don't feel you're getting any more of a grip on this fatherhood thing and still can't get him to sleep or bring up gas, don't worry.

REMEMBER

Good things take time and babies are quite random. Sometimes what works one day won't work the next. All you need is a bit of determination to stick with it. Don't give up being an involved father if you haven't had the amazing experiences we describe in this book. Your baby hugely benefits from every moment you spend with her, whether you feel you are making progress with her or not.

Keeping things flexible

Doing the same thing day in and day out is boring for adults, but babies love routine. If you haven't established some sort of routine or rhythm to your day with baby, establishing a routine soon is a good idea. We highly recommend having some sort of structure to your day so you and your little one know what's coming.

A pattern of sleeping, feeding, changing, having some playtime or awake time, and then back to sleep is pretty standard. You don't have to run things on a clock if you don't want to, but some people love that rigidity. As he approaches his three-month birthday, your baby can stay awake for about one and a half hours before getting tired and needing a nap (again, every baby is different so we are simply going by averages here).

Here are some thoughts about routines and how they may work for you:

>> Anticipate how long you have out and about before baby gets tired and cranky.

>> Arrange visits from friends and family around your schedule, not theirs.

>> Organize your day around your baby's naps, including getting some sleep while she does.

>> Schedule time away from the baby each day, or time together as a family.

>> Work out when to do those pesky chores, like laundry, cooking, and going to the doctor for baby's checkups, around when you think baby will be awake, asleep, or need a feeding, keeping in mind that your ideas and your baby's may differ considerably.

TIP

Even if your baby is on a strict schedule and seems to have settled into his timetable well, try to take each day as it comes. Babies love to keep things interesting by filling their diaper as you step out the door, spitting up just as you've got them into a smart new outfit, or demanding an early dinner when you're out without mom or a bottle to give them. Try not to see the world falling down around your feet if she doesn't conform to your idea of what she should be doing. Take a deep breath and get used to life on baby's time. Things will settle down again into a new routine soon.

Dealing with everyday disasters

You're not alone in thinking that babies are a bit mysterious. They can't talk, so if there's something wrong, they can't tell you straight out what's going on. They have different, unfathomably fragile bodies compared to an adult's body and are sensitive to things adults wouldn't even notice, so babies suffer from "problems" different from adults. By taking time to get to know your baby, you get more of an idea about what makes him tick. You may even have solved the mystery of what kinds of cries your baby makes to communicate with you. Trial and error is often the only way to work out what's going on with your baby or what to do to achieve a particular outcome.

Here are some suggestions for dealing with common problems experienced by babies (and parents) during the first few months of your baby's life.

Clearing up jaundice

A common condition in newborns, jaundice refers to the yellow color of the skin and whites of the eyes. Jaundice clears naturally in around one to two weeks. If the jaundice continues for any longer, your physician may recommend *phototherapy*, which is treatment with a special light that helps rid the body of bilirubin, a byproduct of broken down red blood cells and the cause of jaundice, by altering the bilirubin and making it easier for your baby's liver to get rid of it.

Fluid helps wash the broken down red blood cells. Breastfed babies are more likely to experience jaundice because it takes a few days for breast milk to really come in.

Passing gas

Your baby lets you know he has gas by wriggling after a feeding or arching his back. He may get upset and cry too. See the three main burping positions in Chapter 6 to help him get rid of gas; if this doesn't work, ask your doctor about giving your baby simethicone drops that help break up the gas bubbles, making them easier to bring up.

Coping with colic

Doctors often disagree about what causes infantile colic or which parts of the body are affected. Some doctors say colic is caused by trapped gas; others say a nerve condition is to blame. You will know if your baby suffers from colic. Your little one usually gets pretty cranky in the evening, crying inconsolably for around three hours. Colic generally starts at a few weeks of age and typically disappears when your baby is three or four months old.

There is no magic cure for colic, we're sorry to say, but you can try various tricks to distract your baby so she falls asleep. Movement sometimes helps a colicky baby settle down.

TIP

Some babies seem to be comforted by being held tummy down on laps or forearms. Colic doesn't seem to have any long-lasting effects on the baby, but hearing their baby scream night after night can be terribly traumatic for parents.

REMEMBER

If the crying is getting to be too much for you, put baby in a safe place like her crib or bassinet and take a breather. Take turns getting out of the house, and if you're really afraid the baby's crying might push you over the edge, speak to your doctor about medications — for both of you — that could help you through a rough time.

Surviving colic is really hard on parents, but the love and patience you show during this time won't be forgotten by your little one. Hang in there. Seek help from your healthcare provider if you think there could be some other problem.

Getting rid of cradle cap

Cradle cap is a kind of baby dandruff, a condition in which flakes appear on the scalp. Cradle cap's not harmful and won't cause your little one any distress. You can get rid of cradle cap by massaging the scalp with almond oil or olive oil and rinsing with water. Cradle cap can sometimes become dark or crusty, or spread to the face, in which case you should talk to your healthcare provider about more treatment options.

Dealing with reflux

The valve where your baby's esophagus and stomach meet should close to keep food and stomach acids inside. In babies with reflux, this valve doesn't close properly yet. Most feedings end with your baby's milk and stomach acids coming back up again, either by being vomited up or catching in his throat and hurting him. Nearly all babies experience some spitting in their first three months, before the valve closes tightly.

Your baby may have reflux if he

>> Has sour-smelling breath.

>> Has a wet sound in his throat, or has wet-sounding hiccups. This is caused by regurgitated milk in his throat.

>> Writhes, arches his back, vomits, and cries after feedings.

Parents of babies who suffer from reflux worry about whether their baby is getting enough to eat or suffering a lot of pain from the reflux. Here are some ways you can minimize reflux symptoms:

>> Avoid bouncing your baby, especially after meals.

>> Change your baby's diaper by rolling her to the side rather than lifting her legs higher than her head.

>> Feed your baby in an upright position to help the milk stay down.

>> Give your baby a pacifier to suck. Sucking a pacifier can help him swallow and clear the milk from the esophagus.

>> If using formula, try one of the anti-reflux varieties on the market. Talk to your doctor before trying anti-reflux formula.

>> Keep baby upright as much as you can to help gravity keep the milk and stomach acids in her stomach where they should be after meals.

>> Put baby in a baby chair at an angle rather than placing her flat on the floor under a play gym when she's awake.

>> Raise the mattress in baby's bed so her head is slightly higher than her stomach and the mattress is on a slight

angle. Don't raise the mattress too much or she will slide down the bed, which could be dangerous.

Reflux can be the result of an allergy to cow's milk protein. In some instances having mom change to a dairy-free diet if she's breastfeeding, or switching to a non-dairy formula such as goat or soy, may help. Speak to a medical professional or a dietician first.

Treatments for reflux include thickeners that hold milk down, such as infant Gaviscon. Medication may be prescribed if your baby's case is particularly severe and she isn't putting on as much weight as recommended.

REMEMBER

Your baby will remember the love and comfort you give her as she deals with reflux long after she's forgotten how reflux felt.

TIP

See what the U.S. Department of Health and Human Services has to say about infant reflux at `www.niddk.nih.gov/health-information/health-topics/digestive-diseases/ger-and-gerd-in-infants/Pages/overview.aspx`.

Handling sneezes, coughs, and runny noses

Even though you've bundled up your little precious and protected him from everything you can think of, he'll still fall prey to a common cold. Until he's two, there's not a lot you can do for a baby with a cold except give him infant pain relief (always check the right dosage for your little one's age), extra feedings, and lots of cuddles. You can also try the following:

>> Clear the mucus out of your little one's nose with a bulb syringe made especially for infants. Squeeze the bulb, insert the tip gently into the end of each nostril, and release the bulb. Clean it very thoroughly after each use. Don't overuse it or you could cause irritation that makes things worse.

>> Keep up the feedings so he doesn't get dehydrated. If he's been sleeping through the night (which would be a miracle at this age), expect him to wake up more — top him off with more fluids when he does.

>> Saltwater drops can help unblock her nose and sinuses. Dissolve some salt in warm water and apply up her nose, drop by drop, with an infant medication dropper.

>> She may have to stop to breathe when feeding if her nose is blocked, so take your time and let her control how much she takes.

>> Use a cool-mist humidifier to moisten the air, which can reduce baby's congestion.

REMEMBER

If your baby suddenly comes down with a fever, or your instincts tell you something more than a cold is going on, call your doctor. If nothing else, a trip to your healthcare provider can rule out anything more serious and put your mind at ease. A temperature of 100.4 degrees Fahrenheit is considered a fever.

Clearing up infant acne

Some babies develop a pretty unfortunate pimply face in the first days and weeks after birth. The spots are caused by hormones from the mother and fade away once those hormones are out of your baby's system. You can't do anything to make them go away, but keep baby's hands under wraps (for example, in mittens) to stop her from scratching the spots accidentally. A gentle wash of warm water will keep the spots from becoming infected. Pat dry afterward.

Preventing diaper rash

Diaper rash is a flat red area on your baby's bottom or genital area caused by ammonia from urine and stool staying on his skin. Diaper rash is very uncomfortable, and you may meet some resistance at diaper changing time if your baby has diaper rash.

The best cure for diaper rash is prevention, so make sure his bottom is washed with warm water and a soft cloth every time you change his diaper. Gently pat everything dry and apply your diaper cream or powder before the diaper goes on. Give him some time each day without a diaper to expose his skin to the air and sunlight.

If your poor baby should come down with a case of diaper rash, a zinc-based cream can help heal the skin. Be vigilant about baby hygiene. Wash cloth diapers in hot water and dry them in the sun to kill any bacteria lurking in the fabric. Some babies react badly to disposable diapers, while others flare up at the sight of a cloth diaper, so be flexible and experiment with different products in your diaper routine until you figure out what works for your baby.

Diaper rash may flare up when your baby is teething, but not all babies experience this.

If diaper rash persists despite all your efforts, see your healthcare provider for more advice and treatment.

Teething

Most babies younger than three months old haven't started teething, but some babies are eager to grow up and may have a few teeth bothering them. Some babies are even born with a few gnashers!

See Chapter 9 for tips on helping baby deal with teething.

Treating skin irritations and scratching

If your baby's skin is dry or she's scratching herself, soothe her skin with olive or sweet almond oil and put some mittens on her hands. You can get shirts and sleepers with fold-over ends that become mittens. Try not to use these too often; your baby needs to use her hands to explore her world.

Taking care of business

Like you, babies have growing nails and snotty noses, and get stuff in their ears and eyes. Babies need ongoing body maintenance. Funnily enough, that's often when a frustrated mom hands over baby to dad. Just roll up your sleeves and do it. By the way, if, as part of your fatherhood journey, you haven't been vomited on, had poop squirted on you, or been christened with pee yet, you're not trying hard enough.

A compilation of jobs for real men includes the following:

>> **Administering medicine:** After vaccinations or during an illness, your baby may need pain relievers or antibiotics. Medicines for babies are usually prescribed as a liquid suspension and are most easily given in a plastic syringe

(no needle attached). Dosages are typically measured in milliliters (mL), and getting the dosage right is important. Get your healthcare provider to show you the correct dose when your baby's given his vaccinations or he's prescribed medicine.

» **Cleaning ears:** Earwax is a good thing because it protects the ear canal, so don't get too worked up about it. Wiping the outer ear and neck area where milk can collect should do the trick, but be careful not to get water in the ear canal. If you're concerned about the cleanliness of your baby's ears, leave it to the professionals and see your doctor.

» **Mopping up poop explosions:** Every baby has at least one bowel motion that truly tests the limits of what you thought a small person could excrete. Babies also get the odd bout of diarrhea if they eat something that disagrees with them or if they catch a gastrointestinal bug. The result is the mother (or father) of all poops, also called the "backsider" as stool goes all the way up the diaper and into the sleeper. If your little one has a tummy bug or diarrhea, you can minimize the mess by doubling up on diapers. You may want to invest in an apron to protect your clothes at these times, even if you think it makes you look ridiculous.

» **Trimming finger and toe nails.** Get yourself one of those dinky little manicure sets for children, which include a pair of scissors with rounded ends, a tiny pair of nail clippers, and some emery boards. Approach your baby when she's asleep or feeding so she's not focused on having her fingers dealt with. The clippers are probably easiest to start with, but failing that, try special baby scissors. If you've done a pretty rough job, smooth off craggy nail edges with an emery board so she doesn't scratch herself with them. This job is likely to get harder as your baby gets older, so get some early nail-cutting training in while she is still pretty helpless and can't move about much.

» **Wiping away sticky eye:** Many babies have a buildup of mucus at their eye corners, and this can be easily removed by wetting a washcloth with lukewarm water and gently wiping away the mucus.

Being a Real Hands-On Dad

The days of fathers coming home from work and disappearing behind the evening paper while mother tended to the baby are long gone. Twenty-first-century dads are rolling up their sleeves and are fully involved in all things baby, which doesn't just include chores. In this section we explore ways to have fun with your new playmate and pick up new skills along the way.

Baby massage

We're not talking about being pummeled by a masseuse, but a gentle rub with a light oil, much like a hairdresser shampooing your hair or giving you one of those funny head massages. Baby massage has lots of benefits, not least of all getting his skin nicely moisturized. Touch is the most developed sense in a newborn, and sensory receptors in his skin help him learn about his body. He's not really aware of where his hands, feet, and tummy are yet.

Baby massage is a gentle way to express care and nurturing for your baby and is a time for you to engage and chat, or sing a song. Baby massage is total bliss for your little one and helps his development tremendously. So if you can give your little guy a massage a day, that's fantastic!

A good time to massage your baby is after his bath and before bed. He'll be warm from the bath, and massage will further relax him for a good night's sleep (fingers crossed).

Here's how to massage your baby:

>> Make sure the room you're in is warm and that your hands are warm as well.

>> Set up a flat, comfortable surface, like a changing table or firm mattress.

>> Use a moisturizer made especially for baby, or an edible, unscented oil such as coconut or safflower oil. Some essential oils, diluted for infants, are also soothing for baby massage. Test a small amount on your baby's skin to make

sure his skin isn't sensitive to it. Warm the oil in your hands before touching baby.

>> Take your time. This isn't a chore like washing diapers or getting dinner on the table. Use this time to connect and enjoy being with your baby.

>> Talk to your baby or sing a song, but keep the tone of the massage calm, peaceful, and low key. You can also name the body parts you are massaging. Although speech development is a while off, naming the body parts establishes vocal patterns your baby will recognize over time.

>> You can roll baby over and rub her back. First, roll her onto her side, then put a hand under her torso and the other hand on the leg closest to you. Ease her onto her chest by removing your hand as she turns over.

>> To massage feet, have baby on her front and use slow gentle circles on her tootsies.

>> To massage legs and arms, hold baby's foot or arm with one hand while massaging the limb in one long, gentle stroke with the other from the hand or foot and up.

TIP

Avoid massaging baby right after he's eaten. Pressure on his belly may not agree with him.

REMEMBER

Try to have one hand always touching your baby while massaging, even when reaching for more oil.

Baby activities

You can encourage brain development by playing with your baby. Try these activities:

>> **Laying him on his tummy.** Also known as "tummy time," a few minutes a couple of times a day on his tummy helps strengthen his back and neck muscles. On the floor you can do some visual activities like blowing bubbles or slowly moving a ball in front of his eyes. Place some objects such as toys just out of reach. He'll try reaching them as he develops his physical skills.

>> **Moving him around.** Movement is good for getting those synapses or brain connections firing and linking with other parts of the brain. Try some gentle rocking, or have him lie on your lap facing you as you move your legs up and down. Or you can have baby on your shins while you lie on the floor. Hold his hands and lift your legs. He'll love it.

>> **Reading to her.** You can't start the book habit too early. Picture books with clear, contrasting colors are a big hit.

>> **Talking to him — a lot.** He can't understand your words, but he's listening and learning and picking up language faster than he ever will again. You don't have to discuss Shakespeare or politics; just talk about what you're doing or seeing.

TIP

Even a mundane task like changing a diaper is an opportunity to learn for your baby. Repeating phrases like "lying down" or "off comes your diaper" each time connects the words and action for your child. As his language skills develop, you may find him pointing to his diaper or lying down when you ask him to.

Keeping baby safe and sound

Your baby is pretty helpless physically and oblivious to danger. Keeping baby safe is up to you. The buck stops with the parents; nobody else keeps your baby safe for you. So keep up the good work by always

>> Checking the temperature of formula by sprinkling a little on your wrist.

>> Ensuring your baby's breathing isn't obstructed by objects such as blankets in the crib, crib toys, or bumpers. While all these things are cute, they're also safety hazards in the crib with young infants.

>> Maintaining a smoke-free home and car.

>> Keeping a hand on her when she's on elevated surfaces like a bed or changing table.

>> Keeping your cups of tea, coffee, and other hot beverages well clear of the baby (see the nearby sidebar "Scalding").

>> Providing age-appropriate toys. Toys for older children have small parts that may break off and choke your little one.

>> Supervising the baby when she's in the bath, even if she's using a bath support.

>> Using an age-appropriate car seat for car trips.

TIP

Right now, he can't move or prod his fingers into electrical sockets, so you can get a head start and baby-proof your house now for when he's on the move. A good place to start is to get down on your hands and knees for a baby's-eye-view of the terrain and see what jumps out at you as potentially dangerous. Table 7-1 provides ways to help you rectify any trouble spots.

TABLE 7-1 Baby-Proofing Room by Room

Room	What to Do
Living areas	Secure bookshelves and other unstable furniture like tall CD racks to the wall with anchors to prevent them from toppling on your baby.
	Put childproof locks on china cabinet doors to prevent your sweetie getting into Grandma's heirloom china.
	Use a guard around your fireplace or heater. Teach your child to stay away by saying "hot" when he is near the heat source.
	Tuck away cables or put cushions and furniture in front of them.
	Hide any remote controls you don't want baby to slobber on.
	Put barriers across any stairs or steps.
Kitchen	Keep appliance cords from hanging over the counter or stove. Your baby could easily pull a kettle of hot water on herself.
	Keep pot handles tucked in over the stove.
	Use guards on your stove elements and around the top of your stove to prevent hot food spilling onto your child.
	Erect a barrier across your kitchen's doorway to prevent your child entering while you cook.
	Forget using tablecloths with really small children — one tug and everything goes overboard.

Room	What to Do
	Keep cleaning products and detergents in a cupboard — preferably a high one — with a childproof lock.
	Never store poisons in food containers. Junior can't tell the difference between disinfectant and a bottle of juice.
	Use a childproof lock to secure any cupboard or drawer that has precious china, knives, or equipment you don't want becoming one of your baby's favorite toys.
Laundry	If you use a diaper pail, make sure the lid is securely fitted and the pail is always stored out of baby's reach.
	Keep cleaning products and detergents in a cupboard — preferably a high one — with a childproof lock.
	Make sure all buckets are left empty.
Bathroom	Make sure your hot water thermostat is set no higher than 120 degrees Fahrenheit.
	Keep all electrical appliances out of the bathroom to prevent accidental electrocution.
	Consider getting a lock or keeping the lid down on your toilet to prevent anything, like your car keys, being deposited in the toilet.
	Keep a lock on the medicine cabinet, and keep cleaners and detergents — even your shampoos — in a locked cupboard, preferably out of reach.
Outdoor areas	Make sure pools and balconies are fenced with childproof locks. Fences should have gaps of no more than 4 inches between pickets to prevent baby becoming trapped between them or falling through.

SCALDING

Did you know that an average-sized cup of tea or coffee can cover up to 70 percent of the skin surface of your baby? This means up to 70 percent of the skin of your baby could be scalded if the liquid is accidentally spilled on the baby. Unfortunately, scalding is a common occurrence as any emergency room worker will tell you. So always place hot beverages on safe surfaces (not near the edge) and well away from the baby.

Understanding Your Baby's Development

Watching your offspring transform from a curled ball of wrinkled, angry-looking baby into a wide-eyed, smiling bundle of delight is a joy. In the first three months of life, your baby changes so fast that you may have forgotten what he was like in those first days.

Growth and weight

Newborns typically lose up to ten percent of their body weight in the days immediately after birth, but they can put that back on in the following one to two weeks. Your healthcare provider will keep track of your baby's weight and plot it on a growth chart, usually kept in your baby's medical chart. Unless baby is not putting on any weight, is distressed or lethargic, or seems undernourished, weight is not usually a cause for concern but is a useful way to track his growth.

Babies usually have growth spurts at around 6 and 12 weeks, when they wake more at night for feedings and take more food during the day.

During the first three months, your baby will

>> Blow lots of dribbly bubbles.

>> Coo — baby's first form of non-crying verbal communication.

>> Learn to lift her head without help — the result of all your tummy time endeavors.

>> Reach out and try to bat objects in her vision.

>> Smile. The first heart-melting smiles usually appear around six weeks.

Hearing, sight, smell, taste, and touch

Your baby's senses, just like the rest of his body, need time to develop. He learns by experiencing the world and interpreting what's going on, using his senses to gather information. Here's the lowdown on what your baby can sense already and what you can do to encourage further development of his senses.

Hearing

Your baby can hear before she's born. Already she's had months listening to mom's stomach gurgle and the distant rumble of you talking to her. Your baby may settle to the sound of the vacuum cleaner or washing machine because those noises are like the white noise of being in the womb.

Your baby will respond to the high pitch of baby talk, which you'll find yourself automatically using when you talk to him (some say we are genetically programmed to speak this way, so don't worry about handing in your man card when you hear yourself talk like a girl). Your little one can't understand English yet, but she can understand your tone and is soothed by soft, gentle sounds. She listens when you speak and even though your speech is gibberish to her, keep talking — it's good for her language development.

If you live in a household where more than one language is spoken, your child is in for a treat. Not only do children with a multilingual upbringing perform better academically (across all subjects), but seeing a child master two or more languages with absolute ease is great. In some cases multilingual children come in very handy as translators between various parts of the family. So by all means, speak to your child in as many languages as you can. A baby can produce any sound of any language in the world. If she's exposed to a particular language before she reaches about nine months, she'll be able to speak it like a native tongue.

Your healthcare provider does a simple hearing test during the first few weeks. If for some reason this hasn't happened, have your child's hearing tested right away because hearing problems can be diagnosed early. As your child grows, hearing checks are important, because hearing loss can be caused through things like ear infections, trauma, and high noise levels.

Sight

The world is fuzzy for a newborn, whose eyes are only just figuring out how to do their job. Your newborn sees best at a distance of 8 to 10 inches, which is a good distance to check you out when she's in your arms. In the early weeks, she'll gaze at contrasts like the folds in your curtains or car lights shining on a wall as it passes your house. She'll look at something for a short time and then look away. Looking at something for a long time — apart from you and her mom — is hard work for newborns. You and your partner are your baby's favorite sight.

In these early weeks, your baby learns how to focus both eyes and follow a moving object, and likes to look at contrasts rather than similarly colored objects.

TIP

You can help your little one's vision by showing her a variety of brightly colored and contrasting images. Use one item at a time so she isn't overloaded. A nice game to play is to move in and out of your baby's focus range. She'll smile when you come into focus and concentrate on your face.

TIP

The saying "out of sight, out of mind" is particularly true for babies up to the age of around four to nine months. If baby can't see something, it doesn't exist, which comes in handy when he wants something, such as a toy, but you need him to focus on something else. Hide the toy and you're good. However, baby eventually works out that things continue to exist even when they're not in sight. This signals the beginning of establishing a short-term memory. For example, if mom leaves the room, baby starts crying because he remembers his mom and she's no longer there. This phenomenon is referred to as object permanence.

Smell and taste

Baby comes equipped with a pretty developed sense of smell and taste. He knows you by your smell as well as your voice and what you look like, and can recognize changes in the taste of breast milk or a different brand of formula. Baby can already taste salty, sweet, sour, and bitter flavors. When he's introduced to solids in a few months, you'll learn even the blandest foods can taste wild and exotic to a baby.

Touch

At birth, your baby's sense of touch is fully developed and she loves to be in close contact with you as much as she can. Your baby's favorite thing is to be cuddled or snuggled by you, and you can't cuddle her too much. Your baby's sensitivity is also why baby massage (covered earlier in this chapter) is such an effective tool in bonding, nurturing, and settling.

One of the first ways your infant discovers the world of touch is through his mouth. Even in these early weeks, he investigates rattles, blankets, his fingers, and all manner of objects by gumming and gnawing them with his mouth.

TIP

The flipside of this incredible sensitivity is that babies can feel pain and are sensitive to scratchy clothing labels, temperature, and uncomfortable diapers, so if baby is upset, check to see whether she is uncomfortable or overheated because of her clothing. A baby's skin is several times more sensitive than an adult's skin, so an unintentionally firm grip can be quite painful. Rough and tumble dads — watch the pressure you apply.

Your baby's amazing brain

By three months of age, your baby is almost unrecognizable from the helpless little bundle you first met at birth. As new connections, called *synapses,* form between different parts of her brain, she displays new skills and understands more of what's going on around her. Synapses are formed very quickly in the first six months of life, but as the brain works out which are worth hanging onto, those synapses that aren't used frequently are abandoned. Repetition of words, songs, sights, sensations, routines, movements, sounds, and tastes helps your baby's synapses develop and makes sure they're retained.

Research shows that stimulation in these early months and years of your child's life enhances brain development. Conversely, no stimulation leads to a loss of brain function. Researchers who study brain development found that brain development happens in patterns but not at the same pace. The researchers generally talk about "development windows" being open for a particular period. During this time your baby is particularly interested in developing a certain sense or skill, or grasping a concept. If you find your baby is particularly interested in something, such as rolling over, give him lots of opportunities to do more of it and ensure he can explore his interest safely.

Stimulating your baby's brain is easy. Give him lots of safe opportunities to explore what he's interested in and keep offering new experiences. See the earlier section "Baby activities" for ideas to get your baby's brain abuzz with new information.

REMEMBER

Babies learn new skills at different stages and ages, so don't worry if your baby isn't doing what everyone else's baby in your coffee group is doing — he'll get there. If you're concerned, talk to your healthcare provider. There's a big "nature versus nurture" debate about how and to what extent you can stimulate or influence your child's development. Nobody knows how much influence nature (the genes your baby has inherited) and nurture (parental input and the learning environment) have. However, neither nature nor nurture is 100 percent responsible for your child's development; they both have a certain degree of influence.

The next few months are about your baby discovering that he has a body. Newborns don't recognize their limbs or body as their own. Hands are a particularly big part of your baby's life in the coming months. Make sure any toys he has contact with are suitable for his age, because toys for older kids may have parts that can break off and become a choking risk. Toys with different textures and surfaces expose your baby to different sensations when he plays with the toys in his hands.

Between one and three months, your baby is probably

>> Discovering her hands, perhaps sucking her thumb or fingers.

>> Smiling in response to your smile.

» Uncurling her fists to grasp a rattle. She probably won't be able to look at the rattle, as she won't connect what her hands and her eyes are doing yet and the rattle may be too close for her eyes to focus on.

Looking at Male and Female Postpartum Depression

Feeling "the blues" is one thing, being in a black hole is another. That's how some people describe postpartum depression (PPD). The condition is associated with mothers for the most part, with an estimated 10–15 percent of mothers suffering from postpartum depression. What's less well known is that three to ten percent of fathers can suffer from PPD too.

While many men report feeling left out of their partners' lives as mothers deal with the constant needs of their babies and their own exhaustion, others feel overwhelmed by the demands of work and hectic situations at home. At worst, you may even have negative or guilty feelings about your baby and feel you're a bad father or partner.

TIP

If everything's becoming too much for you, take time out from your partner and baby, go into another room or leave the house for a bit, and let it all hang out. Scream in the room, house, or street if you want. This works wonders at releasing tension, and you'll feel like a new dad. Doing a quick, high-energy exercise like push-ups to release excess adrenalin can also be really useful.

Listening to a baby crying is one of the most stressful things you can expose a human body to; it's nature's cunning way of making sure the offspring is well looked after and gets priority treatment. So don't be surprised if the baby is stressing you out.

REMEMBER

All your baby wants to do is please you. You are a rock star in his world; you're the bee's knees. When things are getting tough, you're sleep deprived, damp diapers are hanging on the clothes rack, it's 2 a.m., and baby won't settle down, remember that your baby isn't crying for the hell of it.

Recognizing the signs

Knowing about and recognizing some of the signs of PPD can assist you to seek help for yourself or someone else with PPD. Some of the signs of PPD to look for include

>> Anxiety or panic attacks

>> Feelings of hopelessness

>> Frequent crying spells

>> Loss of energy and appetite

>> Loss of enjoyment in everyday activities and in your baby

>> Loss of sex drive

>> Mood swings

>> Problems sleeping even when baby is settled

>> Prolonged feelings of sadness and hopelessness, with nothing to look forward to

>> Suicidal thoughts

Every case is different. If you feel you or your partner may have PPD, talk to each other about how you're feeling and see your doctor.

Getting help

If your partner has PPD, supporting her may seem like a pretty impossible task, and you may feel out of your depth. You can help in lots of ways. Try some of these ideas:

>> Arrange things so you can spend time together with your partner — alone. Regular "us" time helps de-stress both of you and helps you to find and share some common ground again.

>> Let her talk while you listen, or involve a friend she feels comfortable talking to.

>> Take over more of the housework and baby care, and try to let her get some sleep. If you can't take on everything, call in some support like family and friends so you're not swamped as well.

>> Treat her in some way, like with a night at the movies, a massage voucher, a bunch of flowers, or a special gift.

>> Make sure she's following up with any therapies, doctor's appointments, or medications needed.

Postpartum depression in men, though not as common as PPD in women, is just as serious. Admitting there's a problem is difficult. You may find the following helpful:

>> **Talk to your doctor:** He can offer you a range of options including counseling and medication.

>> **Talk to family and friends:** This step can be a biggie, but you're likely to be amazed at how anxious people are to help. Chances are some of your friends have gone through the same thing.

>> **Find support in your community:** Many hospitals host groups dealing with postpartum depression. Online groups such as www.ppdsupportpage.com/ can also be a lifesaver.

>> **Get some exercise:** Feeling fit and active can lift your mood. Around 30 minutes of daily activity is all you need to release mood-enhancing hormones.

TIP

Your doctor may know of local sources for PPD groups. Check the website www.postpartumprogress.com/ppd-support-groups-in-the-u-s-canada for a list of groups that meet in each state and in Canada. Also see *Postpartum Depression For Dummies* by Shoshana S. Bennett, PhD (published by Wiley).

REMEMBER

Postpartum depression is temporary, and you can find a way through it. If you feel lost, take stock and get some help.

Chapter 8

Months Three to Six

Congratulations — you've survived the first three months! Remember those first days when you didn't even know how to hold your precious new baby? By now, things in your household are probably settling down a bit, and the adrenalin rush (read "chaos") of the first weeks is dropping away behind you. Your baby is spending longer periods awake and is engaging with you and her surroundings. So now you two can really get to know one another!

The next three months are also a period of great change developmentally, as your "helpless" three-month-old, who can barely hold up her head, transforms into a six-month-old bundle of activity, capable of moving around, downing solid food, and using her hands for all sorts of things (some of which you don't want her to do). Hey, she may even have a few teeth already!

In this chapter, you find out what you can do as a dad during the next three months to interact with your little person. You also get the scoop on any paperwork required for your baby, what you need to know before you can leave your baby with others, and doing things with your partner as a couple.

Watching Your Growing Baby

Your baby is changing — and fast. Commonly, at around three months, he undergoes a growth spurt, and if he's been suffering from colic or other problems with digestion, these may mercifully start to subside over the next few months. Check out Chapter 6 for more information about burping a baby and Chapter 7 for more about digestive problems.

Baby's new tricks

Over the next three months your baby will start to

» Clasp objects, bring his hands together, and reach for toys

» Develop stronger neck muscles and be able to hold his head up more steadily

» Gnaw on everything she can get her hands on

» Make babbling sounds

» Recognize familiar objects and people, and start to look for toys

» Roll over from her back to her front

» Sleep for longer stretches at night (in some cases)

» Smile (intentionally) and squeal

If your baby isn't doing these things, don't panic. All babies are unique and develop at their own pace. If you're concerned with delayed milestones, talk to your healthcare provider.

New challenges for dads

After the first three crazy months, you and your partner are probably more confident parents and are getting your heads around how your new family works. But, as with every stage of being a great dad, you get a few more hurdles to jump.

Handling postpartum depression

Postpartum depression (PPD), a form of clinical depression that can affect women and men following childbirth, doesn't necessarily disappear when your baby outgrows the newborn period. See Chapter 7 for lots of useful information about PPD.

REMEMBER

Riding out the storm of your partner's depression can be tough, so your patience, communication, and support are vital. She may be irritable — mad at you one minute for trying to do too many things with the baby, and then mad at you for not doing enough. Stay strong and make the effort to listen to her. Offer to take the baby off her hands for a while, even if she protests, and be patient. Encourage her to talk to you and others, or to find professional help from her healthcare provider. This is where you can really demonstrate that you're super-star dad material.

Dealing with sleep deprivation

Even if your partner is breastfeeding and you're not getting up at night, you may still wake up when she tends to the baby. So, broken sleep remains a given for dads in these early months when your baby is growing and feeding like an insatiable beast. If your partner is the main caregiver and you're back at work, having to get up in the morning as well as spending eight hours with a new boss when you haven't had a good night's sleep can really get to you.

You need to do something about this situation (other than drinking lots of coffee), so get organized. Take turns, sleep when the baby sleeps during the weekend, or sleep at a friend's house for one night. Don't forget to give your partner a break as well — things often start to look up after you get a decent night's sleep.

TIP

To help you stay asleep when you really need your zzz's, try using ear plugs (or headphones with white noise playing) to cancel out the baby's crying.

REMEMBER

Your baby waking in the night for feedings is a good thing — she needs fuel to grow. The trade-off is coping with the lack of sleep, which is temporary. Baby sleeps for longer during the night as she gets older.

Missing out when you're at work

The first time your child rolls over, works out a toy, or takes some other momentous step toward independence is probably going to happen when you're stuck at work.

TIP

Stay up to date with your little person's development. Have your video camera or digital camera parked in the living room or baby's room so your partner can capture a few minutes of your child's day for you to watch when you get home. Even better — get a webcam going: They're really easy to set up and operate these days.

New adventures for dads

Now that your baby is spending less time sleeping or napping, you, dad, get to have some fun with your wee one. Okay, you may have to wait a few more years until you can kick a ball around the backyard with junior, but you have plenty of things that you can do together right now.

Research shows that playing with your baby, even when he's this size,

» Develops his social skills

» Enhances his relationship with you (and vice versa)

» Helps with hand–eye coordination

» Raises his self-esteem

» Stimulates his brain development

Best of all, playing with your baby is great fun!

Here are some ideas for spending time with your baby:

» **Moving around:** Movement helps your baby establish and grow connections between different parts of the brain. These connections are vital in fine-tuning your child's senses, learning new physical skills, and developing the ability to think and reason.

A good way to do simple movement is by rolling your baby over. Help junior roll over from his back to his front by laying him on his back and crossing one leg over the other so he slowly rolls onto his tummy. Ideally you would do this on the floor on top of a blanket so he can't fall if he rolls suddenly. Make sure his head is supported if he's still a bit unsteady.

» **Singing:** Okay, so everyone else holds his hands over his ears when you sing, but your baby won't. With your baby in a bouncy or baby chair, she loves being sung to along with lots of touch. Songs like "Twinkle, Twinkle Little Star," "Itsy Bitsy Spider," and "Head, Shoulders, Knees, and Toes" can delight your little one. Make corresponding movements when you sing; for example, touch her shoulders when you sing that word.

One thing you never have to worry about with all babies is your level of vocal talent — they enjoy any attempt at singing. Humming or whistling is also a great alternative if your singing voice really grates on everyone's nerves.

» **Stretching and growing:** Blowing bubbles during tummy time helps your little one's eyesight and gets him looking up, strengthening that neck. You can also place toys just out of his reach so he looks up or stretches his body trying to reach them.

» **Taking tummy time:** This activity is about laying your baby on her tummy so she can learn to push up and lift her head. This exercise is so important because it strengthens the muscles in your baby's back, neck, legs, and arms in preparation for crawling and walking.

Some babies really don't like tummy time (and can heartily let you know about it), so be prepared to be as entertaining as you possibly can be — lying on the floor next to her, if necessary — to keep her in this important position several times a day. Try lying down and having her on your tummy facing you, or raise her up on your shins as you hold her hands.

The best place for your baby (and you) to play and explore is the floor. Being low makes it very safe from falls, and floor contact teaches your baby about his body because he can feel a firm surface at each touchpoint.

Adjusting to your baby's changing needs

Looking after your baby is great fun — seems that every time you finally master a particular situation, he just moves on to the next challenge. Welcome to nature's way of ensuring you're not bored as a parent! Now that you're through the first three months, keeping up with your baby's development and adjusting your parenting skills accordingly is very important.

Looking a bit famished?

As your little one moves toward the six-month mark, you start to notice she's chowing through the milk and starting to look for something a bit more substantial. Your baby may be ready to start eating solid food. Until now, breast milk or formula has sustained her, but now her digestive system is more developed, and her growth needs have a bit more oomph.

Your baby's probably ready for solids if

>> He's taking quite an interest in what you're eating. Look for little chewing motions or for him to be reaching out for your mouth.

>> She's able to take food onto her tongue from a spoon and swallow it. *Note:* She's not ready if she pushes food away with her tongue.

>> He still seems hungry after a milk feeding.

>> She's a bit more unsettled at night, maybe requesting an extra night feed.

TIP

Be patient with introducing solids and don't force-feed, ever. You can try introducing the same food several times over until your baby likes it. Don't offer too many different foods at a time — stick to one new food every few days in order to check for potential allergic reactions. First foods can include the following:

>> Baby rice or cereals

>> Cooked and pureed carrot, pumpkin, avocado, or potato

>> Mashed banana

>> Strained and cooked apple and pear

The same old routine?

Most experienced dads agree on one thing — just when you think you've got a handle on things, everything changes. Got junior going for a nap every three hours? Sleeping through the night? Don't get used to it — it's bound to change! Growth spurts, mastering a new skill, or teething can unsettle your baby, and just as he gets ready to start eating solids, he may wake more often at night.

Your baby loves predictability; it gives her a sense of comfort to know what's coming up in her day. So if you haven't got your prince or princess into a routine, introduce one now. You don't have to do everything by the clock; rather, just have a cycle (or a rhythm), so that your little one knows what's coming up next. Repetition is also a primary mechanism for how babies learn, so routines and repeating things help on many levels.

REMEMBER

If a strict schedule stresses you out because you don't work like that or your baby doesn't adhere to it, relax and do whatever works for your situation and your family. Trying to introduce some structure to your baby's life is a positive step, but not at the cost of your sanity. Your stress can also affect your baby, so anything you do to reduce stress for both of you will make family life more pleasant.

TIP

Having a solid bedtime routine can help settle your baby for a good sleep pattern at night. The most popular version of a bed-time routine goes something like this — and if mom's not breast-feeding, you can be in charge of the whole thing:

>> **Bath:** A nice warm soak in the bath can lull most adults to sleep, and it works pretty well with babies too. Your little tyke will like it even more if you're in the tub with him for some good ol' skin-on-skin time — make sure the bathroom is nice and warm. Hold your baby on your chest or tummy, or on your propped-up thighs so junior can get a good look at you. Babies are slippery little beings, though, so hold on tight — and make sure mom's on hand to scoop up your little one when it's time to get out.

>> **Massage:** Babies love touch — it's the first sense they develop — and spending a little time soothing your baby with massage and engaging her with smiles and songs can be a pretty magical time of the day for both of you. Make sure her room is warm and be ready with the sleepwear so she can be wrapped up warm and cozy soon afterwards. Natural oils such as almond, olive, or calendula are great to use. If you have any fears about nut allergies, skip the almond oil. (See Chapter 7 for more on massaging your baby.)

>> **Last feeding:** This is where you need mom if she's breast-feeding. If your little one is on formula, get in touch with your nurturing side, grab that bottle, and tank her up for a long sleep — another slice of "dad time" your baby can't help but love.

>> **And into bed:** With a little song, a rock in the rocking chair, and a final kiss, your little one soon learns that after a bath, a massage, and a last feeding, it's always time for some serious sleeping.

A bedtime routine works even when you're on vacation, going to friends' houses, or staying at grandma's.

You can adjust your baby's sleep-time routine as he gets older, with reading stories, taking favorite toys to bed, or singing a special song together. It's never too early to read or sing to him. (You'll be amazed at what he picks up in the early days and "plays back" at you when he's a bit older.)

Toys, toys, and more toys

No doubt your baby was given mountains of toys when she arrived. Now that she's a bit older, she may enjoy playing with them even more. Make sure you keep some all-time favorites handy:

>> Fabric books or Lamaze toys

>> Rattles, squeaky toys, and bells

>> Small balls and hoops — make sure they're too big to put into your baby's mouth!

>> Stacking toys, boxes, and wooden rings

REMEMBER

You don't need to buy lots of toys — less is definitely more at this stage. Make sure your baby is exposed to different materials and surfaces. Plastic toys and battery-operated toys should be last on your list because they typically don't offer a variety of textures and don't encourage inventive play. They're also expensive, and you then need to buy batteries constantly.

TIP

Many objects your baby will be interested in at this stage can actually be found in your household. A set of keys on a key ring, empty cardboard boxes, wooden clothes pegs, or fruit and vegetables can keep your little one entertained for hours. Remember, though, that most babies put everything in their mouths; make sure your baby's "toys" are too big to fit into his mouth. Choking is a real hazard for children.

Getting On with Life

Life doesn't stop just because your sweet little babe has joined the world. You still need to go out, visit friends, or frequent the odd café from time to time. The more people your baby meets, places he sees, and surroundings he experiences, the better for junior's rapidly growing brain. So, get out there!

Out and about with your baby

Choosing the gear is a lot more fun than picking out fancy outfits for most dads! You get to choose from a wide range of options for carting your baby around, and you can try all of them, depending on your situation. Popping junior in a sling can work for a quick stroll to the convenience store for the paper, but a jog through the park may be better taken with baby in a stroller.

Strollers

During the first three months, your baby lies reasonably flat in the stroller. Now that she's a bit older, you can prop her up a bit so she can see what's happening. You may also want to invest in a lightweight umbrella stroller, which is great for short trips and traveling. Check the model to make sure it's suitable for your baby's age. Check out Chapter 4 for the lowdown on getting the right gear.

Slings and baby carriers

If you haven't already, check out baby slings and baby carriers. They're great for short trips around town. Proponents of baby-wearing, like those who practice attachment parenting — in which a caregiver maintains contact with the baby at all times — swear by the benefits of having their baby in a sling or baby carrier. Babies carried in slings often sleep wherever you go, and you don't have the potential hassle of trying to find a spot to park the stroller in a restaurant or store.

TIP

A ton of different baby carrier models are out there, each with different pros and cons — so shop around. Get your salesperson to fit them correctly to ensure you're not squashing your precious bundle and that your back isn't damaged.

The following are the most common types of slings and baby carriers:

>> Asian slings are a rectangular shape with straps around both shoulders that can be worn in front or behind.

>> Front carriers are like the backpacks you take hiking, only you put a baby in them! They have lots of padding and are usually made of canvas with adjustable straps. They can be worn with your baby facing in toward you or out to the world.

>> Open- and close-tailed ring slings are adjustable and fit over one shoulder.

>> Pouches are pockets of fabric worn over one shoulder and are very easy to get babies in and out of. They aren't adjustable, though, so they can be worn only by the person they fit.

>> Wraps are a piece of fabric that ties around the body. They take some getting used to, but they are said to be more comfortable in the long run than other slings.

Ask yourself these questions when choosing a sling or baby carrier:

>> How well is the weight of the baby spread over my back and shoulders? Will I get tired after wearing it only a short while?

>> Will it just be me using the sling, or is my partner getting in on the act?

>> How easily do I need to be able to get junior in and out of the sling?

Some baby carriers have caused injury or even death, either from baby falls or from holding the baby in a position that impeded his breathing. Never use a second-hand carrier; it may not meet current safety standards.

Traveling by car

In general, when taking your little person with you in the car, the American Academy of Pediatrics recommends that you use the rear-facing car-seat position until your baby is at least 2 years old. Check the instruction manual for details of your model and check out Chapter 4 for a list of different types of car seats for infants.

Getting social

So you've got the latest stroller, your baby is in his flashiest gear, and you're all ready to go. What can you do together?

>> Music and movement classes, like Gymboree, mommy and me (although these really should be called "parent and me") classes, infant swim times, and other group activities are great for getting those brain connections going, but they can be expensive.

>> Playgroups are community-run groups of parents who get together to let their kids play while the adults mingle. Some have music sessions and provide lots of books and toys. They can be invaluable for perking you up on a bad day — having other people ooh and aah over your baby goes a long way toward putting a big grin on your face. The cost depends on who is running the class; informal groups organized by a few neighbors won't cost you anything and can provide potential friends as your baby grows.

>> Story time and music and play sessions at your local library are another tonic for isolated parents, and babies adore them. There is nothing like sitting among 30 other parents

and babies singing "Row, Row, Row Your Boat" and having all 30 babies laughing in delight. And these sessions are usually free.

Don't be intimidated by female dominance in some of these social settings — you're just as much a parent as the next mom. So wear your "dad and I'm proud of it" face and enjoy the attention.

Baby-proofing the house

Your little one is only just beginning to get her moves on, but watch out — in just a few short months she is going to be crawling and pulling up on everything, and open season will be declared on cupboards, bookshelves, and cables. What was out of reach one day is fair game the next. So now's a good time to take baby-proofing to the next level and ensure everything dangerous and precious in your house is either locked down or locked up.

We don't want to sound like molly coddlers here, but household injuries are one of the main causes for emergency room visits for kids under age 3. And 70 percent of children who die from unintentional injury at home are under age 4. So child safety at home is something to take seriously. Check out Chapter 7 for more about common safety hazards by room or area in your baby's adventure playground and what to do to make these hazards safer.

You can never take your child's safety for granted:

>> Keep any potentially lethal substances like pet litter, garden fertilizers, cleaners, pesticides, alcohol, fire starters, and paints in a high cupboard with childproof locks.

>> Young children can drown in a small amount of water, not to mention the hygiene risk of touching dirty areas like the toilet, so you're best to keep the bathroom out of bounds.

You may not think so now, but when your baby is crawling and walking, she can move very, very quickly and get herself into trouble fast. The time spent baby-proofing your house (continuously) can save your child's life or prevent her being seriously hurt.

IT'S ONLY MONEY

Babies and children have a unique way of exposing you to different points of view. For example, you're sure to come to a different understanding of what's valuable to you, mostly because your baby may eat, destroy, pee on, or draw on something that you hold dear. When that momentous event happens (and yes, it is "when," not "if"), remember not to blame your little one. Until he's much older, your baby isn't going to understand the concept of material value — so if something is really, really precious, make sure you keep it out of reach (using a bank vault isn't a bad idea!).

TIP

To make sure you've got everything covered, get down to your baby's height and see what is likely to tempt your curious child.

Wading through the necessary paperwork

By now you most likely have registered your baby's birth, but you still have other bits and pieces of administration to take care of.

Insurance

Give some thought to getting life insurance if you haven't already. If something happens to you, you're going to want your family to be taken care of financially. Shop around for the best deal and to understand the various types of personal insurance. You can try your bank or home insurer as a first approach.

Give your health insurer a call to add your baby to your policy. Check before your baby is born to find out how long you have after her birth to add her to the policy.

Savings accounts

Many parents set up bank accounts for their new child and start saving for big purchases like a new bike or sports fees, or for far-off expenses like college tuition or a deposit on a first house. Most banks have savings accounts for children with low or no fees.

Taxes and benefits

Kids serve as a hefty tax deduction in the United States, and certain expenses, like child care, are also available as a credit to help working parents. Talk to a tax specialist to make sure you're taking all the deductions you can to offset the cost of raising your child.

Wills and guardians

Make sure both you and your partner have updated your wills to take into account your new status as parents, and have thought about who can look after your baby should something happen to you. When thinking about who should be guardian if you and your partner die or are unable to look after your baby, make sure you ask the person(s) first before naming them in your will, and check whether they're equipped financially and emotionally to add a new child to their family.

TIP

You may want to make special mention in your will of any sentimental belongings that you want to hand down to your child, like special clothing, photographs, or family heirlooms.

Immunization records

Keep a record of your baby's immunizations — they may be required when your child starts childcare, kindergarten, or school. While your healthcare provider's office will maintain these records in your child's medical chart, it never hurts to keep a back-up copy at home.

Doing things together: You're still a couple

Your relationship as a couple impacts your little one. Happy parents, happy baby, they say. As a role model to your child, the relationship you have with your partner acts as a guide when he embarks on his own romantic endeavors.

But all your energy these days seems to go into baby, and with the lack of sleep going on right now, just collapsing on the couch at the end of a long day may seem like the easiest way to recharge. And, with all the attention your new bundle is getting from mom, you may not be feeling the love. So both of you have to work hard to ensure your relationship isn't forgotten about.

TIP

Make an effort and make time for each other. Schedule some time in the evening when baby is asleep and prepare a special dinner, or hire a babysitter and head out for the night. It doesn't have to be anything fancy; just do something you both enjoy.

You're probably wondering when sex returns to your relationship. Chances are you're both pretty exhausted most days or the baby is actively preventing you from getting it on. Your partner may also not feel like having sex at the moment. The aftermath of the birth on her body combined with leaky boobs and that all-consuming tiredness may leave her feeling less than "bootilicious" right now. Well — basically, you just have to take it easy. Definitely bring up the subject and ask her how she feels about sex. Ask her to let you know when she's ready to resume relations again. You may have to be a bit patient, but pressuring her is unlikely to speed things up.

Leaving Your Baby with Others

Inevitably the time comes when you and your partner need to hand over your precious baby to others. You may just need a break from the baby routine, or you may want to get back to working. This is a big deal, and many dads feel unsure about leaving baby with someone else (even grandparents or close relatives). Don't panic — you can put your mind at ease (or at least you can try) with advance planning.

As with most things, the key to making this process work is effective communication. A key principle is to make sure the person who looks after your baby knows how you want things done.

Let your baby's caregiver know the following:

>> Your baby's routine, generally.

>> Your baby's bedtime or naptime routine including any songs or stories that are part of putting your child down to sleep.

>> Which foods are allowed and which aren't.

>> Any specifics about your little one such as tired signs, and signs that junior's got a full diaper or is overstimulated. You're an expert on this, after all.

>> What creams or lotions you use (and, of course, any medication, if applicable).

>> How you deal with the baby crying.

>> Any potential safety issues around the house.

>> How to get in touch with you; include alternate numbers just in case your cellphone dies. Every sitter should also know to call 911 in an emergency and to get the baby out of the house in case of fire. If your sitter knows CPR for infants, even better!

Family and friends

Those closest to you are possibly the easiest choice of caregiver if you need to take some time out and/or attend appointments. Make sure you feel totally comfortable with this arrangement, and be sure to brief them in the same way you would nonrelated helpers. Family members are most likely going to be stoked to spend some time with junior, and some one-on-one time is a great way to build an attachment with relatives.

Just ask the relatives how often they may want to do it, because you don't want babysitting to become too much of a chore for them. Not all grandmas today want to spend all their free time babysitting — they've got their own full schedules!

TIP

Create a babysitting club with likeminded parents, especially if they're friends you already know well, where you take turns looking after each other's babies.

Nannies

A nanny is a professional who is trained to look after children in your home, and hiring one can be expensive — you're paying the person's income. Some nannies look after multiple children in one house, so you can team up with friends and split the cost.

REMEMBER

Make sure you go with a reputable agency that has done all the necessary checks on the nanny and can guarantee your nanny has qualifications, knows basic first aid, and has been vetted by the police. If in doubt, ask to see your prospective nanny's paperwork. Most importantly, check references.

A written contract is the most professional way to ensure that you and your nanny are on the same page about her duties, her pay, her use of a car, and other issues that may arise. If you have specific requests, for example, that she take your baby to the park daily, put it in the contract. You can't argue with a signed document!

A nanny should

>> Take care of your child's physical, intellectual, emotional, and social needs — that is, feed him, play with him, and be someone he feels safe and secure with.

>> Take care of your child's laundry (not yours), cloth diaper cleaning, cooking, and bottle washing.

Hiring a nanny can be complex, especially if you're providing a room for her to live in and paying her healthcare insurance. You'll need to keep good records so you can properly file paperwork at tax time. A nanny can cost between $16 to $20 per hour, plus fees to the agency who places her. Live-in nannies are paid slightly less, because you're supplying them with room and board.

Some agencies can also provide nannies from abroad (in some cases they're referred to as *au pairs*). This may be a good way to expose your child to another language. However, au pairs usually stay with you for only up to 12 months.

While nannies are experienced caregivers, make sure you leave special instructions about your baby and the house. Also, nannies aren't maids, so don't expect them to do your washing and cleaning or to look after your household at the same time.

When choosing a nanny, interview the person with your baby there, and see how they interact together. The nanny should spend more time chatting and playing with the child than talking to you.

Some questions to ask prospective nannies include the following:

>> What's your family situation?

>> What are your qualifications?

>> How do you feel about me working from home from time to time?

>> Why do you like children?

>> What do you dislike about looking after children?

>> What is your philosophy on boundaries and discipline?

>> What is your philosophy on play and stimulation?

>> What do you do when a baby is sick and you can't wake her up? (Correct answer: Call 911!)

Babysitters

Babysitters are different from nannies in that they usually look after children just for a few hours — that is, a morning, afternoon, or evening. The majority of sitters are cheaper, too, than nannies. Expect to pay anywhere from $10 to $20 an hour. If you go through an agency, you have to pay a placement fee and will probably face higher hourly charges as well.

In most cases you don't need to worry about being late getting back (but check beforehand) — after all, they're paid by the hour.

Teenage babysitters may be cheap, but they should still have access to adult help and a car with an approved safety car-seat restraint, in case of an emergency.

PUTTING IN A NANNY CAM

You trust your nanny or sitter — at least you want to. But this is your most precious possession you're talking about, so how far should your trust go? On the other hand, you probably wouldn't want someone filming you without your knowledge, although if you work in a hospital, a federal building, or any one of a million other places, you're probably already being filmed, at least part of the time.

It's legal in all 50 states to film without informing your nanny that you're doing it, with some exceptions. You can't film private areas like her room or, of course, the bathroom. In some states, you also can't record audio, unless you tell your nanny you're doing it.

If you can, it's probably better to tell your potential nanny that you have cameras set up, so she doesn't find them by accident.

REMEMBER

Interview your prospective babysitter just like you would a nanny (refer to the previous section). You're leaving this person in charge of the most important person in your world!

Day care centers

Sending your little one off to day care can be a heart-breaking experience for a dad. It can be really hard on mom, too, so be there with a supportive shoulder and some reassuring words — and a box of tissues — if she's upset.

You're essentially entrusting your child to strangers in a strange place, so don't hold back from getting to know your day care center well. The more confident you are about the place, the more confident junior is likely to be as well. Make sure to visit the center more than once to get a good feel for what it's like at different times of the day.

You can find a range of different types of child care facilities — community, not-for-profit, and commercial. Many churches run day care centers, but many take only toddlers or preschoolers, not infants.

Centers must have special programs for each age. Some take babies from 6 weeks old, and others don't take children under age 2. Some have half-day attendance; others don't. Some provide meals; others don't. Shop around for what works best for your family. In the United States, day care centers charge an average of around $1,000 per month for full-time care.

Child care in some areas is in high demand. So register your interest early if you want to make sure of a place for your little one when you need it. Waiting lists in bigger cities or popular neighborhoods can be up to two years.

Here are a few things to look out for with a day care center:

>> Do their opening hours work with your schedule?

>> Do they charge if you're late picking up your child?

>> Do they check a permissions list for whomever is picking your child up? Do they ask for identification?

>> Do they open during holidays, and if so, how much do they charge?

>> What are the teachers like? Are they bubbly and fun to be with? Do they have a rapport with the children — remember that your child will most likely be continuing in day care for a few years — and communicate with them well? Is one particular teacher assigned to look after your child more than the other teachers?

>> What qualifications do teachers have, and are they trained in first aid? Is there an AED (automated external defibrillator) onsite, and have staff been trained in how to use it?

>> What philosophy does the center have on activities, play, discipline, and behavior issues? How do they handle children's behavioral problems such as hitting other children?

>> What medicines do they have on the premises, and what is their policy on giving medicines to children? What happens if your child is hurt?

>> Does the center have fire extinguishers, exits, alarms, and smoke detectors? What are their policies in case of emergencies such as earthquakes or fire?

>> Do they have a webcam, where you can peek in on your child?

>> What foods are the older children given? Can you request special food, like gluten-free or organic? Is the center nut-free?

>> What happens at sleep time? Does the center have a policy on pacifiers, or special blankets and toys? What happens to children who don't have a nap? Most centers usually have a dedicated sleep room, with a teacher checking on children every few minutes. Some centers provide bedding; others encourage you to bring your own.

>> Is there a service for picking up children after school (looking ahead to the future again)?

>> What activities are available at the center?

>> Does the center take the children on trips outside the center?

>> Are children separated by age once they become toddlers, or do they all play together after a certain age, say 2?

>> Who should you speak to if you have any concerns?

>> How do teachers keep track of your child's progress? Most centers have a book with stories and pictures of your child's activities.

TIP

Ask if the center is accredited by one of the national accreditation programs (see the following sites: www.naeyc.org/academy/, www.earlylearningleaders.org/?page=accreditation, and www.necpa.net/index.php). If not, ask why. Each state also has its own requirements for day care centers; make sure your center knows the regulations and complies with them.

TIP

After a few weeks, assess how well your child has settled in. Does your baby seem clean and well kept, and is she generally happy when you pick her up? Does the center have a bad habit of losing her extra outfits or blankets? Also, drop in unannounced to see what your child is up to. Make a regular appearance at lunchtimes — most centers offer days where parents can come in to eat with their children.

In-home care

In-home care with a trained caregiver looking after several children at the same time in her own home is a different set-up from a day care center, but, in principle, you can still ask the same sorts of questions. With in-home care, also known as family day care, your child is usually placed with one caregiver, who looks after your little one (and other babies/children) in the caregiver's own home.

Because you're dealing with just the one caregiver, you can often get to know the person better than the teachers at a day care center and can sometimes be a little more flexible in drop-off and pick-up hours.

REMEMBER

To avoid both you and junior feeling anxious about the daily routine and other issues, you're best to take the time and energy to build rapport with the caregiver.

TIP

Go with a reputable company when choosing in-home care; they will have vetted your caregiver's house for safety, given them training, and done police checks. Get references, talk to other parents, and spend time there at different times of the day.

So what's important when choosing in-home care?

>> Does your child get one-on-one attention?

>> What learning program is in place? Is TV time limited?

>> What foods are provided when your child gets older?

>> What are the sleeping arrangements? (Single bed, bunk beds, floor space: Be sure you're happy with the safety aspects, and make sure all cribs are newer and meet current safety standards.)

>> What are the other children under the caregiver's wing like?

>> What happens if my sitter gets sick?

>> What happens when my child is sick?

>> What happens if I'm late picking up my child?

>> Does the main caregiver know CPR?

Chapter 9
Months Six to Twelve

You've firmly got a handle on this fatherhood business now, haven't you? The next six months are all about your baby becoming more aware of her body and using it to get around, from rolling on the floor to getting up on her feet and doing that amazing thing babies do, walking. Witnessing your small, vulnerable child set out on the path to independence is amazing.

Of course, she needs you, her dad, to hold her hand as she makes her way. So keep up the good work; you're doing a fantastic job!

But wait — there's more to discover! In this chapter we show you how to cope with your baby's ravenous appetite and what you need to feed her now that milk's not cutting it anymore. And speaking of cutting, we let you in on tips so teething is less of a trauma for your baby. We show you the amazing changes your baby is going through to become a mover and shaker, and how to manage a trip or vacation with baby in tow. And last but not least, we conclude with a little party — your child's first birthday.

Keeping Up with Baby

If you thought your baby changed a lot in the first six months, hold onto your burp cloth, because things don't slow down just yet.

Your baby's evolving diet

Until now, breast milk or formula has been all the food your baby needs. But to keep up with her growth, she needs to move on to solid food. Most health professionals and breastfeeding organizations recommend waiting until baby's around six months old before trying solids, which aren't really that solid, more like puree and mush. But you may find your little one is ready to start a few weeks earlier than the six-month mark.

Signs that your baby is ready for solids

Your baby gives you some signs he's ready for solids by

>> Looking a bit famished after a milk feeding — he's waiting around for more.

>> Paying attention to what you eat, perhaps following your fork going into your mouth and making little chewing faces.

>> Pointing at food on the table or trying to grab food that's within reach.

>> Being able to hold his head up for long periods at a time and take food onto his tongue. If he's not ready for solids, he'll push the food out again, called the *extrusion reflex*.

First foods and how to feed them to your baby

As your baby's digestive system is still pretty undeveloped and he doesn't have any teeth with which to break down food, first solid foods have to be pureed or mashed thoroughly so they're almost runny. Some good first foods to try include

>> Cooked and pureed apple, pear, apricot, peach, carrot, pumpkin, potato, peas, sweet potato, or green beans.

>> Iron-enriched baby cereal or baby rice. You can use breast milk or formula to mix these.

>> Uncooked and mashed banana and avocado.

Here's how to feed solids to your baby for the first time:

>> Give your baby a milk feeding first. Solid food comes after milk feedings until about eight months of age.

>> Try one food, such as carrot, for three to five days in a row to make sure your baby has no reaction to that food.

>> Try your first food when baby seems relaxed and happy, not when she's super hungry, tired, or grumpy. Lunchtimes or early afternoons are often good times.

>> If she's not into her carrots at first, that's okay. Try again tomorrow and if she's still not into it, give her a few days before trying again. It can take ten attempts before your princess discovers her passion for a particular food.

>> Let baby decide how much she needs to eat. Force-feeding her is not likely to make eating vegetables something she looks forward to. Let her appetite guide you. It may be only a few teaspoons at first.

REMEMBER

A few things to remember about feeding solids to your baby are

>> A baby's sense of taste is very sensitive, and he won't need salt, sugar, or spices to flavor a food.

>> Some people insist on heating their baby's food, but this is more a matter of adult taste than baby's. If you do heat your child's food, test it yourself before spooning it to him to make sure the food's not scalding hot.

>> You'll need a highchair, a lot of bibs, and some sort of protective plastic matting for your floor — unless you like orange patterns on your kitchen floor.

>> You can buy plastic feeding spoons, which are gentler on baby's gums and smaller than teaspoons. They look huge compared to your little one's tiny mouth.

>> As your baby gets older, food can become more textured and less runny.

Adding new foods and routines

Once your baby has the hang of solid food, try mixing different foods for a range of flavors. Introduce meat into her diet, because at six months old she needs more iron to support the growth of her rapidly developing brain.

WARNING

Cooked liver can be given to boost her iron supply, but only once a week as it contains a lot of vitamin A, which your baby can get too much of.

Try adding these foods to the menu:

>> Cooked meat like beef, chicken, liver, and lamb; meat must be pureed, minced, or served as a broth so it's soft and fine enough for an infant to eat

>> Egg yolks (from hard-boiled eggs)

>> Uncooked melon, plum, and nectarine

>> Finger foods such as toast, cereals, and crackers

REMEMBER

Try each food for three to five days to make sure your champ isn't allergic to it. If he is, he'll have a bloated tummy, a rash, or a hard time breathing. Call 911 right away if he's having a severe reaction.

WARNING

Honey is potentially lethal for babies up to 12 months of age. Honey can contain bacteria that release botulinum toxin, a neurotoxin that can lead to severe food poisoning. Honey is safe to eat by toddlers from about 1 year of age because their digestive system is fully developed and can neutralize the toxins.

After eight months you can introduce these foods into baby's diet:

>> Cooked creamed corn, cabbage, and spinach

» Fish, unless your family has a history of fish allergy, in which case wait until your baby is a year old

» Pasta and rice

» Smooth peanut butter, unless there's a family history of nut allergy, in which case wait until baby is 3 years old

» Soy foods like tofu and tempeh

» Uncooked kiwifruit, orange, berries, pineapple, and tomatoes

» Yogurt, cheese, custard, and ice cream, unless there's a strong family allergy to dairy, in which case wait until your baby is a year old

At eight months, your baby can also start exploring finger foods such as slices of soft fruit, cooked vegetable pieces, grated cheese, and cooked pasta pieces. Avoid anything small and hard that may choke your baby, like hard nuts, popcorn, and hard candy.

If you're not sure about when a particular food is okay to feed to your baby, check with your healthcare provider.

After eight months, solid food takes on more importance in baby's diet and can be given before a milk feeding. Move baby onto three meals a day, with breast milk or formula snacks mid-morning and in the afternoon, if your doctor agrees.

Encourage family meals from the start. Pull the highchair up to the dining table so the three of you can enjoy your meals together. Your baby learns the mechanics of eating from you by copying, and you teach her that eating is about sharing a meal and eating healthy food together.

Don't pass your food preferences to your baby. For example, if you don't like broccoli, you needn't put it in front of your baby in a way that makes it obvious you don't like it. Why should he like broccoli if you present it poorly? Make encouraging noises, like "Yummy yummy broccoli," when you serve food.

Taking care of teeth

In the coming months your baby gets her first teeth (see the section on teething later in this chapter for more information), so you need a new piece of equipment — a tiny toothbrush. You can instill healthy oral hygiene early by making tooth-brushing time good fun.

Special low-fluoride toothpaste and soft toothbrushes for babies are available. You need only a pea-size dot of paste at the moment, if for nothing else than it provides a bit of taste for baby to think about while you brush his gnashers.

TIP

Brushing teeth with the little one is another perfect dad job. If you're a working dad, you can integrate brushing teeth into your baby's bedtime routine. That way you get even more daddy–baby time in your day.

Keeping up with your little explorer

From rolling over, to crawling, to pulling up, to cruising, to walking — the next six months are characterized by your baby's growing mobility and all the challenges that brings for dads. Of course, you followed our baby-proofing instructions in Chapter 7 to the letter, and your house is a place where your baby can free range and explore to his heart's content once he's mobile. But you can't just let him loose on your house to do his exploring. Instead, help his exploration by exposing him to all sorts of different materials and textures. Use plenty of chatting about what he's experiencing to help develop his language at the same time.

The routines, they're a-changing

All babies are different, but you may be surprised to wake one morning and find the sun's up and baby hasn't even made a whimper. This can be terrifying — you rush into her room to make sure nothing is wrong, only to be met by a sweetly sleeping baby who wakes just as you enter and greets you with a smile. Yep, your baby has slept through the night — a miracle!

REMEMBER

If your baby hasn't slept through the night after six months, don't worry. Teething, getting enough to eat, and not having a developed sense of sleep yet can keep her waking up at night. Also bear in mind that sleeping through the night can mean from

10 p.m. to 5 a.m. Don't get stressed about getting your baby to sleep for 12 hours at a time — this may or may not happen with your little one.

You may also notice that baby is awake more and more during the day and is settling into having two naps a day, one in the morning and one in the afternoon. At six months, your baby needs about 14 hours of sleep in a 24-hour period. By 1 year of age, she may be giving up one of her naps in favor of a nap in the late morning or early afternoon. Let her decide when she naps by reading her tired signs.

REMEMBER

A change in routine can be messy and may result in things being unsettled for a while, but if you roll with it and remember that everything is just a phase, things settle in no time at all. Some health professionals say that pretty much any routine can be changed over a period of two weeks (consistency is important), so don't worry that you're being locked into a schedule you can't change.

With the rate of development your baby is going through right now and all the new skills he's picking up, you may find he's too excited for sleep and tries out his new party tricks at sleep time, such as pulling up on the side of his crib or crawling around his bed. Some babies pull up on their crib and find they can't get down again, so they cry out for your help. Just ease him back down with your well-practiced settling techniques and wait for this phase to blow over. One sure thing about parenting and dealing with babies and kids is that things change frequently.

Adopting your own parenting style

As your baby becomes an active toddler, the way you manage her behavior comes to the fore. The researcher Diana Baumrind defines four different styles of parenting: authoritarian, authoritative, neglectful, and permissive. These parenting styles influence the relationship you have with your child, including how you manage discipline and behavior.

Each style has its own characteristics, and, although you may find yourself changing styles at times, most parents tend to adopt one of the following as their basic parenting philosophy:

>> **Authoritarian:** A kind of parenting in which children are "seen and not heard" and the parent has high expectations that the child follow rules. Parents don't allow for dialogue between themselves and their children, and are not responsive to children's wishes. It's the parents' way or the highway.

>> **Authoritative:** This style of parenting also has high demands on the children to follow rules, but the parents also respond to their children, explain boundaries and limits, and encourage the child's independence. Children know where they stand and are encouraged to have an open dialogue with their parents.

>> **Neglectful:** Also known as *detached* or *uninvolved* parenting. The title says it all — parents don't engage with children, children don't have limits or boundaries, and parents are not responsive to children's needs. This style of parenting has been linked to truancy and delinquency in teenage years.

>> **Permissive:** Also known as *indulgent* parenting, parents have low expectations of the children but are highly responsive to them. The parents may be loving and nurturing, more like friends than parents, with few limits or boundaries for the children. This parenting style is likely to lead to some issues with authority as your child grows.

Your child needs your love and nurturing, to feel safe with you, and to know she has boundaries, which she will keep pushing until she's well into her twenties! Have a chat with your partner about the way you would like to parent your child as she grows older. If you're interested in more about parenting styles and discipline, check out Chapter 10, where we talk about the principles of effective discipline.

Hey, you're getting good at this

Seen the way your baby responds to you these days? With smiles and squeals? He knows without doubt you're his dad, and he thinks you're a bit of a rock star.

Perhaps you'd like to take the reins for the day and spend a day alone with your baby. Send mom out for the day or let her have a day lounging in bed while you and your little one get your groove on together. You may even surprise yourself with how naturally being a dad comes to you now. Isn't it amazing how far you have come on your fatherhood journey? Pat yourself on the shoulder and enjoy your new skills.

Playtime with Daddy

The second half of your baby's first year is characterized by his growing mobility, which is great news for dads. Soon you'll be at the park on slides and swings, or kicking a ball around. But you have to learn to walk before you can run, and you can help your little guy get the strength he needs to be on his feet.

Sitting, crawling, and walking

All babies are different and develop at different rates, but generally you can expect your baby to be

- ›› Rolling over from her back to her front between three and six months
- ›› Sitting unsupported between six and eight months
- ›› Crawling between 8 and 11 months
- ›› Walking between 11 and 17 months

Each stage of mobility is pretty exciting. The first time he rolls over, you may praise him like he's just discovered a cure for cancer, and taking his first step is a moment to treasure. Activities and games you play together at all these different levels of mobility encourage your baby's strength and learning.

REMEMBER

Your baby is a little parrot and loves to mimic you. You help her move and learn just by being there and having time to play. She watches you sitting, getting up, and walking, and wants to copy what you're doing.

Some activities to help your baby get the strength to reach these milestones include

» **Sitting:** To sit, your baby needs good head control and good balance, both of which are encouraged by tummy time. By lying on the floor on her tummy, she instinctively lifts her head to see you or any interesting toys nearby. You could even have a mirror in front of her so she can see another baby — and a miracle — two dads! You can encourage her balance with some gentle rolling, which helps develop the vestibular system in the ear that controls balance.

» **Crawling:** Once your baby is sitting unsupported for a while, he'll start to want to reach out for things around him and then work out how to get back onto his tummy. From here he'll work out how to move his body forward and commando crawl by almost slithering along the floor! As he builds strength in his arms and legs, he'll get up on all fours and work out how to propel himself forward, and voilà — he's crawling.

You can develop your baby's strength by putting things out of his reach that he can move toward, like blocks, or by rolling a ball near him. When he is crawling confidently, challenge him by giving him tunnels to climb through or chairs to crawl under. Get down on your hands and knees and chase him along — babies love to be chased! Don't forget to give baby lots of different textures to try out, like crawling on grass, carpet, your bed, or at the beach.

» **Walking:** As she gets stronger, your little one will figure out that she can pull herself up to standing on solid objects like walls, her highchair, or her crib. She may want to hold your hands and walk everywhere, using you for balance. After some months of practicing, she'll have the confidence and balance to stand by herself and take a few wobbly steps on her own.

No doubt she'll have a lot of falls and there will be tears, but falls and tears are all part of the learning process, and she will gain confidence, balance, and strength. Be there with a kiss and a cuddle for those bumps and scrapes.

People may say to you that once your baby's walking she'll be into everything, and you won't get a moment's peace. That's a very limited view of parenting, because there's a huge upside to it. Your baby can now explore much more of the outdoors, kick balls around in the yard, and explore just about everything much more easily, without being dependent on you. This is a huge step toward independence and should be celebrated. When your child is walking, she can do things like greet you at the door when you get home from work or hold your hand as you walk together to the park, and express her preferences and personality more. Of course this new freedom does come with a need for extra vigilance for parents.

WARNING

When your child is walking, be prepared for her to run away (and expect you to chase her). Be vigilant — she can disappear in a flash when your back is turned. Take extra care around roads, dogs, and water. Double-check your baby-proofing now that your toddler is upright. Make sure that gates on stairs are secure, cover all sharp edges (such as those on brick fireplaces and coffee tables), and put childproof coverings over outside door handles.

REMEMBER

Not all babies develop in the same order. Some miss crawling and shuffle along on their bottoms, like little crabs, or go straight to walking. If you're concerned about your baby's development, talk to your healthcare provider. And don't compare your kiddo with the neighbor's kid — even if they were born within five minutes of each other. Each child has her own developmental timetable.

Talking the talk

Just as the first year is shaped by baby's growing mobility, the second year is shaped by language and emotional development. But just because your baby isn't talking yet doesn't mean she can't understand you. In fact she's soaking up what and how you're saying things to her. When she's figured out how to get her lips and tongue and mouth coordinated, language tumbles out of her mouth.

Your baby's babbling and raspberries, shouts and whoops are all attempts to communicate, although she hasn't mastered language yet. Observing her attempts at language is often hilarious. She may turn to you with a serious face and deliver a speech in what sounds like Mongolian or some ancient language, which you can't make heads or tails of. If you respond with "Really?" or "Is that so?" she'll keep going, and eventually words you recognize will start emerging.

Babies learn by repetition, so reading the same book over and over, or using the same phrases for activities like changing a diaper or making her cereal, all sink in. Your little one is learning to associate words or phrases with activities, objects, and situations. So don't be surprised if you hear her say things exactly the way you do (and that goes for everything, so if you don't want your child to use certain words, hold your tongue when she's around).

Talk to your child and let him know what is happening today: "Today, honey, we are going to see Brian, and then we are going to the supermarket and then home for a snack." He may not say anything in response, but he's soaking up those words.

Children use different speech sounds at different ages. When your child will make certain speech sounds depends on how difficult they are to make. For example, some sounds such as "m" and "b" are easy to say and these will probably be some of the first sounds your little one makes.

TIP

For more information about when to expect your little one to start using certain speech sounds, go to www.nidcd.nih.gov/health/voice/pages/speechandlanguage.aspx#1.

WARNING

Along with "duck," "ball," and "dog," your baby will pick up the less savory words that he hears around the house. Censor yourself early on — you don't want junior announcing to the world he can swear like a sailor when grandparents come to stay. This also goes for what you say about other people. Kids have a remarkable way of remembering all the things you said about Brian a few days ago and telling Brian everything you said the next time he sees him.

Introducing your baby to water

One of the joys of having a baby over six months old is that you can go swimming in a pool together! Before then, his immune system is probably not up to it—he's not able to control his temperature well, and his neck muscles aren't strong enough to allow him to control his head. Public pools often have separate pools for babies and toddlers, and it can be worthwhile taking swimming lessons with your little one, as much for your own confidence handling your baby in the water as for baby's sake.

Instructors can show you how to glide your baby through the water, help him float on his back, and eventually put his head underwater. At this age, being in the pool is all about having fun and becoming confident in the water.

TIP

You can buy special swimmer diapers that hold in any urine or stool that junior may do while in the pool. Many pools insist that young children wear these.

WARNING

If your baby has had diarrhea, keep her out of a public pool for at least two weeks. If baby has eczema, chlorine and water may irritate it, so put the swimming on hold until the eczema has cleared up. Avoid going to the pool altogether if your baby is unwell, particularly if he has an ear infection.

REMEMBER

Instilling a sense of confidence around water in your child now is a good idea, so start teaching basic water safety. Always supervise your child around water. Children ages 1 through 4 have the highest drowning rates. A child can drown in *any* amount of water. See `www.cdc.gov/HomeandRecreationalSafety/Water-Safety/waterinjuries-factsheet.html` for more information.

These tips can help keep your child safe in and around water:

» Empty the bath or paddling pool as soon as you've finished with it.

» Fence your pool. Check your town ordinances to see whether your fencing meets the requirements.

» Stay within arm's reach of your child in or near the water. If the phone rings when junior is in the bath, either ignore it or take your baby with you to answer it. If you have a cordless phone or cellphone, take it to the bathroom as you're preparing the bath.

>> Keep your eye on your child every minute while he's in or around water. Many drownings occur even when a parent is "right there" because he took his eyes off the child for a minute. If more than one person is "watching the baby," be very clear about which of you is actively watching; never assume other eyes are on your child.

Connecting with playgroups

No matter how much fun you're having with your baby at home, there will be days when you just have to get out and see adults. Going along to a playgroup can be a good way to entertain your little one and get some much-needed adult company at the same time. One of the great things about playgroups is that there's a whole range of ages and stages, and plenty of other dads and moms to talk with about what's happening in your little one's world and what's coming up next.

Playgroups are usually a group of parents getting together in a community center, church, or other public space where children can play safely and parents can meet other parents. Playgroups can also meet at homes, with everyone taking a turn in hosting the group. You could even start your own playgroup if one isn't in your area. Some playgroups organize musical sessions, have arts and crafts available, and provide morning or afternoon snacks for a small donation.

Children love being around other children, even if at this age they don't really interact with each other. Playgroups at churches or other community centers often have bigger toys, better books, and lots more activities than you could fit into your house — all good things for challenging your little one.

Before you join a playgroup in your community, ask yourself these questions:

>> Are there activities suitable for my child's age?

>> How safe are the facilities?

>> Is the playgroup convenient for me? Does it work for baby's sleep time, is it easily accessible for strollers, and does it cost much?

>> What is the policy for dealing with other people's children? Am I allowed to pick up another person's child? How is conflict between children handled?

>> Who is running the playgroup? Is there a commercial interest behind it?

TIP

Check out `www.parenthood.com/article/how_to_start_and_run_a_successful_playgroup.html#.VreUa11oThU` for ideas on how to start and run a playgroup.

Who needs toys when you've got wrapping paper?

If you like gadgets, you'll love the toys that are on the market these days. You may find yourself piling up the shopping cart with battery-operated products that do all sorts of funny stuff or claim to turn your child into a genius. As well as the toys you buy, toys also turn up as gifts, your baby inadvertently steals them at playgroup, or you receive toys free with some other baby-related purchase, so you may find gadgetry piling up in your house.

But apart from the few toys we mention in Chapter 4 — cloth books, soft toys, teething toys like car keys and rattles — your baby doesn't really need most of the battery-operated toys for his development.

You certainly don't need to buy a lot of toys at this age to stimulate development, because you already have lots of really cool toys in your house right now. You just may not realize they are toys.

Here are a few examples. Babies love things that they can

>> Explore, like wrapping paper, pieces of cloth, a set of keys (best to use keys you don't actually need), or old books to gnaw on. Watch out for small pieces that present a choking hazard.

>> Make noise with, like pots and pans. Give baby a wooden spoon and let her drum happily away.

>> Mouth, like wooden pegs, wooden spoons, and those plastic spoons you're feeding him solids with (be vigilant about choking hazards).

>> Shake, like a plastic container with a tight-fitting lid half filled with rice, or a plastic milk bottle with pasta shapes inside. Glue the lids on with hot glue or Super Glue.

>> Stack, such as food containers. Small cardboard boxes or plastic bottles (which you can fill with confetti, rice, or pasta) can also be stacked.

Many babies find everyday objects, such as remote controls and cellphones, far more interesting than their toy version. A toy version will be thrown aside for the real thing any day. Take the batteries out of an old remote or phone and let your little one push all the buttons she likes without risking a call to Brazil.

If the temptation to try lots of different toys takes you, you can avoid spending a small fortune by buying costly items like an ExerSaucer (an activity station that you sit your baby in) or dress-up outfits used. Or organize a clothing and toy exchange with other families in the neighborhood or in your church or other social groups.

Toys with small parts are still off limits for little ones. Anything with parts smaller than a film canister are considered a choking risk, so wait until your baby is at least 3 years old before letting him play with toys with small parts.

Here Come Some Milestones

As we approach the end of the first year, the stay-at-home parent has usually returned to work as obligated under the terms of his employment. Time to sit back and reflect on the past year as your baby approaches her first birthday and becomes a toddler.

Preparing to return to work

Dads are not necessarily the ones bringing home the bacon these days while baby is small. Increasing numbers of fathers are staying home with their babies while mom goes back to paid employment. But sooner or later, most dads also find themselves joining the rat race and returning to work. Check out Chapter 16 for more on stay-at-home dads.

Before you head off with your briefcase, though, sit down with your partner and think about these things:

>> How will you manage days when your child is sick and can't go to day care, or days when her nanny is sick? Who will take off work?

>> How will you manage your time? Will you have time to juggle work and family? Will you have time to spend with your partner?

>> Who'll take care of the baby? See Chapter 8 for more about other people taking care of your child, such as day care and nannies.

>> Will the costs of child care outweigh the benefits of both of you going back to work?

TIP

Waiting lists for some day care centers or nursery schools can be up to two years long, so call around and get yourself on waiting lists as soon as you can.

Keeping work and family time separate is a struggle in this high-tech age, when employees and business associates expect to reach you 24/7. However, you can set a few rules for yourself so that you're not burnt out by work or short-changing your family. Make it a rule that if you have to bring work home, you wait until your baby is in bed before bringing out the work, or that your phone is switched off when you walk through the front door at night.

Likewise, when you're at work, the more productive you are the less likely you may be to have to bring work home. Keeping in mind that time spent working is time you can't be with your child helps keep you focused and value the time the two of you have together.

Going on vacation

The idea of taking a demanding, pooping, sometimes crying child who is wholly dependent on you for his survival on vacation sounds a little like an oxymoron. There's nothing vacation-like about looking after a baby! Vacations aren't the same with children, but at some stage in the first year you may want a break from staring at the same old walls.

Going on a short trip isn't such a big deal, but if you're going anywhere farther away than a couple of hours' drive, you need a few strategies to stop everyone going mental on the journey.

Driving without going crazy

Imagine if you were strapped into a car seat with a full harness at the front. You'd get pretty uncomfortable after a couple of hours, and if you couldn't stretch and move around of your own free will, you'd get a bit grumpy too. So will your baby if you don't stop every now and then to let him have a breather, some food, or a diaper change.

Here are some more ways to manage a long car trip with your baby:

>> If you're traveling during summer, keep baby lightly dressed, as he can get pretty sticky on his back or anywhere that is touching his car seat. Use visors on windows to keep glare out of his face and to protect him from the sun. Make sure he has a cup or bottle of water on hand to stop him becoming dehydrated. Avoid driving in the heat of the day if you can.

>> Make sure you've got some snacks prepared for the trip. You wouldn't want to get caught out miles from anywhere with a hungry baby who won't be satisfied with a breastfeed or bottle. It also means you've got food for baby should you break down, heaven forbid.

>> Plan your trip around when baby is due to sleep because, with any luck at all, the motion of the car will send him off to sleepyland.

>> Take plenty of toys or objects to keep your little one entertained while awake. Books or his favorite teddy bear are also great. If you can, bring a new toy or something he hasn't seen before. That way you can keep him interested for longer.

REMEMBER

Drive safely at all times. Your most precious person is in the back with you, so don't take any chances. Never take the baby out of the car seat, not even for "just a minute" or for a feeding. Pull over if you need to take him out.

Up, up, and away

The idea of air travel with a baby can strike fear into the most experienced dads, especially today, when children (and their parents) are getting kicked off flights, seemingly just for being children. The perils of confined space and air pressure issues coupled with the idea of sitting within smelling and screeching distance of other passengers aren't to be taken lightly, but they're manageable.

Here are some ways to make flying with your baby easier:

» Have plenty of books and toys to keep her entertained. Organize new things that your little one hasn't seen before. A great strategy is to wrap toys, books, and other things your baby is used to as if they were presents. Unwrapping the "present" is fun and adds to the excitement.

» If baby's restless, take him for a walk up and down the aisles. Seeing other people cheers him up and gets you out of your seat as well.

» If other parents with babies are on board, make contact with them. They may come in very handy if you need an extra pair of hands or for keeping an eye on baby while you eat or go to the toilet. Most parents of young children are quite helpful as they know what traveling with babies is like. The grandma in the next seat may even be more helpful!

» Don't expect much, if any, help from the crew. The days of helpful crew members holding your baby or even heating a bottle have pretty much gone by the wayside.

» If you're traveling on a long flight, book the bulkhead seat that most major airlines offer. You will at least have extra leg room for your baby to play on the floor at your feet.

- » Pack a drink because the swallowing action helps your baby equalize her ears. If mom's on hand, breastfeeding during takeoff and landing can help too. If mom's not available, give your baby something to drink or eat during takeoff and landing.

- » Bring your baby's airline-approved car seat. Your baby will be more comfortable and also safer in it.

- » Stay calm. If you're calm, baby will most likely be calm too.

- » Take a fully packed diaper bag with diapers, a changing mat, wipes, plastic bags for dirty diapers, diaper cream, spare clothes, and snacks or jars of baby food. And lots of toys — lots.

- » When you check in, hold onto your stroller until you board and then gate-check it. Navigating through airports and departure lounges and carrying all the bags is a lot easier when you've got a safe place to put baby.

If you're traveling overseas, your baby needs his own passport.

If you're staying overnight somewhere, you need

- » A crib for baby to sleep in, with appropriate bedding. Most hotels and motels have portacribs, but check when you make your booking. When you get there, make sure the model you're given is safe and in good condition.

- » A mini first-aid kit of teething remedies, pain reliever, and any lotions and potions your baby needs.

- » A stroller or baby carrier, depending on how much walking you plan to do.

- » Diapers and diaper-changing accessories.

- » The usual clothes, toys, and books.

Wow, that's strange: Addressing your concerns

By now, you know your baby well enough to know when something's not quite right. You may discover something unexpected, such as a rash, or your baby makes a fuss at something specific, or something just doesn't feel right.

Father knows best

Sometimes it may be easy to figure out the problem; other times, if you ignore it, it will likely go away on its own. Or you can do some research and deal with your concerns. This doesn't mean buying every book in the store about childhood illness, but observing your baby's body and moods and acting accordingly.

Nobody expects you to know everything about your baby, but you are the best judge if something's not right. Trust your instincts and don't be afraid to ask for help if you need it. Healthcare providers are there to provide help.

REMEMBER

Get involved in your child's healthcare. If something's wrong, don't leave it to mom to work out or take him to the doctor; get in on the act as well. You'll be prepared for when the problem happens again.

Teething

Teething is the biggest issue for babies aged 6 to 12 months. Having a sharp tooth cut through her gum can be very upsetting for your child, especially because she won't understand what's going on.

Signs that baby is teething include the following:

>> Her cheeks may be bright red.

>> She drools a lot.

>> She puts objects in her mouth more than usual.

>> She may get diaper rash.

>> She's more cranky and clingy.

>> She may run a low-grade fever. Doctors' opinions differ as to whether this is a "normal" part of teething, so ask yours.

Here are some simple ways to help relieve her discomfort:

>> Teething necklaces can help teething babies. These are special necklaces that can sometimes be chilled in the refrigerator to make them more soothing for swollen gums.

>> Chilled apple slices wrapped in a piece of muslin cloth tied with a band are soothing and healthy for her too. Baby sucks and gums the apple, but bits can't come free in her mouth. Chill fruit in the fridge, not the freezer.

>> Some parents swear by commercial teething gels, but make sure you're happy with the ingredients in them first.

>> Toys with some "give" in them and texture can help numb pain when baby bites on them by causing counter pressure. Some toys can be filled with liquid and chilled in the fridge.

WARNING

As tempting as it may be, don't put teething toys with gels in the freezer. This may make them too cold, which can cause more pain for your little one.

If all else fails and baby is just too upset with all these remedies, some infant acetaminophen or ibuprofen can be given. Check with your healthcare provider about the correct dosage for your child's age and weight.

TIP

When baby is teething, he needs more cuddling and may be a bit clingy. He may wake up at night more and be difficult to settle. Try to be patient — teething is not much fun. The love you show your child when he needs you like this builds trust and security in your baby.

How time flies

Now that you're a dad, time seems to evaporate in front of your eyes. Fatherhood is like a whirlwind tour of your favorite places in the shortest time possible. If you don't take photos and keep a diary, you soon forget the journey. So much happens in the first year. Not only does your baby transform into a toddler, but you and your partner are also transformed into completely awesome parents.

So how can you capture this first year?

>> Keep a diary. You could even do it online with a blog.

>> Take lots of photos of your little one. Pictures paint a thousand words.

>> Start a book for your child where you can record her first words and foods, and the dates when she first rolled over, crawled, and walked. You can also keep photos and mementos in the book.

REMEMBER

None of this makes any difference if you're not interested in recording these memories. Be interested in contributing to a diary and your photos and spend loads of time having fun with your baby when you take them. When your child becomes interested in his past, he'll really appreciate the effort you put into recording him as a baby.

One year old today!

What, already?! Your baby isn't a baby anymore — she's a toddler now. How did that happen? Didn't you only just bring her home from the hospital brand-new, like, last week?

Congratulations to you and your partner. Marking this milestone is just as much for you, the parents, as it is for your child — in fact, probably more! One year ago your baby was born and turned your lives upside down.

So gather your family and friends and celebrate your baby turning one. A birthday celebration is an excellent way to thank those around you for all the support they've given you over the last year and to cement your child's place in your family.

Your baby won't remember or even understand that today is her birthday, but if you want to mark the day with a child's party, here are some tips to make it memorable:

>> Plan well in advance to allow yourself enough time to get everything done.

>> Plastic cups and plates make cleaning up easier and, with little ones around, make breakages less likely.

>> Provide food for adults as well as safe food for children. Avoid nuts and hard foods that may choke little ones. Have a balance between healthy and treat foods.

>> Take lots of photos! Baby won't turn one again.

>> Time the party around sleep times. You don't want the superstar of the day to be grumpy because he should be sleeping. Other parents will be working around their children's sleep times too, so expect people to be late and leave after only an hour or two.

TIP

Start the day with quiet family time so you, your partner, and your child can look back on the past 12 months and marvel at what you have now in front of you.

The Toddler Years

Chapter 10

Toddling Toward Two: Months 12–24

However challenging toddlers can be, the second year of life is also a delightful age. Language, social, and motor skills are all developing, and toddlers can surprise you with what they understand and repeat back to you as they grow. Your little eagle-eye will remember where you hid the cookies, can figure out what the remote control does, and will mimic your gestures and movements in such a sweet, naïve way that it will make you crack up with laughter.

Your child's first words may be a little predictable — Mom, Dad, ball, dog, more. But be prepared for some unexpected words — noisy, heater, dinosaur, or even toothbrush. Kids this age are often called sponges and that's what they are, sucking up knowledge like you wouldn't believe. The kid who just celebrated his first birthday is going to be quite a different boy when he turns 2.

In this chapter, you find out all about his development, as well as how to cope as he deals with frustration, anger, and all manner of emotions he can't figure out. We also take you through the changes in your child's eating, sleeping, and health and safety needs.

Hey, You Have a Toddler Now

Once your child starts to walk, she magically transforms from a baby into a toddler. Just the word *toddler* can strike fear into a dad: Toddlers have a reputation for getting into trouble. Your little one is also a ticking tantrum time bomb now. You've probably heard the saying "terrible twos," meaning that at the stroke of midnight on her second birthday your formerly perfectly pleasant baby turns into a monster of unequalled horribleness.

It doesn't quite work like that, thank goodness. And as your toddler creeps toward being an independent little person, she'll be struggling between needing her dad every step of the way and wanting to do things her own way, thank you very much. This means she will sometimes have little meltdowns when what *you* want her to do and what *she* wants to do collide. This can start as early as right now.

REMEMBER

If your toddler suddenly starts resisting diaper changes, getting into her car seat, or having to sit in a shopping cart, she hasn't turned into a monster, she's just continuing her struggle to become an individual and have her own free will. We talk later on in this chapter about how to deal with taxing toddler behavior.

Sleeping update

Most dads by now are enjoying a good night's sleep as junior is no longer getting up for feedings in the early hours. That said, don't expect your toddler to sleep through every night. Teething, colds, being too hot or too cold, having just mastered a new skill, or simply needing some cuddle time will still have him calling out for you in the night. Often this is just temporary, and you'll be getting 40 winks again in no time.

Some toddlers also start to have nightmares and night terrors, where they wake up screaming or lashing out at you. Be there with comforting arms and some soothing words. Make bed a really happy, attractive place to be with soft toys and special blankets, which toddlers can get very attached to. Make sure there's lots of love and good feelings at bedtime.

Most toddlers go through some sort of *separation anxiety* in the first year, and it often comes back in the second. Your toddler may cling to you more, need more reassurance, and object to you leaving the room. Explain to your toddler that you're not going far or will be back soon, and some other lovely person will look after him while you're gone.

At about the one-year mark, many children go from two naps during the day to one nap, which is usually taken in the middle of the day. Let your child work out how much sleep he needs by watching for his tired signs — yawning, becoming a bit clumsy, gazing into the distance, and becoming a cranky bear — and putting him down for a nap then.

At some point he will start missing a nap, needing only one. Sometimes he may seem tired in the afternoon but will resist going to sleep and by early evening will be exhausted and falling asleep in his dinner plate, so try moving his bedtime forward a bit until he gets used to his one-nap-a-day routine.

Eating update

The start of this year will see a change in your little one's diet. As she grows more teeth, she'll be able to handle a bigger variety of foods and foods with chunkier textures. With her digestive and immune systems maturing, your toddler can handle foods that were once off the menu, such as cow's milk, honey, and egg whites.

WARNING

Small, hard foods like popcorn and nuts are still off the menu until junior is at least 3 years old, because of the choking risk.

Offer your child a variety of foods. What he doesn't like one day, he may love the next, so keep trying with things he has turned his nose up at before.

A typical toddler needs the following:

>> At least five servings of fruit and vegetables a day. A serving is the amount that fits into your child's hand. Vitamin C helps your child absorb iron, so include some vitamin C–rich fruits like citrus fruit or kiwifruit.

>> Iron from red meat, chicken, or fish, or vegetarian options like spinach and broccoli.

>> Dairy, but not low-fat. Young children need fat to grow, but keep the French fries and burgers for special treats. Toddlers need about 3 cups of dairy a day, which may be given as milk, cheese, yogurt, and the like. Don't allow your toddler to fill up on dairy and miss out on other nutrients. This is the age to eliminate bottles and switch to sippy cups. Breastfeeding toddlers will probably begin to nurse more for comfort than for nutrition.

>> Breads and cereals, but not heavy whole grains or bran until he's at least 2 years old.

WARNING

Limit the number of sweet snacks such as dried fruit, candy, and cookies because of their tooth-damaging sugar content. Additives and high sugar content in "junk" food have been linked to altering children's moods and making them possibly even more energetic than they typically are anyway, although studies have never proven this. Unfortunately, juice boxes — a staple of many toddler diets — are also very heavy in sugar content and should be limited or saved as a special treat.

TIP

Toddlers don't need to eat as much as they did in their first year of life and often become picky eaters, besides. One way to get your toddler the nutrients he needs is to offer a smorgasbord of foods in a muffin tray or other dish with small compartments. Put a little fruit in one, a little cereal in another, peanut butter on a cracker, a few pieces of cheese, and soft veggies to round out the variety, and let him pick what he wants.

Now that your toddler is able to experience more texture and variety in her meals, she can have toddler versions of your meals and eat with you. This is a good time to teach your child about the social aspects of eating, with all of you around the table talking about your day and about the food in front of you. Make sure the TV is off and just hang out together as a family. Seeing you eat good, healthy meals encourages your child to eat healthily too. The American Academy of Pediatrics supplies some guidelines for healthy eating at www.healthychildren.org/English/healthy-living/nutrition/Pages/Childhood-Nutrition.aspx.

The toddler years are often when children start to show signs of food allergies. Rashes, hives, and gastrointestinal upsets are the most common signs of a food allergy; more serious reactions, such as wheezing, shortness of breath, collapsing, or turning blue, require immediate medical help. Six foods — milk, eggs, peanuts, tree nuts, soy, and wheat —, cause around 90 percent of all allergic reactions. Introduce these foods one at a time, with several days between each introduction.

Lactose intolerance is not an allergy and rarely affects children under the age of 2. Lactose intolerance — more common in children of Asian, African American, or Hispanic/Latino descent — causes gastrointestinal upset. This usually occurs within 30 minutes to 2 hours after ingesting foods containing lactose, which includes most dairy products.

Health update

Try not to forget that your child, even though she's not a baby anymore, still needs to keep up-to-date with her immunizations. To immunize or not to immunize is a hot debate in the United States today, with most pediatricians solidly in favor of immunizing. Many will adjust the schedule if you don't want your toddler getting too many vaccinations at one time. See the Centers for Disease Control and Prevention's recommended immunization schedule at www.cdc.gov/vaccines/parents/downloads/parent-ver-sch-0-6yrs.pdf.

If your child is now at child care, he's likely to pick up every germ on the planet, and will have between 6 and 12 colds a year — which is why it seems as if he constantly has a runny nose. Even kids who aren't in child care are vulnerable to the viruses flying around, and it may sometimes seem as if junior's only just getting over one cold before another one comes along.

Children have the same symptoms of a cold as adults — runny nose, cough, headache, sneezing, and swollen glands. He may also run a low-grade fever. He'll probably wake up more often in the night for comforting and be a bit miserable during the day. Unfortunately, you can't give your child any cold medication, but you can give extra fluids, the correct dosage of acetaminophen or ibuprofen (by age), and lots of cuddling to make him feel a bit less miserable. A cool-mist humidifier may also help.

TIP

At this age, you can also show your child how to blow her nose, or at least wipe it, or blow it while you hold the tissue. Most children get a great sense of satisfaction and achievement in then putting their dirty tissue in the trash bin. Give your child heaps of praise when you show her how to do it, so blowing her nose is not a chore but a fun thing to do.

REMEMBER

You can use nonmedicated means to lessen your child's discomfort and congestion. See Chapter 7 for some tips.

Mingling with other children in the wider community also brings your little star into contact with germs that are nastier than the common cold. You may find she's come down with one of the following infections:

>> **Bronchiolitis:** An inflammation of the bronchioles (lungs' airways). Your child will have a nasty cough and may have trouble breathing. Take her to your pediatrician.

>> **Chickenpox:** Starts with a fever and cold symptoms. After a day or two, your child gets red, itchy blisters on her skin. You can calm the itch with calamine lotion or other lotions available from your pharmacy and give your child lots of soothing baths. A vaccination is available to prevent your child getting chickenpox. Talk to your pediatrician about having her vaccinated. While chickenpox is generally mild and mostly annoying, in rare cases it can cause very serious and life-threatening complications.

>> **Croup:** A cough caused by a viral infection. It starts out as a cold but becomes a pretty nasty and wheezy cough, similar to a barking seal's, that comes on suddenly. Call your pediatrician. In rare cases, croup can interfere with your child's breathing. Call 911 if he's turning blue or is unable to catch his breath.

>> **Ear infection:** If your child has an ear infection, she'll be cranky and tug at her ears or rub them. A trip to your

pediatrician to check your child's ears thoroughly is in order. She may need antibiotics to treat the infection.

>> **Gastroenteritis:** Most children have a "tummy bug" at some stage, which usually involves a lot of vomiting and diarrhea. A number of common viruses can be responsible for your child's illness. Gastro bugs can cause dehydration, so make sure your child gets plenty to drink. Gastro bugs can take a week to disappear, but if you're concerned, see your pediatrician, especially if your child can't keep anything down and is running a fever.

>> **Strep throat:** Your child may have a high temperature, tug at his throat, or act exhausted. Go to your pediatrician.

REMEMBER

If you're at all worried about how unwell your child is, take her to your pediatrician. Checking with a healthcare professional is best, especially if she's running a temperature that doesn't go down after giving her acetaminophen or ibuprofen.

To take care of a child with a fever (a temperature over 100.4 degrees Fahrenheit), try the following:

>> Give her a dose of children's acetaminophen or ibuprofen suitable for her age.

>> Keep her clothing light, and use only a sheet to cover her in bed.

>> Give her lots of fluids.

>> Keep her bedroom cool but not cold.

REMEMBER

If her temperature stays high, or you're worried about her illness, see your pediatrician. You know your child best, so if she seems not to be her usual self — for example, she's less active, quiet, or sleepy — checking with your pediatrician is a good idea. In general, look at the child, not the thermometer. The degree of fever isn't always an indication of how sick a child is.

Safety update

Of course you've completely baby-proofed the house by now, as we suggest in Chapter 7, but there's an issue to consider as your baby turns into a toddler to make sure he's safe — the walking issue.

EXPERIENCING FEBRILE SEIZURES

Few things are as frightening as watching your toddler have a febrile seizure — a seizure that occurs only when he runs a fever. Between 2 and 5 percent of children under age 5 experience one or more febrile seizures. Most last only a few minutes and do not cause any lasting harm. Stay calm, turn your child on his side, and don't try to force anything into his mouth. Call your pediatrician after to let her know. If your child turns blue or a seizure lasts 15 minutes without stopping, call 911.

Once toddlers find their feet, they're off — and fast. Leaving the front door open may spell disaster, as your child can be out of the house and down to the road in seconds. You may want to invest in safety gates for stairs, making sure that back and front yards have toddler-proof fencing and that any rooms you don't want junior visiting are closed off and out of bounds — at least until he can reach the door handle. Some parents find a playpen handy at this age, but be aware that an 18-month-old can learn pretty quickly how to get out of a playpen — and could hurt himself in the process.

In the first half of his second year, your little one will be canny enough to use other objects like chairs, boxes, and large toys to climb and get into cupboards, benches, and other places you assumed were out of reach.

WARNING

Pay particular attention to your kitchen. Take knives off the countertop. A curious toddler can work out how to grab pot handles, so keep handles tucked in toward the stove and away from inquisitive little hands.

Conscious Fathering

As parents, you have the choice to find out and educate yourselves about your children, or to not bother and rely on what you know from your own parents. While grandparents are a great source of child-rearing information, things have changed in the last 20–30 years, and you will want to change with them.

You may have heard about *conscious parenting*, which means thinking about what sort of parent you want to be and what you want for your children. Conscious parenting is also about actively taking part in learning about how children are developing. So for guys, this means conscious fathering. We believe being active in your child's life is important so you can understand and manage the different stages she's going through, rather than being dumbfounded by her behavior.

Parents realize that learning to walk is a huge developmental achievement, but so is having a tantrum. Understanding what's behind these developmental milestones makes all the difference. Reacting appropriately to your child's behavior is much easier when you know what's going on.

If you look at your toddler's new tricks (especially the challenging behavior) from the point of view that this is a phase of her growth and development, managing the way your child behaves is much easier and less stressful for both of you. That said, the environment and situation plays a big part in your toddler's behavior as well; for example, toddlers and young children act up and are difficult to manage when they're tired, hungry, or in pain or discomfort — just like most adults.

Children need

>> Consistency and consequences

>> Guidance and understanding

>> Limits and boundaries

>> Love and warmth

>> A structured and secure environment

>> To be talked to and listened to

Taking into account your child's developmental stage and temperament when you're interacting with her is also important. Read on to find out about developmental stages for toddlers.

Your toddler is learning that she has her own will and can assert herself. She's a curious little creature who doesn't know yet what the rules about living are, and she needs you to show her what her boundaries and limits are.

A Busy Year for Your Little One

Remember how much your child changed in the first year of life? She may have slowed her rapid rate of physical growth, but not her development. She's speeding toward ever-increasing abilities, skills, and independence.

Toddler development

This year is characterized by your little one taking her first steps and speaking her first words, and by her social and emotional development. By the time she's 2, she'll be able to say about 50 words, if not more.

At this time, she's developing the following physical skills:

>> Being able to see into the distance and spot things like the moon, planes, and birds in the sky

>> Climbing objects like ladders, steps, and chairs to get higher, so watch that safety!

>> Feeding herself with a spoon, then a fork, and then adding a dull knife to the equation, with much more dexterity and skill than before

>> Making attempts to run, albeit with knocked-knees

>> Performing little tasks such as "find Dad's slippers"

>> Stacking objects on top of each other, such as blocks and little chairs on tables

>> Taking her clothes off and putting on some simple clothing, such as her hat and jacket

>> Throwing and kicking a ball (however, catching is pretty advanced)

Her language skills are growing too. During this year, she's learning to

>> Listen to and understand conversations

>> Say approximately 50-plus words, although not clearly and perhaps not in coherent sentences, but rather like "Daddy gone" or "sock where?"

>> Understand simple instructions

As for her social and mental development, you'll find that she's

>> Able to feel jealous, and may object if you and your partner show affection for each other or if you're close to other children.

>> Able to remember things, and may talk about them or find things that she's left somewhere (see Chapter 7 for more information about object permanence).

>> Able to say "no" more often than you'd like and can be possessive of favorite toys.

>> Excited by presents or events, or the anticipation of seeing someone special like grandparents.

>> Incredibly curious and wants to be involved with everything that you're doing.

>> Involved for longer periods with specific toys. Tell her when you want to start a new activity, such as changing her diaper, because she may not object so loudly then.

TIP

If you announce what you're going to do next or what you'd like your little man to do next, you'll probably encounter less resistance. We all want to feel we're in control (at least a little bit) and know what's happening, and toddlers are no different, so comment on everything you're doing and tell him what's going to happen next.

>> More interested in books, and will want you to read them over and over again. Repetition is good for children's learning, so even if you've read her *Goodnight Moon* 500 times already, just keep reading it if she asks. You may find she also knows the words by heart and will call you out if you skip phrases or pages.

>> Objecting to changes in her environment or activity. If she's really enjoying playing with blocks, she may object to having a bath, even though she loves bathing.

>> Perhaps afraid of dogs, water, heights, the dark, and all manner of things, including things she used to enjoy.

>> Recognizing herself in a mirror, as well as family and friends in photos.

>> Showing more determination to do things her way or the highway. She's also showing her independence by refusing your help with tasks.

>> Very attached to mom and dad, and gets upset if you leave her alone.

Playing with your child at this age is really fun. Unlike a baby, your toddler can make full use of playgrounds and go outside and explore the landscape, and you can really talk to each other! Here are some simple things you two can do together that he'll really love and that will encourage the development of skills:

>> Play with building blocks. They fascinate toddlers and help develop fine motor skills. Try making some towers or castles together.

>> Get outdoors. Climb a tree together, get on your bikes, or head to the park or playground.

>> Let the music play. Some toddlers really love listening to music and dancing. He wants to do everything you're doing, so dance along with him. It doesn't matter if the neighbors see you.

>> Let your toddler explore. If he gets into your closet and tries on your shoes, let him go for it! What harm can it do? He may just learn the motor skills to put on his own shoes.

>> Play chase around the house. Stay just a little bit out of his reach so he has to catch you.

>> Play in the sandbox. Sandbox play helps your toddler develop fine motor skills and dexterity, as well as experience sand running through his fingers.

>> Play with water. Toddlers love pouring water into objects, so if you're washing the dishes, he can "help" by standing on a chair at the sink with you and pouring water from one cup to another.

>> Read stories together, sometimes dozens of times over. You can change things a bit by reading the story in a silly voice or asking your child questions about what's on each page as you go along.

>> Roll around on the floor together. This helps with your toddler's sense of balance and prepares him for rough and tumble play when he gets a bit older.

Toddlers can get pretty excited when rough-housing or playing and forget themselves, so you and mom need to set some rules around play. Some suggestions include no throwing balls in the house, no hitting, and no snatching toys from other children. However, children don't fully understand the concept of sharing and inflicting pain until they are much older, so they will still snatch toys and hit other children.

Be patient and consistent. When things get a bit out of hand around the playground, remove your child from the scene, distract him, or give him a cuddle as a simple intervention.

Talk about everything that you and your little one are doing. His mind is a sponge, and he'll soak up every word.

Say "daddy"

Hearing your child talk for the first time is like your cat suddenly speaking to you. For the whole of your child's life he's done nothing but coo and babble and cry, and then voilà! Words! Some of the first words he'll say won't sound like much until a light goes on in your head and you recognize "ball" or "truck" or "dog" — an amazing moment.

Communicating is more than just about words and speech; it's about body language, gestures, and the tone of your voice when you speak, which is how you can help your toddler connect ideas with spoken words. For example, the way you say "hot!" in a sharp tone indicates to your child that hot things are to be avoided, and the way you say "good boy!" with applause and a kiss helps to connect those words with good feelings.

Toddlers understand pointing, gestures, and tone before they understand words, so you can help expand your little one's language by connecting those things with words. Try to describe what you're doing so he connects that action with the words you're saying.

Unlike when you tried to learn a language at school, picking up language is really easy for young children. All your child really needs is lots of talking from you and help to connect ideas, like pictures in books, and actions, like getting dressed, with words in order to get those language synapses firing.

Toddlers typically go through a *word spurt* from 18 months onward, where they may learn a word from hearing it only once. Children who have been through their word spurts already can deduce or *fast map* what the word for a particular object is by eliminating objects they already know. Show your child three animals, such as a duck, a lion, and an animal he has never seen before. Ask him which is the duck, which is the lion, and which is the aardvark, and he'll be able to pick the aardvark because it's the animal he doesn't know.

Enthusiasm is infectious. If you're talking about how gorgeous your little petal is or how well she's put away her toys, your tone communicates how you feel about her, and that's what will hold her attention and motivate her to work out what you're saying.

Repetition of words and phrases is important, so keep pointing at the rabbit picture and saying "rabbit." Any day now you'll hear your toddler mumble "wabbit" when you point at the picture.

As we mention in Chapter 7, keep exposing your child to different languages if you can. This exposure helps his pronunciation later in life, and he will also enjoy hearing different words that describe the same thing. If you don't know any other language, learn a few words for common items — many kids' shows are great for this — and throw them into the conversation now and then.

Dad, I need to pee

Toilet training is a subject close to the heart of many fathers — those who are cheering for an end to diaper changing and those who can't bear the thought of having to clean poop out of the carpet again.

Toilet training is another of those sticks that people measure their children's success by. Most children are diaper free by 18 months to 4 years old. Some parents may brag that little Jimmy was toilet trained by 2 years as if that's some mark of his genius, but some perfectly normal, bright children aren't ready to go potty by themselves until they're 4.

Try not to get too hung up about toilet training by a certain age. Like other milestones, such as rolling over and walking, your child will toilet train when she's ready. You can lead her to the toilet, but you can't make her pee.

You know your toddler is ready to give the toilet a go when

>> She's interested in watching you go to the toilet yourself.

>> She has dry diapers for a couple of hours or more. This shows she can "save up" urine in her bladder.

>> She has the language skills to tell you she has soiled or wet her diaper, or can tell you she wants to pee or poop.

>> She starts to dislike wearing a diaper and tries to take it off.

>> She can pull up and pull down her pants or tights.

>> She can walk steadily and sit long enough to urinate or have a BM.

>> Her bowel movements are soft, well formed, and fairly predictable.

REMEMBER

Your child doesn't need to demonstrate all these signs to show he's ready to toilet train. Like starting solids, starting toilet training is something you can judge and try out. If it doesn't work, just wait and try again when more signs pop up.

In France, parents believe you shouldn't start toilet training before the child can walk up and down stairs upright and unassisted. Apparently this means the child's muscles are ready to control bowel movements. See if it works for you!

Some tips for starting toilet training are as follows:

>> Choose a settled time in your child's life to begin toilet training, not the week your parents are coming to stay or when he's due for immunizations.

>> If your child has a regular routine, find a time to try the potty that can become part of that routine.

>> Be prepared for toilet training to take a few months. Have patience if things go backward. There will be setbacks, but like everything, setbacks are just a phase. If toilet training isn't working after three months, stop and wait a month or so until giving it another shot.

>> If she's watching you use the toilet, tell her what you're doing.

>> Let her push the button to make the toilet flush to reduce the fear that comes when she hears the flush.

>> Go slowly. Don't expect her to be dry at night for a while after she has gotten the hang of the toilet in the daytime. There will be daytime accidents too, so be a patient dad.

>> Encourage her to eat fruit and drink fluid to avoid constipation.

Forcing your child to toilet train when you want her to is bound to fail. Let her guide you to when she's ready developmentally to go to the toilet. And having a potty-trained kid doesn't always make your life simpler. You can be sure he'll need to visit every restroom in every big box store you go into for the next year or two.

Here's how to start toilet training:

>> Get a plastic potty or a toilet trainer that sits on the toilet seat or on the floor. One that sits on the floor is easier for most children to manage.

>> At a specific time of day when you think junior needs to go, put her on the potty with her clothes on so she can get a feel for the potty.

>> When she's used to being on the potty each day, try it with her diaper off.

>> Change to training pants or a combination of training pants and diapers for nighttime. Training pants are designed so that junior feels wet. The idea is to help your toddler develop a cause-effect link between a wet diaper and the muscles in her body that are responsible for urinating or having a BM.

>> Give a big cheer when she produces anything at all in the toilet or potty.

REMEMBER

Don't forget to show your little one how to wash and dry her hands after using the toilet — may as well start developing good habits now.

Can we play football yet?

Any father knows that the possibilities for playing with your toddler open up dramatically once he's mobile. As he develops his throwing, kicking, and running, you may be tempted to see him as the next rising star in soccer or football or whatever you're into. That's great, as long as you don't pressure your child to perform.

The idea that toddlers, not known for their teamwork or sharing, can play team sports seems a little ridiculous at first glance, but not so. Creating structure, rules, and team spirit is a great way to introduce your child to sports, not to mention an awesome way to burn off excess energy. And sports are yet another way to encourage some dad-time with your child by giving him encouragement, helping out with practice, or even coaching.

Playing in team sports is important because

>> Children this age love to be around other kids, and being in a group helps them socialize and develop interpersonal skills.

>> It encourages your child from an early age to participate in physical activities and learn a skill with other children his age.

>> It helps develop gross motor skills such as throwing and kicking.

It's All about Me, Dad!

The newborn who didn't recognize himself in the mirror and had no idea he even had hands has left the building. Your toddler not only knows who he is, but thinks he's the only kid on the block and acts like nothing else matters — not the instructions you give him or the cat he's chasing. Now is the time to get serious about discipline.

Understanding discipline

Toddlers don't know the rules to the game of life yet, so you dads and your partners need to teach the rules to your children. Another word for this is *discipline.* Discipline's not about laying down the law and punishing your child when he doesn't conform, but about giving your kids the tools to know what's right and wrong and helping them on the way to becoming independent young people. Developing a warm, loving relationship with your child where he feels safe and secure with you is the best place to start, because he'll know you're always there for him and love him, even when he's just painted his room with toothpaste.

Children need boundaries and limits so they know where they stand and know the consequences of crossing those lines. Children are challenging in the respect that part of their nature is to push those boundaries.

Here are some tips for making discipline work:

>> Be consistent with your boundaries. If snatching a toy from a friend is not okay one day, but okay the next, junior will be confused. He needs to know from day one that snatching's not okay. At the same time, giving warmth, talking, guidance, and encouragement so he doesn't feel alienated as a result of his behavior is also important. Time-outs and more drastic consequences are more appropriate with slightly older children, such as preschoolers.

>> Be realistic about what your child can do. Children can't do everything perfectly right away and can't control their emotions or understand their bodies the way adults do. We get grumpy when we're hungry or tired, and so do children, but children don't know how to control those emotions yet.

>> Model the behavior you want to see in your children. If your son sees you punching the wall when you're annoyed, in all likelihood he'll repeat that behavior when he's annoyed. Saying you're sorry to your toddler encourages him to say it too when he needs to.

>> Communicate with your toddler, even if she isn't really speaking well yet. It may take a few explanations to show her the rules, but she'll get there. You don't need to give complicated explanations for why hitting the cat is not okay. Simply telling her he may scratch is enough.

>> Try to be patient with your child. It takes time for toddlers to learn their boundaries and to understand consequences.

>> Kids aren't naughty for the sake of it, or to wind you up. There's usually a reason. Your toddler is trying out new things every second of the day, like throwing bits of banana around the car, for the experience of it. She may also be less well behaved when she's tired or hungry, frustrated, or shy. Work with your child's routine: Don't go shopping at lunchtime or to a busy, crowded place at nap time.

>> Remember that your child just wants you to love her and to please you, which may be hard to do on a day when she's thrown bits of banana around the car. Be patient and use distraction to divert her attention while removing the banana from sight.

>> Reward good behavior with lots of love and praise, but try not to withhold love when she's behaving badly. Let her know you love *her* (the little person), not the behavior.

>> Say more positive than negative things to your child. Reword phrases; for example, "no running in the house" becomes "slow down, please."

>> You and your partner need to work out what action to take when junior is doing something undesirable. Think about the "naughty step." Distracting your child from a behavior, showing her how to clean up if she's made a mess, or taking away a toy that's being fought over are all techniques to discipline a child. Smacking a child, in our opinion, is not acceptable. Smacking has been found to be ineffective in changing behavior, and it confuses children: How can dad love me when he hits me?

We recommend using a framework for effective discipline that starts before any issues arise. It goes like this:

>> Be consistent and explain consequences.

>> Establish limits and boundaries.

>> Guide and understand him.

>> Show love and warmth to your child at every opportunity.

>> Talk and listen to him frequently.

The result will be a structured and secure environment to grow up in.

REMEMBER

If your child is really pushing your buttons with his behavior, yelling at him won't make things any easier. In fact, it may just make things worse. So try to be calm, take a deep breath, and sing a song, like "Itsy Bitsy Spider," to yourself.

TIP

When you feel yourself getting really wound up, check how you're feeling and what your day has been like. It may be that the behavior of your little one isn't actually that bad; you've just had a tough day. It may be a good idea to remove yourself from the situation to let off some steam, or lift your spirits by listening to a good song in the car.

REMEMBER

Understand the difference between discipline and punishment. Discipline is derived from "disciple" and refers to a particular code of conduct given to a person to follow. Punishment is the practice of imposing something unpleasant or aversive on somebody. Punishment doesn't involve any instruction or code of conduct, and as a result, it is typically not effective in changing behavior. Use discipline with your children rather than punishment.

Tantrums, biting, and hitting

When you first met your seconds-old baby all those months ago, you probably didn't imagine that she'd be having a full-on hissy fit in the middle of the supermarket over not being able to grab a bottle of bleach from the shelf. But it happens to even the nicest babies, with the nicest, most nurturing parents. Not only do children have tantrums, but they hit other children (or you), pull hair, bite, and scratch because they aren't yet able to control their emotions, frustrations, and physicality.

Tantrums

Although 2-year-olds are infamous for being tempestuous, even children under 2 have tantrums. Tantrums can go on into the fifth year and beyond. You've probably seen a child mid-tantrum in the street or shop, with an embarrassed, stressed-out parent standing nearby, trying to reason her little one out of it or ignore the whole thing. You probably said that your kid would never do that. But tantrums are almost inevitable.

Tantrums happen when your child is overloaded with stress or frustration. He has an idea of what he wants to do, such as running around like a crazy thing in the supermarket. If you want him to do otherwise, such as staying by your side as you shop, he's going to get pretty fed up with you holding him back and have a tantrum.

He may also be tired and hungry, or feeling vulnerable or insecure, which makes all people's tolerance for things they don't want to do much lower, even you big, grown-up fathers.

Here are some pointers on how to stop tantrums happening:

>> Make sure junior isn't tired or hungry before setting out on an activity.

>> Talk to your child about what you're going to be doing or who you'll be seeing so there aren't surprises for him.

>> If you're at the playground and it's nearly time to leave, let him have plenty of time to get used to the idea, so he understands when it's time to go.

>> Get your child involved in what you're doing so he's engaged with you rather than wanting to behave in a way that requires you telling him off.

If a tantrum is on its way, the best strategy is to ignore it. Keep close by to make sure your little one doesn't feel completely abandoned by you, but understand that trying to reason with or distract him is usually pointless. Just let him get it all out, and when the tantrum's over, give him a hug and a kiss and keep on with what you were doing. Don't get upset, as that usually just intensifies the tantrum. Keep breathing!

Talk to your partner about how you plan to manage tantrums and activities that may involve tantrums, like shopping, long car rides, or visiting people. Consistency is important in helping your toddler grow up, so the two of you need a consistent approach to handle tantrums or discipline in general.

Hurting others

Having your child come home from day care with a bite mark or scratches on her face is horrifying. Finding out that your child's the person doing the biting and scratching is also horrifying.

Your toddler hasn't gotten the hang of *empathy* (the ability to feel how others are feeling) yet, and hitting someone else hasn't registered on her list of things on the "not okay" list. Hurting others is often a sign of some underlying emotion, such as anger, fear, insecurity, or frustration. By finding out what is behind this behavior, you can address the problem directly and let her know plainly that hurting another person is never okay. Your little one doesn't necessarily grasp that her hitting or biting hurts the other person. Empathy is a complex concept that most children master only when they are around 5 years or older.

Labeling your child as a "biter" or "hitter" leads to more biting and hitting. Your child is a person, not a behavior.

Here's how you can deal with your child hitting or scratching another child:

>> Acknowledge how your child is feeling — "I know you're angry . . ."

>> Explain that's not how you deal with problems — "We don't hit people when we're angry. Hitting hurts people."

>> Give her an alternative for dealing with her anger, such as stomping her feet.

>> Show her how to touch people with kindness rather than anger.

Bear in mind that your child is still pretty young. It may be that all the behavior management is a bit too overwhelming for her at present, so try again in a few months. Be patient and gentle, and keep showing her a better way to handle conflict or frustration. This is another area where you can be a shining example as a dad — show her how it's done.

Sharing — what a nice idea

Toddlers are territorial creatures whose favorite word after "no!" is "mine!" Your sweet little boy doesn't yet understand the feelings of others and thinks only about himself. Sounds awful, but it's true.

Even kids who are best buddies at day care or cousins who adore each other's company will fight over possession of a favored toy and lay claim to what they think is theirs. Play dates, playgroups, and child care can be rife with conflict. This conflict is all part of your toddler becoming independent and learning he has some control over the universe.

But if you want to stop your child from turning out like Veruca Salt from *Charlie and the Chocolate Factory*, teach him how to share. Hearing your 3-year-old tell you "we're sharing" and knowing your good fathering got him there is amazing.

Here are some ways to help your child become the sharing type:

>> Make it clear that not sharing, such as snatching a toy away or hogging a toy that another child wants, is not okay. Even if your child *owns* the toy, snatching the toy from another is not okay.

>> Praise your child whenever she gives a toy to another child and reinforce the behavior with "good sharing!"

>> Step in if your child and another child are tussling over a favored toy. Explain that when you share, you take turns playing with something. Give the toy back to whoever had it first.

>> Show your child how both she and a playmate can use or play with the toy together.

TIP If you're hosting a play date, don't make it too long. An hour or two is long enough. Make sure you keep both children topped up with food and drink. Being hungry or thirsty can make them grumpy and less likely to play nicely.

Sharing is also a complex concept that most children don't fully grasp until they're much older (around 5 or 6 years old). However, explaining sharing to your little one from an early stage is still important. Patience is required, but eventually she'll understand why sharing is a useful concept.

Setbacks

Dealing with setbacks is a part of fatherhood. All great fathers have setbacks. Your little angel has been glorious company for a week, but one day you come home from work to find he's transformed into a monster, ignoring everything you tell him and chasing the cat like crazy. Letting fly with a few choice words may be easy but won't help anyone.

You'll almost certainly have to face a few setbacks on your fatherhood journey. Maybe setbacks are nature's way of keeping life interesting for parents, or perhaps every so often children have to take a step back to make two steps forward while they're developing. In most cases there don't seem to be any logical explanations for why setbacks occur, so you have to take them as they come. Stick with your parenting approach and don't be distracted by temporary setbacks.

These strategies can help:

>> Be consistent with your discipline.

>> Divert the energy of the annoying activity to something else that can be more easily managed, such as introducing a different toy, game, or rule.

>> Keep your cool. Take some deep breaths. Think of Monty Python's "Always look on the bright side of life" and see the funny side of it. Walk outside if you need to.

You're always going to have setbacks — they're part of being a father. Your child, even though he's acting like a demon, really only wants to be loved and to make you happy. Try to remember that when he's smearing jam on your suit jacket.

Chapter 11

Charging Toward Three: Months 24–36

H aving your child turn 2 is quite a milestone for a lot of dads — you've put some serious miles between now and when you first met your baby. Now that your little one is 2 years old, he's no longer an infant, but a fully fledged toddler. At the end of this year when he's 3, he'll graduate from toddlerhood and become a preschooler. Your little tyke may have been through a whole lot of firsts in these two years — first smile, first step, first word — but the experience of being a dad just gets better. Now you can kick a ball around, have real conversations, and share your first joke together at mom's expense.

Two is also a challenging age. Junior's getting some strong opinions about things and won't hesitate to tell you about them, although the only expression he knows for "I'm not very fond of this" may be very similar to a full-on scream. Tantrums can also really come to the fore this year.

Luckily for you, in this chapter we're here with tips for talking to your toddler in ways that may bypass the whole tantrum situation, encouraging his interests with play indoors and out, and keeping on top of discipline. We also look at the possibility of starting nursery school and changing your work to fit your new lifestyle.

Exploring the World with Dad

Your toddler is quickly getting better on her feet and really comes alive in terms of her physical ability around 2 years old. She'll be up for more sliding, swinging, bike riding, and more of everything physical. This increased physical ability is great, because it's good for her learning and good for dads to do something other than shake rattles and stumble through nursery rhymes.

Helping your toddler grow up

You can have all the DVDs in the world to teach your toddler this and that, but what really gets a little person's brain going is contact with other people, most importantly his parents. Children learn best from direct contact with other human beings. The closer the relationship with the person they're learning from, the better they pick up new skills.

Even though junior's vocabulary is expanding by leaps and bounds, he's still got a long way to go with his development. Children need stimulation to grow and learn, and the first place they look for stimulation is with parents. Keep challenging your little one to try new things out — even though you may think he's not capable yet, let him try a new skill. Learning is about taking risks (within reason) and being challenged.

TIP

Everything you do around the house is an opportunity to learn. Even washing the dishes can turn into a chance for your toddler to practice pouring water and wiping down the counters, two simple activities he may be interested in and feel really good about when he masters them. You may find you have a budding chef in the house if you involve him in making his own lunch or getting dinner ready in the evening. Kids this age love having little tasks to do and want to contribute, so let them, even if they make a bit of a mess at times.

When your child is struggling with a task or activity, try to hang back and see what happens rather than stepping in to do it for her. Moms are (generally) guiltier of this than dads, but some dads are also just too quick to step in to help. If you're always stepping in, you deprive your child of the chance to figure things out for herself and overcome obstacles, and enjoy the confidence and self-esteem that working out obstacles brings.

Developing skills and confidence

The third year of your child's life is another whirlwind of development. If the second year was all about finding her feet, the third year is about finding her voice, and she will — usually in a shopping mall or other public place, yelling "No no no" at you, but that's another topic. Her language skills are growing daily and so are her physical, emotional, social, and cognitive skills. You can help develop her skills by

>> **Challenging:** Every day, give your child an opportunity to dress herself, walk up steps by herself, wash her own face, and take other little steps toward being independent. Of course you can't expect her to master all these skills, but cheering on the progress she makes each day gives her the confidence to keep trying. Not long from now she'll be telling you she can do it all by herself, thank you very much.

>> **Drawing:** Your toddler's fine motor skills are at work when she draws pictures, or rather, scribbles. And there's nothing to stop you from joining in. You can have little draw-offs with your child, where you challenge her to draw something for you and in return you draw something for her. Get your child to explain what her pictures are about, rather than giving empty praise for her work. Ask lots of questions about what she's drawing and repeat back to her in your own words what you're looking at; for example, "Okay, I can see a house, a cat, and a dog" (which will probably look like three circles on paper at this stage). Remember — the accuracy of her drawing doesn't matter; the effort and her explanations are what count.

» **Hanging out:** If your child doesn't go to day care, you'll need to arrange some social situations for her to meet other children and play with them. This helps your child learn about sharing, cooperating, and language. She'll also see other people her age. See Chapter 9 for information about playgroups and Chapter 10 for tips on handling toddlers' interaction.

» **Making stuff:** How many cereal boxes did you believe were rocket ships when you were a kid? Resurrect your imagination (that thing you gave up when you became an adult), and use it to help your child create all sorts of toys and playthings from everyday objects. See the section "Fun and games" later in this chapter for some ideas.

» **Reading:** You can't read too much to a young child. Bringing your enthusiasm for reading to each story session encourages a love of words; stimulates your child's interest in the topic being read about; and creates a warm, secure bond between the two of you. While your toddler wants you to read the same story over and over, mix it up a bit with different authors, styles, and topics that challenge her. Buying every *Thomas the Tank Engine* title — and nothing else — isn't giving your child variety.

» **Talking:** Your toddler learns her language from hearing you talk to her. Though she hasn't mastered getting her lips, mouth, and tongue to do exactly what adults can do, she's on her way. Table 11-1 provides a guide to your toddler's speech development for her age. See www.children.gov. on.ca/htdocs/English/topics/earlychildhood/ speechlanguage/brochure_speech.aspx for more on developmental milestones for children's speech.

» **Waiting:** Like time, toddlers wait for no man — or anything else. Patience doesn't come naturally, so provide examples of good things that take time, such as cooking food in the oven, or planting seeds and keeping tabs on their growth. Doing jigsaw puzzles is another excellent way to help her develop patience and persistence to complete a task.

TABLE 11-1 **Language Ages and Stages**

Age	Your child can
2 years	Use two words together; for example, Daddy gone, more drink, no shoes
	Use words to request something, rather than just name it
	Ask questions
	Name objects without prompting
	Do a two-part task, like put the cup on the table
	Say no (a lot)
	Identify parts of the body when asked
3 years	Make a sentence of three or more words, such as "me wear shoes"
	Use several hundred words (not all at once)
	Talk about things that happened in the past
	Use adjectives like "big" and "fast"
	Talk about things that aren't present
	Ask even more questions
	Answer questions like "What's Dad up to?"
	Say her whole name
	Listen attentively for short periods

TIP

Try not to get too hung up on having little Jimmy recite the alphabet or count to 100. Memorizing isn't the same as actually understanding. You'll have plenty of time for rote memorization when he gets closer to school age.

REMEMBER

Lots of genuine praise when your toddler does something awesome, like trying to say a new word when you point at a picture, or completing an activity like putting her cup on the bench, builds her self-confidence.

Fun and games

Here are some more ideas for playing and having fun with your little one:

>> **Go camping in your living room.** If you've got a tent, you can set it up in your living room and fill it with pillows, toys, and sleeping bags. Snuggle up, sing songs, watch some fun movies, and eat some junk food. Skip the campfire, though. If you don't have a tent, organize a large cardboard box (a supermarket, retail store, or furniture shop may be able to provide you with one) and make a little house out of it.

>> **Make a roll-around bottle together.** Cut two big plastic drink bottles in half and use the top end of each. Put some interesting shapes inside and thread a shoelace through the bottle tops on either end. Seal the middle with tape. Knot the shoelaces together to make a line that your toddler can drag around.

>> **Make lunch.** Toddlers love to help and seem especially drawn to helping out in the kitchen. If you get your toddler his own stool or box to stand on so he can reach the countertop, he can help with simple tasks like peeling boiled eggs and stirring ingredients with a spoon.

>> **Create an obstacle course.** Make tunnels by placing a blanket over the tops of two chairs with their backs facing each other. Add other elements with low tables to crawl under, stairs to climb, and boxes to climb over. You can buy commercial plastic tunnels, but why, when you can make your own and change it from day to day?

>> **Get dizzy.** Have your toddler hold onto a towel and spin it around on a slippery floor slowly so that he doesn't fall. You can also try sitting in a spinning chair like an office chair with junior on your lap whizzing around and around. Kids love to get dizzy — you, maybe not so much, but this is what parental sacrifices are all about. These activities help your toddler's balance.

>> **Play chase.** Toddlers love being chased, peeking through curtains, and a bit of rough and tumble play when they're caught. Just don't go overboard on the rough stuff, and stop if your kiddo is more scared than having a good time.

> **» Sing!** There are so many great children's songs and nursery rhymes. Little ones really love songs with hand actions like "This Old Man" or "Itsy Bitsy Spider."

Some words for worried moms

If your partner has a seriously worried look on her face while watching you tumble around with the little one, talk to her about *rough and tumble play* (she can even look it up on the Internet — rough and tumble play is a well-known concept of child play). Dad's natural way to engage with his child is often to challenge him physically and "play a little rough" — at least by mom's standards. There's nothing wrong with this as long as junior still has a smile on his face and is squealing with delight. In fact, rough and tumble play is good for kids — it develops their social and physical skills, uses their imaginations, and introduces the ideas of good and bad, justice and courage. Just make sure no one gets too squished in a rough-housing session, and explain it to mom so she's comfortable. And by the way . . . why not ask mom to join in? This is not the place to work out any relationship frustrations you're having at the moment, however.

You've Created a Genius

Your child's brain is constantly developing, and rapidly. Some areas are coming along faster than others. Speaking and motor skills are getting up there, while emotional and social skills develop fully further down the line and over a long period.

Development update

As your child grows, the things he's capable of doing change, along with his behavior. As great dads, you really need to know about your child's development so you understand his behavior and interests and know how to respond to them.

Between the ages of 2 and 3, your child

>> Can feed himself, remove and put on clothing, and undo zippers and large buttons

>> Can remember people, places, and stories

>> Enjoys creating things

>> Has a sense of ownership over his toys and belongings, saying things like "mine!"

>> Is able to use two- to three-word sentences, ask questions, and follow an instruction with two steps

>> Is confident enough on his feet to try running, jumping, and hopping

>> Is developing a sense of humor

>> Likes to pretend to be someone else

>> Knows his full name and gender

>> Matches objects, such as shoes and animal pictures

REMEMBER

The way your toddler behaves is part of his growing up. One of the fundamental aspects of disciplining your child is to have realistic expectations of what he can and can't do. At 2 years old, he can't manage his emotions well, express how he feels, or remember all the rules. Consequently during this stage you need to muster some extra patience. He'll get there in his own time!

Giving your toddler choices

Getting tired of saying "no" yet? No, you can't open that cupboard! No, you can't go outside. Saying no all the time gets boring, doesn't it? Imagine what it sounds like to your toddler, hearing that all day long.

The answer to avoiding being stuck in the "no" loop is choices. Junior wants to go outside but it's pouring rain? Instead of saying no, offer him a couple of other activities he can do inside, like drawing with crayons or building with some blocks or snap-together models. Tell him, "We can't go outside because it's raining, but we can draw." Offering your child a couple of things to choose from means you still have some control over what he does, but he also feels like he has some say in his life.

Distracting your child by giving him something else to do instead of the thing he can't do is a great technique for stopping the no's.

Say your toddler is pulling out clothes from the dresser to put on in the morning. Instead of saying no to the nightshirt he wants to wear to nursery school that day, give him the option of a green shirt or a blue one. He'll feel like you take his opinions into account and will be more receptive to putting on a shirt. Less is more when it comes to giving a toddler choices.

Giving your child a choice also works with eating. Instead of plying your toddler with lots of vegetables, give him a choice: Broccoli or carrots? He may even end up eating both. Also, not forcing a decision helps. Sometimes you can simply say "I'll do something else while you make up your mind whether you'd like broccoli or carrots." In some cases your little champ might start eating one of the choices when you're not looking — after all, he's hungry.

At bedtime, letting your child choose a couple of stories before bed gets him interested in the idea of stories and what he wants to hear, rather than having him focus on resisting bedtime.

Setting boundaries and rules to match

Imagine you've landed on planet Wafunkle and you have no idea about the local etiquette, the way people talk to each other, what the customs are, or the way people live. You don't know whether smiling is considered rude or doing underarm farts is a way of showing appreciation. You also don't speak the language well, so the best you can do is bumble around, trying things out and being shown the rules until you get the hang of things.

This is the situation your toddler finds himself in right now. He doesn't know that wrenching your glasses off your face is wrong or that sticking a knife in an electric socket is dangerous. He needs a guide to show him through the sometimes confusing maze that is modern life and society. And that guide is you. The method by which you guide him through that maze is called discipline.

Discipline's about showing him the rules and having patience and strategies to help the rules stick.

REMEMBER

Discipline isn't about punishment, but about guiding your child to learn what the boundaries and rules in life are. You and your partner decide what the rules are depending on your personal beliefs, morals, and way of life. Discipline is about finding a balance between letting your child run wild exploring things that can be dangerous for her or inappropriate, like hitting and biting, and not letting her try anything out and hindering her ability to learn.

Here are some ideas for rules and boundaries you may want to instill in your child:

>> After two stories, it's into bed.

>> No going outside without dad or mom.

>> Plugs and appliances are off limits.

>> We're gentle to animals and other people.

>> We don't scream or throw balls in the house.

>> When we're upset we use our words rather than our bodies to express how we feel.

>> When we make a mistake or hurt someone, we say sorry.

>> When we ask for something we say please, and when someone is nice to us we say thank you.

You may also like to come up with some rules and boundaries for yourself as a dad, including all of the preceding and a few more.

TIP

Be consistent with your rules and boundaries. Although you've told your little princess not to draw on the walls with crayon but only on paper and she keeps drawing on the walls, she'll understand and get the idea one day, so hang in there.

Some parents like to use a strategy called *time out* when their child pushes the rules, such as refusing to say sorry when she's hurt another child or snatched a toy. This means removing her from the situation and putting her in a designated time-out area, like a corner or her room, for one minute per year of her age. Most toddlers won't stay put, but it breaks the cycle or tantrum that's about to erupt and lets them know in a nonviolent way that their behavior isn't okay.

Telling your child for the millionth time not to run out onto the road can push your buttons, and make you angry and frustrated that the message isn't getting through. However scared and angry you are, hitting your child isn't the way to deal with it. Find another way to deal with *your* frustration — take a couple of deep breaths and make a mental note to use your favorite way to let off some steam later on. When you raise your voice to say "STOP" (as she's about to run onto the street), give her a hug afterward and explain to her why running onto the road isn't okay. The message *will* get through!

A key aspect of effective discipline is consistency and appropriateness of your behavior management to your child's developmental stage and temperament. The older your child gets, the more you can use rational arguments, rules, and consequences. So keep talking to your child about the same rules, outline consequences, stick to your rules, and follow through with consequences.

Stimulating your toddler's interests

Every child is different, and different things will catch his eye. One thing that all children have in common is their interest in playing. If you notice your toddler doing something over and over, he's exploring a new concept and he can become almost obsessive about it. Child-care professionals usually refer to this behavior as a *schema*. Your child may pour water from one cup to another cup over and over, or paint a picture and then cover the whole thing in black paint, or cut up everything he can get his hands on. These are different types of schemas.

Some kinds of schemas can be destructive or against the boundaries you've set for your child and household, such as flicking the light switches up and down again and again. From your child's perspective, he's exploring a *vertical schema*. If your champ tears pieces of tissue into little pieces, he's exploring a *separation schema*.

If you aren't happy with the way he's exploring a particular schema, try to offer another way he can explore it. For example, get together a box of things he's allowed to rip up or cut (with your supervision, of course), or encourage him to explore vertical schema by bouncing on a trampoline or drawing. You could also demonstrate your DIY skills in front of your child by making a board of old switches (which aren't connected to an electrical source) so your little one can safely flick switches all day.

TIP

You may also like to take an interest in the things he seems to really enjoy playing with, like a Lego project he's been plugging away at, or a favorite set of shoes he's been trying on, and have these at the ready for when you need to offer your child a tantrum-distracting choice.

Talking to your child so he understands

Sometimes it feels as if you're beating your head against a wall as you try to communicate with your toddler. She won't listen, you get angry, and both of you end up frustrated and in a worse spot than you were before. Take heart — here are some techniques you can use now that will help build good, open communication between the two of you as your little one grows:

>> **Acknowledge how she feels.** You can easily walk all over your little one's objections or opinions with your words when you're talking to her. As fathers, with all good intentions, you frequently think you know best. When your child falls over and cries, you say things like "Oh, it doesn't hurt." You may offer a hug and some comfort, but your words are denying the way your child feels. Kids need to have their feelings acknowledged, just like adults do. By denying your child's feelings, you're kind of setting yourself up against her, rather than encouraging her to open up and find solutions. When your child is upset about something, rather than offer advice or a phrase to downplay her feelings, say something obvious like "You're upset," or agree with her by saying "Oh really?" and let her do the talking.

>> **Describe the problem.** This technique avoids laying blame on your child for something she's done. Blaming can make your toddler feel helpless and wrong all the time, and she'll become defiant whenever you open your mouth. Say she's spilled milk on the carpet. Rather than berate her about the mess she's made, tell her there's milk on the carpet, which describes the problem, and that she'd better get a cloth to clean it up.

>> **Give information.** Junior has just drawn on the wall for the thousandth time. Instead of yelling at him for his misplaced art, show him that drawing is for paper, not walls.

>> **Offer choices.** You want your little one to clear up her toys. Rather than order her to clean up, offer her a choice of which toys to clean up first.

>> **Use a single word or gesture.** You've already asked every day for a year that toys be cleared up before bedtime, so your toddler should be getting the hang of that concept by now. Instead of a nightly "clean up your toys, like I've asked you a million times," simply say "toys." Leaving out the blaming and ordering should get a better result. Kids dislike long explanations for things. Your tyke still has a very short attention span.

TIP

The underlying principle of most of these techniques is to avoid laying blame or criticism on your child. Making her feel wrong will make her defiant and scared, rather than open and willing to take risks. Ridiculing your child for a mistake is also unlikely to get her to take responsibility for her mistakes in the future because she'll be afraid of your ridicule.

REMEMBER

When talking to your child, imagine the way that you like to be talked to by your boss, for example. You don't like to be blamed, yelled at, made fun of, or ordered around. Neither does your toddler.

TIP

Check out pediatrician Dr. William Sears's suggestions for communicating effectively with kids, starting from the toddler years, at www.askdrsears.com/topics/parenting/discipline-behavior/25-ways-talk-so-children-will-listen.

Exploring Different Opportunities

Your role as a dad is simple — be there for your child with love, food, and shelter. And until now, that's been enough. Traditionally this may well have meant that you took care of your child by "bringing home the bacon." But in our modern lives, there are other avenues you can explore as well.

The fathering road less traveled

If you're finding, like many dads do, that keeping all your plates in the air — work life, home life, time for yourself — is just too much, there are options you can look at to reduce some of the stress. These options include the following:

>> Become a stay-at-home dad (SAHD) while your partner works.

>> Reduce your hours and work a four-day week or go part-time.

>> Start your own business, do what you love doing, and organize your work life around your family (for example, by having a home office).

>> Take a break from work, such as three months, especially if you feel you're stuck in a dead-end career or job. Many career coaches recommend you change careers if your current job is a dead end, so use this time as a transition phase to spend some more time with the family.

>> Talk to your boss about flex schedules, which means you can have flexible start and finish times while remaining in work full-time.

WARNING

Money and your financial position dictate which of these options is available to you, so before you walk into your boss's office with your resignation letter, do your math and work out what you can afford.

TIP

If you work from home, you can already work quite flexibly by scheduling your work around nap times or times when your partner or family can take care of your toddler.

TV, videos, computers, and games

We live in a media age, where there are literally hundreds of TV channels to choose from; where people communicate via email, Twitter, and Facebook rather than with an old-fashioned letter; and where elementary school children have cellphones. Unless you live in a jungle or a cave, the media's impossible to avoid.

To deal with the volume of media coming at your child, which at this age she's becoming increasingly aware of, it may be a good idea to think in terms of moderation rather than banning your toddler from the TV. Watching a little bit of TV for half an hour or so isn't the worst thing in the world and may help keep her out of your hair while you prepare a meal or have a shower, but letting her stare passively at cartoons all morning isn't doing her a whole lot of good. Watching lots of TV isn't encouraging interaction between the two of you or encouraging any of those synapses to keep connecting through movement or using her body, which is what she needs most right now.

Here are some techniques to help prevent your child turning into a TV addict:

>> As your toddler grows up, he may be interested in computers, handheld games, cellphones, and MP3 players. Establish a media-free time during the day — perhaps at mealtimes — when all devices are off.

>> Have a specific time your child can watch TV rather than putting on a show anytime he wants. This can be an effective way of limiting the amount of TV he watches.

>> Keep an eye on what programs your child watches on TV and make sure you're happy with the content. That goes for the advertisements that are played as well. You may want to select a few DVDs from the library to screen rather than just flicking on the TV and watching whatever is playing. DVDs are also a great way to avoid all the advertisements that increasingly target young children.

>> Keep bedrooms TV-free. Computers should be in a central part of the house too, if space allows.

>> Try to provide alternatives to media that force your child to be a passive observer. Exposing your child to a variety of activities like sports, handicrafts, the natural environment, gardening, food preparation, and music can spark an interest that may be lifelong.

>> Watch TV with your child, so you can talk about what you're seeing and hearing, and can encourage participation in any of the songs or dances on the screen.

WARNING

TV is not beneficial for children under 2 years of age, says the American Academy of Pediatrics, whose studies show infants who watched TV learned fewer words than those who didn't.

Next stop: Nursery school

As your child gets closer to becoming a preschooler (when he turns 3), you may want to start thinking about a more formal learning environment for him. Nursery school is traditionally the place children go to transition from being at home with a parent or caregiver, or a step on from child care before starting school. Nursery school is a place where children continue to explore learning through play, work on developing social skills, and begin academic learning, usually disguised as play.

Nursery school used to be for just those aged 3 and up, but some cater to children as young as 2½ years. Unlike school, nursery school isn't compulsory, but in some areas of the country, you'll find it's pretty much the standard.

Some nursery schools are very difficult to get into and have long waiting lists — not just the ones in New York City, either. If you live in a small town, you may find that the *best* nursery school is impossible to get into unless you know the director. Don't worry too much about this; any accredited nursery school can provide your toddler with the experiences he needs to learn and grow.

Of course, you should check out any school before you send your child there; word of mouth, parent recommendations, and online reviews are good, but no substitute exists for seeing a place yourself and assessing whether you think your child will be comfortable there.

If you're thinking about sending your child off to nursery school, consider the following:

» Is she potty trained? This is essential in many nursery schools, and sending your child off in new superhero underwear and pretending he's trained when he isn't is not kosher.

» Do your hours match the nursery school's? If you absolutely can't get there to pick her up before 12:30 and school ends at 12, don't think the teachers will be happy to watch her (unpaid) for another half hour. Some nursery schools do offer after-school day care.

» Is your child developmentally ready for nursery school? Some little ones just aren't ready for nursery school the minute they turn 3. Waiting a few months can mean the difference between a fun experience and a nightmare for all of you (nursery school staff included).

» Is the school convenient to your house or work? The best school may be 20 minutes away, which may not seem like much until you consider winter storms, packing up a sick baby to take her along to pick up your toddler, or the fact that nursery school is often just 2½ hours long. You may just about get home before you have to turn around and go get him.

» Do you like the teachers? The physical layout? The cleanliness standards? The playground equipment? Does the school separate children by age? Do they have snacks? What kind?

If everything looks positive, it's go time for a major event in your child's life: the start of his life away from you. Shedding a few tears — on your part, as well as his — is to be expected.

Chapter 12
Adding to Your Family

O ne of the questions fathers of one child are asked the most is, "So when are you having number two?" Some dads may be ready with an answer — "I've been planning on having seven children since I was little, so any time now." For others, it may be a question of asking themselves whether number two will ever happen — one child is quite enough at the moment, but thanks for asking.

Adding another baby to your family changes the dynamic completely and can be a tricky adjustment period as everyone — including your number one — finds their feet. In this chapter, we take you through making the financial adjustment; juggling the needs of two children at demanding times in their development; and working out how to stop World War III from happening as toys, clothes, and, most importantly, your love are shared between the two of them.

Having Another Child

Making the decision to have another child is, in some ways, as big a decision as having the first. In addition to all your concerns about being a father again — the sleepless nights, supporting your partner, the trials and tribulations of daily life with a helpless baby or rambunctious toddler — you also must take into account your first child's needs, such as his need to feel loved and cared for. You also now know how much time and work a baby takes, so the "ignorance is bliss" attitude you may have had the first time around is probably gone.

Here's what you need to think about if you want to take the rational approach to making a decision about baby #2:

>> Are you expecting life to get easier for you because the children can play with one another? This may be true, but not until your youngest child is 2 years or older. And some siblings never hit it off until adulthood, due to completely different temperaments or interests.

>> Can you afford for you or your partner to not earn a living while caring for a new baby, as well as buying any new equipment you may need?

>> Do you have enough room in your house for four? Will you need to move? What about your transport and travel arrangements — will you need a larger vehicle?

>> How mentally prepared are you to cope with a new arrival? Would you be excited to have another baby, or is having another baby something you feel you have to do to complete your family?

>> How will the practical aspects, such as sleeping arrangements, routines, and child care, work?

REMEMBER

Some parents think that only children are often spoiled, antisocial, and lonely. While having only one child creates a situation that can bring out these tendencies in children, parents can easily counterbalance by involving only children in lots of social settings, such as day care, playgroups, sleepovers, and team sports. You needn't worry your child will turn into a spoiled brat just because he doesn't have any siblings.

Is having another child worth it?

In the end, this is the question you and your partner have to resolve for yourselves. Having two children may not feel worthwhile when both kids are sick and up all night, and terrorizing each other by day. But it may be worth it when they are adults, have children of their own, and support each other in a way only family can.

Having a second child also gives you the opportunity to do things with your new baby differently if you feel you haven't done things the way you wanted the first time around, such as sticking to a routine from early on or trying a different approach to settling baby at night.

REMEMBER

If your partner had a traumatic birth experience or difficulties breastfeeding early on last time, she'll really need your support this time. You have the opportunity to help your partner see your second child as an opportunity to have a very different experience this time around.

What to expect

So you've decided you're ready for baby #2. With baby #2 you'll almost feel like a professional — after all, you've been there, done that. Many fathers of two say they don't feel as wound up and anxious about their baby the second time around, and that mothers are often more relaxed and confident. That said, here are some things you need to know:

>> Depending on the age gap between #1 and #2, you may need twice as many strollers and car seats, which may mean you need a bigger car.

>> Your life will be twice as busy, with both children having different activities and sleep times, and possibly twice as many diapers to change and clothes to wash.

>> Depending on his age, your older child will not necessarily be particularly helpful with the younger child until he is a bit older, but may relish the responsibility of being in charge of the baby when the time comes, even if it's just in name only.

>> You'll need to be a lot more organized and may find yourself spending more time lying in bed at night thinking about the laundry, getting lunch prepared for child care, and pulling your weight with the housework.

Budgeting and finance

Raising a child is an expensive business. Raising a child to 18 years is thought to cost an average of around $250,000 in the United States. While some things can be passed down from one child to another, you can assume that raising two children will nearly double your expenses for the next 18 years. The good news is that after having raised child #1, you now know what is really useful and essential, and what is just fluff. So our suggestion for #2 is to cut out the fluff and focus on essentials. You may also take heart from an old Spanish saying: "Every baby is born with a loaf of bread under their arm." In other words, you'll find a way to make ends meet.

TIP

You can have another baby and not have to get a third job. Here are some ways to do so:

>> Stick to the essentials. You don't need another flashy Moses basket or $20-a-tub diaper cream. And you didn't need half of all those clothes you had first time around, did you?

>> If you don't still have your first child's stuff sitting in his wardrobe, ask for hand-me-downs, go to swapping events (where you can swap clothes and toys), or check with friends who have kids. Check Craigslist, eBay, and other online sites for pricy items like cribs.

>> Don't buy anything until after the baby shower, or register for baby shower gifts at a store. That way you won't double up on anything you already have.

>> Keep an eye on specials at supermarkets and baby stores to start stocking up on consumables. When there's a good sale on diapers, stock up — you know you'll use them eventually.

FRUGAL DAD

So you're having another baby and you're strapped for cash? Try these cheap homemade versions of baby stuff that will save you money. Hey, if they were good enough for our grandparents, they're good enough for us.

- **Wipes:** Cut into quarters some cheap, soft facecloths. If you're really crafty, you can sew up the edges with a sewing machine to stop fraying. Fill a clean container with water and add a little almond oil. Use it to clean junior's backside. Pat dry with a clean cloth afterward. Wash wipes with the diapers (if you're using cloth diapers) and hang them out to dry in the sun to kill any bacteria.

- **Breastfeeding:** Talk to your partner about breastfeeding, which will save you a fortune in formula, bottles, and all the accoutrements.

- **Coupons:** Yes, it takes a little time, but saving a few bucks a week adds up over time, and baby items are frequent coupon items. Check online sites such as www.retailmenot.com to pick up online discounts.

TIP

In the coming years, child-care costs could be a major expense in your household. Think about how you and your partner could work flexibly, reduce your hours, enlist friends and family in a kind of group babysitting scheme, or work from home to reduce this cost.

Looking After Another Family Member

So there's another mouth to feed, another body to clothe, and another bottom to wipe. If you were stretched by one baby, two may seem impossible right now, but it's not.

Taking a practical approach

All babies really need is love, warmth, food, sleep, and a clean bum. Though having color-coordinated outfits is mom's thing, when you've got two kids, this may no longer be top priority.

Read Part 2 about baby's first year to remind yourself of what's coming up, such as how to avoid diaper rash, how warm your newborn should be kept, and which clothes you'll need.

Get into a routine with your new baby as soon as you can, but don't freak out if it all goes a little awry some days. With two children, you certainly won't get everything right every day, but don't beat yourself up about it.

TIP

Remember to be as hands-on with this new baby as you were with the last. Remember how time flew by with the first one? Well, here's another chance to savor the unforgettable time when she's tiny.

Keeping two or more healthy and safe

Having a second child is easier — and harder. It's easier in the sense that you have previous experience at handling a newborn, but harder in the sense that you now have to wrestle your toddler into his car seat with a baby demanding your attention at the same time. If you thought one child was enough to keep you occupied, two will show you that you're capable of a lot more!

Here are some ways you can avoid your life becoming a crazy house:

>> **Get organized.** Think about where the new baby will sleep. Do you need to get another crib, or is your older child ready to move into a bed? Organize chests of drawers and car seats, and work out where you're going to change the baby. Most importantly, look into changing your stroller. Some strollers can accommodate two children, either side by side or by having one behind the other. If your first child is a little older, a stroller where he can stand on the back may be more to his liking.

>> **Get your family and friends involved.** It takes a village to raise a child, so organize someone to take your older child on outings when you need a break, or to cook when you're too exhausted.

>> **Keep healthy.** The last thing you need with two little ones is to get ill. Inevitably your whole family will get sick, and you'll be so busy looking after children all night long that you won't be able to get better yourself. Keep eating well and take every opportunity you can to get some exercise. A fantastic way to find time to exercise is to combine exercise with an activity with child #1.

>> **Prepare yourself to give child #1 some extra love.** It can be a rough transition for him — suddenly he has to share your attention with another person in the house. You need to compensate for that. Read more about sibling rivalry later in this chapter.

>> **Try not to change your older child's routines too much.** If you're currently reading him five stories before bed every night, keep doing that. With a new person in the house, he's going through enough upheaval without losing his time with you too.

>> **Work as a team and make a schedule.** Divvy up chores around the house, talk about when you and your partner can have some time off, and don't forget to exercise! Did we say that already?

Juggling activities

With two children now, both at challenging stages in their development, you'll need to fine-tune some of the activities you have in your life. It may be time to look at flexible work (see Chapter 6), reducing your hours, or prioritizing some of the things you do outside work and family.

You may find life is a bit like a game of Tetris — trying to fit all tasks and people you need to spend time with into a limited amount of space. Scheduling your tasks and making time with your family one of your top jobs helps ensure you don't lose touch with what is really important — your partner and children.

It may pay to get a calendar or keep a list on the fridge of your tasks, so you don't get swamped by them.

Talk to your children all the time. Let them share in what you do at work and be prepared to spend time reading stories, playing, and doing all the dad stuff you've been doing so well anyway.

If you're one of those guys who puts things off all the time, now's the time to break the habit. Leaving things undone will only stress you out and cause you grief when you could be doing something you enjoy.

Sibling Discipline

All children react differently to the news that another baby is coming along to usurp their throne as king or queen. Some rebel and get extremely upset when the new baby is even mentioned. Others relish the chance to meet their new sibling. Some children change overnight from angels into demons, and others develop a new-found sense of responsibility and grown-upness that you never would have imagined. Your child may feel threatened, unloved, or ignored.

Understanding sibling rivalry

So far, your child has been the only apple of your eye, the center of your world and the center of her own world. Suddenly, a new baby is on the scene, taking away time and attention from her. You're busy with the new baby, which means her demands come second and she has to wait when she doesn't want to, share her stuff, and have the limelight shine somewhere else. No wonder she's a little grumpy and jealous right now.

She's caught in a place where she's trying to find her own individuality, but she still very much needs you to boost her confidence and show her the way. If you're giving too much of your time and attention to your new little one, she's going to let you know about it by being angry and jealous, and rebelling against you and her new sibling.

To prepare your child for the fact that another baby is coming into your family, try these ideas:

>> Break the news to your child when the three of you are together. A good time to do this is when mom's belly is starting to stick out, or during the final trimester. Toddlers don't have a good grasp of time, so you'll be bombarded with cries of "Is the baby coming yet?"

>> Keep involving your first child in lots of things you do to prepare for the new arrival. For example, you can take her along to the scans and keep explaining things to her about how the baby develops. She may not understand everything, but making her feel involved is important.

>> Offer some choices to your child when it comes to buying for the new baby, such as asking her to help pick clothes and gear for the new baby.

>> Let her know that the baby is not just for mom and dad; the baby is her brother or sister.

>> If you're moving your older child to a new room, do it well before the new baby arrives, so he won't feel displaced. If he's moving to a big bed, make a really big deal about it. Buy a very cool bed if you can swing it — like a race car bed or a fairy princess bed.

>> Prepare her for the demands a new baby will place on the family: the baby will cry, will need to be fed (explain how that feeding will happen — your child may get upset at mom and baby's new closeness if she's breastfeeding), and will not be able to play with her for a little while until he grows bigger.

Coping with jealousy and fighting

No matter how well your older child copes with the news that another baby is on the way or how brilliantly she accepts the new baby's arrival, she's still that same volatile mix of burgeoning independence and emotional immaturity, so inevitably she'll feel resentful and jealous from time to time.

Here are some techniques you can try to minimize bad feelings:

>> Balance the time that you spend with your newborn and toddler.

>> Encourage your toddler's pride in her new little sibling by showing her how to hold the baby and taking lots of photos. Talk to your older child about when she was a baby and get some pictures out to look at.

>> Make special time to devote to your toddler that doesn't include the new baby.

>> Toddlers love to have "tasks" to do, so you can enlist her help in getting baby's blanket and putting clothes away. Give her lots of praise for doing a good job.

>> Try to keep your toddler's routine as much as possible, so she doesn't feel lost in all the upheaval and resent her new sibling.

>> When your older child meets her new sibling, have the baby in a crib or bassinet or basket rather than in your arms.

If your older child is uninterested in the baby, don't worry. She'll take an interest in her own time.

Fighting and setting boundaries

If you've got your toddler feeling pretty excited about his new sister, fetching diapers for changes, and helping to settle her at night, you're doing really well. But we're dealing with a toddler who hasn't quite worked out how to handle his emotions just yet. Anger, resentment, and fighting are bound to break out at some stage, so here are some suggestions to help manage that:

>> Should conflict break out, act fast. Hitting, snatching, and acting roughly are unacceptable. Use your disciplinary action of choice — a stern talking-to or taking away the object of dispute (the toy). Distraction may also work well in these situations.

>> Teach your older child how to touch the baby without hurting her, just like you do with a pet or with other children his own age. Use the words "gentle" and "nice," and praise him for his efforts.

>> Until you feel that your toddler can safely be around the baby without incident, keep a close eye on them. Toddlers are notorious for snatching. If baby has a toy he wants, your toddler may snatch it straight out of your baby's mouth, which could result in some distress from baby.

>> Your behavior is your child's greatest teacher, and he'll copy what he sees you doing. If you're quick to anger and treat others with disrespect, he'll learn to do that too.

REMEMBER

Behavior management strategies need to relate to the developmental stage and temperament of your child. Try out a few things (and keep trying them as your child gets older), and use what works best for your child. In general, distraction techniques tend to work better with younger children, whereas time-outs tend to work better with older children.

Discovering different personalities

Take a look at your own siblings, if you have them. Are you into the same stuff? Do you have the same temperament or ideas? Chances are, although you were brought up by the same parents and share a heck of a lot of DNA, you've got your own interests and personality. After all, we're all individuals.

And so it is with your children. Chances are both your kids are quite different kettles of fish and require different things from you as a father. Both your children are going to require different ways of stimulation, encouragement, and confidence building. A bit of trial and error may be required.

REMEMBER

Rather than seeing different personalities as extra work for you, think of them as a good thing. You get to explore different interests with your children, and they can learn from each other as they grow up, drawing on each other's strengths to get them through challenging times. Different personalities also keeps things interesting for you — never a dull day!

4

The Preschool Years

Grow with your dad role as your toddler becomes your preschooler.

Keep your child healthy and active with good food and exercise. Discover what to do when common health problems strike.

Enter the worlds of school, sports, and other activities.

Chapter 13

Fun and Games

Your walking, talking child is quite a different bundle from the newborn you first met three years ago. He's a dynamo of questions, words, stories, and kooky ideas. And he needs you to keep up with him. Hang out with your child (a lot) and hang on for the ride!

In this chapter we explore what your preschooler will be doing for the next couple of years as he nears school age. We share our ideas for keeping that inquisitive little person busy and show you some ways to help your child get ready for learning at school and beyond.

Your Active Preschooler

With his third birthday, your child graduates from being a toddler to a preschooler. Preschooler isn't a great term because it describes what your child isn't, rather than what he is, but that's the most well-worn term to describe ages 3 and 4 years old. *Note:* Some people use "young children," but that applies to a wide age range, so we decided to stick with preschooler.

Mapping the next two years

As well as getting more of a grip on his language skills, being able to come up with more complex sentence structures, and increasing his vocabulary, your child is developing in the following ways. Your preschooler

>> Has more control over his emotions, is able to empathize more, and shows concern for others

>> Is able to express more complex emotions like embarrassment, pride, and guilt

>> Likes to take part in imaginative games, like playing doctor or school, or pretending boxes are boats and rockets

>> Can sort shapes, like pegs and shells or buttons

>> Can use alternate feet to climb stairs or steps and, as he gets closer to 5, to skip

>> Starts understanding abstract concepts like "being a hero," confidence, or what it means to be the "good guy/bad guy" in a play

>> Can perform simple tasks and use scissors

>> Can serve himself food, and eat and drink by himself

>> Becomes more invested in friendships as he nears school age

REMEMBER

Your child is also learning to really count; recognizes the letters of the alphabet rather than just reciting them by rote; knows the names of lots of animals, plants, objects, and people; and much more, provided you keep stimulating him with books, pictures, outings, and opportunities.

Building self-sufficiency and self-esteem

Like an athlete training for a big race, or a gymnast for a competition, practice makes perfect. The more you do something, the better you get at it. For a child to master a skill, she must do it again and again with lots of mistakes along the way so that she can improve and feel a sense of accomplishment.

As a father, your role is to provide plenty of opportunities for your child to practice, make mistakes, improve, and master a skill in order to build self-esteem and feel pride in her achievements. Letting your child fall, fail, and pick herself up again can be difficult at times, especially because you can often see in advance what's going to happen and may not want to deal with the consequences of her fall. But giving her the space to mess up is important, and your attitude that you believe she can get better with practice rubs off too.

Between the ages of 3 and 4, let your child take on more tasks that she may not get right at first but will accomplish, with a little time, practice, and patience from you. A great example is giving your child little jobs around the house, or getting her to do personal hygiene jobs herself, like washing her hands or brushing her teeth. (You may have to follow up with a little extra help to make sure these tasks are done effectively.)

Giving healthy doses of praise when your child tries really hard or achieves a goal boosts her confidence and makes her feel pretty pleased with herself.

Praise

Using praise is tricky. Tired fathers coming home from work at night or after a long day minding the children can easily give a glib "that's great, darling" without really looking at the picture their preschooler has drawn. She'll know your heart isn't really in it and feel doubtful about her achievements.

Praise should also be nonjudgmental; that is, rather than saying about a painting, "Wow, that's fantastic, darling," be specific about what it is you like or which skills you see developing. "I like the way you used purple" or "You are really good at coloring her hair" gives your child a sense of her accomplishment, and she will use that praise to tell herself "I'm good at using color" when she approaches a drawing next time. Also, point out specifics in the painting, such as "I can see you've painted a house."

Making out what your child has actually drawn can be hard, but guessing correctly isn't important. Your budding artist will tell you that the "house" is actually a "dog," and you can then discuss with her aspects of how she has drawn her dog.

Active movement

Active movement — that is, getting out there with your child and encouraging physical activities — is an important tool for building self-esteem and confidence.

Children (and adults) learn through repetition. When we do something over and over, it seems to become locked in our brains. Learning things like climbing a ladder takes time and practice for little children to master, and there will probably be some falls and spills along the way. But without that practice, how will she ever get the chance to learn to climb a ladder? Some child-care professionals also believe that physical movement is key to helping the brain develop fully.

Genuine praise for your child's accomplishments as she gains more confidence in her body also encourages her to get physical more often, which can only be good for her and help keep her healthy and confident of her abilities.

TIP

Embrace your inner child and get active with your children. Play on swings, go down the slide, and play on the monkey bars (if you can actually do this). As a dad, you're not only a role model for your children, showing them how to master a skill, but if you also become part of the activity and want to give it a try too, they'll love the activity all the more.

Even if you don't have a playground close to your home where you can let your child practice swinging, jumping, climbing, and balancing, you can encourage active movement at your own place. Here are some ideas:

>> Create an obstacle course in your living room from chairs with sheets draped over them, and boxes and tables to crawl through and under.

>> Dance in your living room — often the emptiest room in the house. Take note of music your child enjoys; it will come in handy when she's fussy or bored.

>> Go on a walk in your area (not too far — you don't want a cranky, tired child you have to carry home) and check out mailboxes, flowers in gardens, birds on telephone wires, and cracks in the pavement.

>> Play chase. You probably know by now that little kids love to be chased and will take off, wanting you to follow. Put a scarf in your child's pants so it sticks out like a tail and chase her while trying to get the scarf.

>> Play hide and seek. If your child can't count, use an egg timer to measure the time passed before she comes looking for you.

>> Roll down a gentle slope, or play helicopters where you spin around and around until you're dizzy. This helps your child's developing sense of balance and is really great fun!

>> Show your child how to jump off low walls, and on and off surfaces you put on the floor for her, like a towel or piece of carpet. Be prepared for a few tumbles at first! (Try to make sure they aren't yours.)

>> Walk like a bear around the house on all fours, play wheelbarrow walk, and make a rope swing on a tree in your yard to encourage upper body development. Don't hurt yourself.

Classes

You can also consider enrolling your child in classes like junior soccer, swimming and water confidence, singing, or music and movement. Follow your child's lead by paying attention to the things she enjoys doing.

Keeping a check on fatherly concerns

Dads have been known to be somewhat competitive and to compare and measure children against one another. Raising children, however, is not a competitive sport, and there's no medal for having a child who is first to spell "encyclopedia" or count to 1,000. Every child moves and develops at his own pace.

Patience with your child's pace is one of the most important things you can give him right now. He's got to have space and time to develop and learn, and expecting him to do what others can do will leave you frustrated, and him less likely to figure it out for himself. It certainly doesn't boost his confidence to say, "Johnny can already count to 100 — why can't you do that?"

Take a deep breath when he spills milk on the carpet for the hundredth time as he learns to master drinking from a glass, or drops his knife and fork as he tries to put his plate on the kitchen counter. He'll get there. By helping, encouraging, and gently challenging him, rather than getting frustrated and doing it for him, he'll learn he can do it by himself and have more confidence in his abilities.

REMEMBER

So you want junior to be a world-class golfer and already have him swinging clubs in the backyard. But he's just not getting golf and wants to water the garden or help with the cooking instead. Follow his lead and ditch the clubs. Remember that old saying, "You can lead a horse to water, but you can't make it drink"? It's the same with children. You can buy your child golf clubs, but you can't make him like playing golf. You may have to get used to the idea that you've got a potential Top Chef on your hands, not a golf champion.

During the preschool years, many children often switch from being very close to mom if she's been the primary caregiver to wanting to be with dad all the time. This is great news for dads! It means you have more opportunities to hang out with your kid and deepen that already awesome relationship you have with him. Make more of your time available to your little champ and enjoy the attention you're getting!

Keeping Your Preschooler Busy

Some preschoolers are always on the move; they're always asking questions and exploring the world. That's a great thing, but it can be a little tiring, and on a rainy day, a high-energy preschooler may be a tantrum waiting to happen. In the following sections, we show you some ways to make the most of the time you and your preschooler have together that are fun and a little educational.

"Dad, I'm bored"

For years to come, you'll occasionally hear the refrain all fathers fear — "Dad, I'm bored." Not only is she bored, but she wants you to fix the problem. Brushing off your child with a computer game or putting on a movie is easy, but the best activities for your pre-schooler are the ones that involve the two of you being together. These are opportunities to read, play, explore, and learn together or to introduce junior to a hobby or passion of yours that she may be interested in.

Here are some ideas for banishing the "I'm bored" blues:

>> Ask a question about a concept your child wouldn't have come across, like "Do you know how bats can fly in the dark without bumping into things?" Then offer to find out with her. Do some research together and make it into a "solving the mystery" quest.

>> Build something together, such as a swing, a bird feeder, or a wooden seat, but be clear about safety around tools. Three-year-olds and saws — along with many other tools — are not a good mix. For that matter, some dads and tools aren't such a good mix either; know your limits! And keep a close eye on both your tools and your child when you're in building mode.

>> Encourage a love of gardening and growing her own food by starting a little garden in the backyard. Pumpkins and peas are pretty easy to grow, and your child will be encouraged to eat them at dinnertime knowing she's grown the food herself!

>> Hide something in the house or garden that she has to find by asking you for clues.

>> Involve your child in a chore you have to do, like vacuuming or washing the car. Let her be in charge of washing the tires or lifting rugs for you to clean under. Helping with tasks like hanging out the washing develops fine motor skills and makes a dull job more enjoyable.

>> Rather than just flicking on the TV, make a point of selecting what your child is going to watch and involve her in the decision making. For example, go to the library to select a DVD, and then watch it together.

>> Read some books. If you're sick of reading the same books over and over, head to the library for some new ones.

>> Remember all the games you used to play as a child like "I spy with my little eye"? Play them with your child.

>> Take a trip to the beach to play in the sand; go for a bike ride; visit the local playground; take a child-friendly trail walk; or wander around the botanic gardens, museum, or zoo. Keep talking with your child all the time about what you see and hear, and ask her questions about what she thinks about things you come across.

>> Visit a local farm. Many farmers are more than happy to open the gates and show you around (provided you arrange a suitable time with them beforehand).

>> Visit some pals. Arrange a play date with other kids your child's age from nursery school, your prenatal group, or other friends with children.

WARNING

Sometimes saying she's bored is your child's code for "I want to watch TV or play on the computer." It can be easy just to let her, especially if you have chores you need to do or you're tired. But try to resist. Perhaps just a quick trip to the local park will give her enough lift to come home and be entertained with doing her own thing for the rest of the afternoon.

TIP

Encourage your child to come up with activities she would like to try to keep on hand when the "I'm bored" blues hit.

Surviving snow (and rain) days

Adults find it difficult not to go stir-crazy with cabin fever when it's raining and cold outside. For children, who have energy to burn, not going mad is even harder.

HOW TO MAKE YOUR OWN PLAY DOUGH

Here's everything you need to make play dough:

2 cups plain flour

2 cups warm water

1 cup salt

2 tablespoons vegetable oil

1 tablespoon cream of tartar

Food coloring

1. Mix all the ingredients together in a pot over low heat. Stir.

2. When the mixture thickens, clumps in the middle, and feels dry rather than sticky, remove from the heat and allow to cool.

3. Turn out onto a counter or tray and knead until the dough's silky smooth.

4. Divide into as many balls as you want to make colors.

5. Poke a finger into each ball and add a drop of your desired color into the hole. This protects your hands from coming into contact with the concentrated food coloring, which can stain your skin. Knead the color through the ball.

This dough keeps for a few days and is best kept in the fridge. Wrap the dough in cling film to stop it from drying out. If the dough does dry out, it can be dampened with a little water.

Voilà! Now you can get really creative. Watch out, Michelangelo!

So what can you do about it? Here are some ideas:

>> Board games are always good fun for an emergency. Perhaps invite some friends over to play.

>> Find out about open days at your local fire station, your local police station, the city council, or a large factory nearby, such as a processing plant. (If you live near a chocolate factory or other kid-friendly and kid-interesting plant, this is a good place to start!) You can also ask about public tours of places that your child shows interest in.

>> Get hands-on by getting out the craft supplies or playing with play dough, all cheap and cheerful activities that encourage creativity and fine motor skills. See the nearby sidebar "How to make your own play dough" for a recipe.

>> Get out some old photos from when you were a child, teen, or student. Organize a family photo session, which can be even better if you have some old slides and a projector. Create a fabulous home cinema experience for your child.

>> Get your little chef involved in baking and cooking.

>> Have a singing and dancing competition in your living room. Prizes for everyone, of course.

>> Make up stories, and then draw pictures to go with them.

>> Organize a trip to a nearby airport, train station, harbor, or dock. Young children are typically fascinated by the hustle and bustle that can be observed at these places.

>> Pretend you're outdoors by making a tent out of chairs or a table and some sheets. You could camp out all day in your tent, with snacks, toys, books, and pillows for lounging on.

>> Visit the local museum or indoor play center. Bring lots of cash for the gift shop at the museum or for all the "extras" at the play center.

Bringing out your child's talents without going OTT

Expecting your child to be super-skilled at something at this age is unreasonable, although you may think the way she kicks a ball means she's the next female David Beckham. Rather, this is a time for giving your child lots of opportunities for her to discover what she's good at and what she enjoys doing. How will your child discover if she loves gardening if she never sees a garden, or enjoys fishing if you never show her what fishing is all about? We don't mean spending thousands on fishing gear, but by exposing your child to ideas, telling her what others are doing, and showing her in books, you'll see what your child takes a fancy to.

Sometimes you can use this opportunity to try out something new yourself and share that experience with your little one. Remember the saying, "Do something that scares you every day." Doing something new with your children is a great way to step outside your own comfort zone.

Being a dad is also about showing your children that you, too, have to learn new things and that you're ready to try something new. Take a keen interest in what your children like doing, even if they're not interested in your favorite sport or activity.

TIP

Follow your child's interests. Let her choose which books she's interested in, what games she likes, and which activities she's into. Forcing your values on her or making her decisions for her isn't going to help build her relationship with you or let her become her own person.

Being a good sport

Preschoolers are more interested in other people than toddlers are, but they still struggle to control their emotions and impulses. While your child may love playing with others, it can be hard for her to accept not having her own way all the time, and playing sports or games where there are winners and losers can be really tricky for a preschooler to deal with. Learning to lose without losing your cool is a skill, like learning to ride a bike. Being able to cope with losing is a step toward being able to admit making mistakes or accepting not getting your way, which are emotions that even adults struggle with. Being a good winner and not gloating is also an important skill to learn.

Here are some ideas you can instill in your child to help her become a good sport:

>> **Be a good sport as a father.** You're a role model, and accepting defeat gracefully encourages the same behavior in your child.

>> **Congratulate the winner.** It takes grace to admit someone else played better on the day. If you're the winner, be gracious about winning by not rubbing it in the other team's face.

>> **Focus on the fact that the performance, not the person, lost.** Your child is not a "loser" because she lost. She's the same person and may beat her opponent next time. She lost because of the way she played, not because of who she is.

>> **Don't make excuses for why your child lost.** Blaming others like referees or cheating from the other side only makes you look desperate, and it means your child has no chance to analyze why she lost and improve her performance for next time.

REMEMBER

Social skills and an understanding of teamwork take a long time to develop. Younger children can generally focus on only one thing at a time (that's why 3-year-olds playing football all chase the ball and don't keep their positions). So be realistic about your expectations when it comes to team sports.

Experiencing nature

Preschoolers are naturally curious, active, and imaginative. And what better place to hook into all those parts of themselves than out in nature?

For a fun day out that will charge his batteries and get those brain connections whirring, try taking your child to

>> **The beach:** There's a reason why parks and nursery schools have sandpits — sand is a blank canvas for a child to play on. Your child can create castles, words, faces, and shapes. Or he can just feel the sand and scoop it up for hours. Most little kids also love the water, so keep a look out to make sure he's safe — and remember the sunblock.

>> **The great outdoors:** Try taking a walk through a park, in the woods, or on local trails for a few hours to get your child's body and mind fit and healthy. Take along a book about native plants or birds and animals, and see what you can find.

Another great thing about using the outdoors and nature is that they're usually free of charge.

Encouraging an appreciation of the great outdoors also encourages an appreciation of the environment. Remember to take only pictures and leave only footprints when you're out and about.

Lifelong Learning Starts Here

The first years of a child's life are critical to his development as a thinking, feeling human being. Forming an attachment to you and your partner, and forming connections between different parts of his brain, is your child's main function at this age.

School is on your child's horizon, and with it comes a more formal way of learning than you've been practicing at home with books, toys, and talk.

Fathers as first teachers

As a father, you are your child's role model and teacher. He'll learn more from you than how to tie his shoelaces or use a knife and fork. Giving your child the opportunity to spend time with you — doing puzzles, climbing trees, and reading together — makes you his first teacher.

The teaching and example you set now shape how your child respects other people, manages his emotions, takes winning and losing with dignity, treats the environment, and manages relationships with those around him.

Your values, attitudes, and beliefs filter down to him, and if you've had a rough upbringing or your experience with schools and authority was not a happy one, you may want to think about ways you can change that for your child, so he has a fresh start.

Starting school on the right foot

If your child hasn't gone to day care, the first time he leaves home for periods of time away from you may be to go to nursery school, also known as preschool. In Chapter 11, we discuss how nursery schools prepare your child for school and teach children skills through play.

If your child is already in day care, talk with the teachers there about whether they have sessions that prepare children for school as they turn 3 and 4. Some day care centers offer preschool programs starting at 2½ or 3 years. If you don't have a day-care option and have to pick a place from many available, see Chapter 11 for more guidance on picking the right school.

If your child is used to a specific routine, you need to work preschool into it. Some kids adapt better to this change than others. Most centers have morning and afternoon sessions, so consider which will work better with your schedule as well as your child's. If your child is a late riser, getting him up, fed, dressed, and into the car before 9 a.m. may seem like more trouble than it's worth. But if he still takes a solid two-hour nap, he may be falling asleep in his snack if he attends an afternoon session.

If your child hasn't been to day care, the stimulation at preschool may tire him, so be flexible about bedtimes and naps, perhaps putting him to bed a little earlier at night.

Leaving your child at preschool can be tough at first as she settles in, but don't feel guilty. Feel confident that the staff have seen it all before and know how to handle it. If your child is upset about you leaving, give her to a teacher, give her a kiss, and tell her that you love her and you'll see her later. Give her a wave and let the staff get on with their job. If you come back two minutes later, you may find your child happily absorbed in an activity, having completely forgotten you were ever there.

Learning objectives

Finding out what your child is capable of learning at this age is a bit tricky, as all children develop at their own speed. But you can encourage her learning by stimulating her with books and images, and with one-on-one time with you.

Here are some objectives you can aim for:

>> **Learning the alphabet:** Use jigsaw puzzles and point out letters when you're reading — for example, "That's A for apple." Use a chalkboard or drawing paper to practice the shapes of letters.

>> **Learning to count:** Lots of books with numbers are available, and when you're at the store or out and about, you can count together the number of things you see. Take it slowly at first. Getting to ten is a major achievement!

>> **Learning about time and the seasons:** Use pictures on your child's bedroom wall, books, and your own backyard to show how time passes and seasons change.

TIP

As your child approaches school age, talk to your local school about things they may expect a new entrant to know and what skills will make going off to school easier. You may also want to talk to your day-care or preschool teacher about your child's progress and which areas he may need help with.

Learning for the whole family

Even though you're the father and you're the one role-modeling and passing on your knowledge to your kids, learning is a two-way street. You can learn a lot from your child too. Your child can teach you the following:

>> **How to be totally in the moment:** Watch your son's delight at running sand through his fingers.

>> **How to see the world for the first time again:** Enjoy the moment with your son when he sees an animal at the zoo he's never seen before.

>> **How to translate the world, later in life:** Just like you did for your parents, your child will be able to explain why what's in fashion looks good and why music on the radio is popular.

>> **How to make the best out of every situation:** For example, you'll learn how unimportant your son rubbing his snotty nose on your suit pants just before work is.

>> **Patience:** When your normally brave little soldier thinks there's a dragon under his bed at 3 a.m., you can muster the patience to convince him he's going to be okay.

>> **What really matters in life:** Is it impressing the boss with long hours, or being home in time to read *Green Eggs and Ham* with your son?

TIP

Another fun activity is to switch roles with your children: Ask them to play "dad" while you play "child." The outcome can be hilarious — or maybe disconcerting — as they play back your own behavior to you. It can give you interesting clues about what you might want to change in how you treat your child. You can, of course, also get your own back by throwing yourself on the floor, screaming, and shouting to explain what your son looks like when he's in tantrum mode.

Chapter 14

Health and Nutrition

Your health is the most important thing you have. Surely the health of your child is equally important or even more important to you. She doesn't yet know how to maintain her health, so you need to ensure that she stays in tiptop shape. The health she enjoys now, and the healthy eating and exercise she does, are good habits to instill in the early years and will stay with her for life.

In this chapter we show you how to encourage and maintain those good habits, not just for her but for you too. We guide you through the difficulties of picky eaters, allergies, and introducing new foods. We also bring you up to speed on the multiple bugs and illnesses your child will inevitably pick up from her environment, which is a rather challenging part of fatherhood.

Food, Nutritious Food

Like you, young children need three meals a day plus snacks and plenty to drink every day to keep healthy and active.

Your child needs a variety of foods from each of these groups:

>> **Breads and cereals:** At least four servings a day, of which half or more should be whole grains.

>> **Dairy products and milk:** Two to three servings a day. Children under age 2 should drink whole milk.

>> **Fats and oils:** Children need fat for brain development. At ages 2–3, 30 to 35 percent of a child's calories should come from fats, preferably unsaturated fats.

>> **Meats, legumes, and other sources of protein like eggs or soy:** One to two servings a day.

>> **Vegetables and fruit:** At least five servings a day (two fruit, three vegetable).

REMEMBER

A serving is usually the size of your child's palm, or a piece of bread, glass of milk, or one-serving-size container of yogurt.

Cooking and baking for busy dads

Getting all these "servings" into your child may seem daunting, but it's not. Don't panic if junior hasn't had exactly what's in the guidelines; his appetite will guide you for the most part. It's important to not force-feed your child because he may develop an aversion to the food you're trying to get into him. He may also get very upset and throw up, which means you'll have achieved the opposite of what you were trying to do.

If you're stuck for ideas, try these:

>> **Breads, cereals and other starches:** Avoid cereals colored to appeal to children; they're often filled with sugar. Instead, offer whole-grain cereals, breads, oatmeal, muffins, rice, risotto, pasta, couscous, or quinoa.

>> **Fruit and vegetables:** Try dried fruit (only occasionally, as the sugars in them can harm teeth); frozen or canned fruit and vegetables, which are just as nutritious as fresh, as long as they're not packaged in syrup; and fruit and vegetables in muffins or sandwiches.

>> **Meat, legumes, and protein:** Offer sliced lunchmeats, baked beans, kidney or pinto beans, peanut butter or other nut spreads, tuna in a sandwich or salad, tofu, or chickpeas.

>> **Milk and dairy products:** Serve cheese slices in a sandwich, yogurt, or a fruit smoothie or milkshake.

TIP

A simple strategy to inspire kids to eat a variety of fruit and vegetables is to point out the colors to them — for example, "You've eaten lots of orange food; how about some green (peas), red (tomatoes), and yellow (sweet corn) food?"

Kids need fluid just like adults do, so keep your tyke topped up with cartons of milk or soy milk, or water in a bottle.

WARNING

Drinking juice is not recommended because the sugar content is very high. If you do want to give your child juice, dilute it, and avoid giving it after he has brushed his teeth at night.

TIP

You'll find more recipes, dietary guidelines, and nutrition information at www.nutrition.gov/life-stages/children.

Avoiding the wrong foods

The U.S. Department of Agriculture decided to replace the Food Pyramid for healthy eating with MyPlate a few years ago. Foods high in salt, sugar, and saturated or trans fat should still be limited, which means you should have them only as occasional treats. Just as certain foods are "sometimes" foods for dads, so they are "sometimes" foods for your children and should be eaten a few times a week at the most.

Occasional treat foods include foods that are

>> Heavy in sugars, like hard candy, cookies, chocolate, and dried fruit.

>> Heavily processed, such as microwavable or frozen meals such as pizza or pies, fruit roll-ups, and sweet cereals.

>> Laden with saturated fats, like fish and chips, or burgers.

>> High in salt and flavorings, such as crackers and chips. Even commercial soups can have a very high sodium count.

We've also become increasingly aware of how food additives, flavorings, and colorings can affect our children; how processing can take away nutritional value; and how cruel some farming practices can be to animals. There's a movement toward eating more organic, less processed foods in order to avoid pesticide residues and get more nutritional value from what we eat. You may want to consider doing the same.

WARNING

If your child is under 3, avoid foods that may choke him, such as nuts, olives, or popcorn. Even after 3, discourage eating while on the move, watching TV, or doing anything that may distract him. Keep cutting food into small pieces to avoid an airway blockage.

Telling your child "no" for the hundredth time to the candy or cookies you have stashed in the pantry is easier said than done, and even if you don't have a private supply that junior knows about, he's going to discover treat foods at school or at friends' houses. So you probably won't be able to keep your child as pure as the day he was born. That's okay. A few animal crackers every now and then isn't going to turn him into Fat Albert. Just keep remembering to fill him full of good stuff whenever you can and encourage him to get active.

TIP

Completely banning "bad" foods makes them objects of desire, so let your child have a few treats now and then, just like you would treat yourself. Children need fat in their diet, but things like chips should be limited to once a week.

Introducing different foods

Putting a plate of never-seen-before food in front of your child can be a little disconcerting for her. She may turn her nose up at something you think she'll love just because it looks funny.

So take some time to introduce new tastes and textures thoughtfully. Here are some ideas:

>> **Do it yourself.** You are your child's role model, and if you dig into your food with gusto, chances are she will too.

>> **Get creative with your presentation.** Make a face, shapes, or patterns with food.

>> **Give her something to dip into.** Low-fat dressing, tomato sauce, mild salsa, hummus, and yogurt dips all provide a fun way of testing out new foods.

>> **Get sneaky.** Put finely chopped pieces of new foods into stews, omelets, mashed potatoes, smoothies, or rice.

>> **Grow your own.** One way to get children into fruits and vegetables is to let them take part in growing it themselves. She'll be enormously proud to dig into those beans she's seen grow from seed and watered every night.

>> **Keep portions small.** Not only will this keep new foods from seeming so overwhelming, but it will also get you in the habit of not overloading your child's plate. And never, ever enroll your child in the "clean plate club"; forcing kids to eat more than they want or need can start bad habits that lead to obesity down the road.

TIP

Forcing children to eat something they don't like is counterproductive. If your child tries a new meal and doesn't like it, that's okay. She'll make up for it by eating others. Punishing your child for not eating makes her more defiant. Remember also that children take time to develop a taste for something. The fact that she turned down broccoli the first time she tried it doesn't mean she'll never like it.

Leading by example

You are your child's role model, and what you eat and how you live sets the scene for how your child will eat and live.

Children who have one obese parent have a 40 percent chance of becoming obese themselves, and children with two obese parents have an 80 percent chance of facing obesity. That's a poor legacy to leave a child. If you've already fallen into the trap of giving your child whatever sugary and fatty processed foods she wants, now is an opportunity to consider a change of course and swap unhealthy food options with healthy ones. Here are some simple ways to make meals healthier:

>> **Avoid processed and pre-prepared foods.** Generally, the less time food has spent going through a factory, the better it is for you. This also goes for basic ingredients like sugar, flour, or rice. Use raw or brown sugar, whole grain flour, and brown rice.

>> **Eat meals as a family when you can.** Turn off the TV and use dinnertime to catch up on your day and enjoy each other's company. Sharing food is an important social interaction for humans, and enjoying food together should be special.

>> **Exercise restraint.** If you habitually have dessert, keep the portions small.

>> **Find out about healthy substitutes to sugar and fat-laden foods.** Try natural yogurt with fruit added rather than tubs of sweetened yogurt, for example. Honey is an excellent replacement for refined, white sugar, after your child is over age 1. Honey is a natural product and complex food that is easier to digest and produces less of a "sugar high" than white sugar.

>> **Prepare meals together.** Let your child have some responsibility over what goes into her food. Get her involved in where your food comes from and how easy it is to prepare. As we get older, making food for each other is another social interaction that shows our family and friends how much we love and care for each other, and this can be a positive activity for your child to enjoy right now.

Handling fussy eaters

Children may go through a fussy eating period. This stage is annoying and frustrating, and all you want your child to do is eat! It's enough to make a grown man cry. There can sometimes be a reason behind it, such as meal times falling at a time when she's tired, too much distraction when she should be eating, or snacking before mealtimes. In all circumstances patience with fussy eating results in better eating than getting angry and annoyed.

Here are some ways to deal with fussy eaters:

>> Avoid arguing about food. Forcing your child to eat mushrooms is unlikely to encourage a love of them in the future, so you're no further ahead next time you serve them up.

>> Avoid giving snacks in the hour before a meal, as she won't be hungry when mealtime arrives.

>> Offer a variety of small servings of food in a meal, with lots of vegetables and other goodies to choose from, so if she doesn't like one food she has others to choose from.

>> Praise your child when she eats, especially when she tries something new and different.

>> Try some of the suggestions from the section "Leading by example" earlier in this chapter, such as getting your child involved in food preparation, making meal times a family time, and growing your own food. Take small amounts and don't feel like you need to polish off your plate whenever you eat.

Try to avoid the following:

>> Cooking another meal to feed her if she turns up her nose at the first

>> Giving your child a treat to make her stop whining

>> Having meals in front of TV or while doing something else, such as reading, playing games, or walking around the house

If you're concerned that your fussy eater isn't getting enough to eat to grow, play, and be active, talk to your pediatrician.

Coping with special dietary requirements

More and more children seem to be developing allergies to certain foods, such as wheat, gluten, eggs, nuts, milk, shellfish, and even some types of fruits and vegetables. Some children may grow out of them; others won't. Managing an allergy can be a matter of life or death.

The recommended practice of introducing new foods one at a time helps with detecting reactions to certain foods. If your child shows symptoms of an allergic reaction, take him to your healthcare provider to have him tested.

What is an allergy?

An *allergy* is a reaction by the immune system when it thinks the food you're eating is harmful. It produces *histamines,* which can cause hives or other rashes, breathing difficulties, a tight throat, nausea, vomiting, and diarrhea. The most dangerous reaction the body can have is called *anaphylaxis,* in which the tongue swells, air passages narrow, and blood pressure drops. Anaphylaxis can cause death.

Recognizing the most common food allergens

Just six common foods cause 90 percent of allergic reactions in children: milk, eggs, peanuts, tree nuts, soy, and wheat. Between 2 and 3 percent of children under age 3 have a cow's milk allergy, although some outgrow it over time.

Children with cow's milk allergy may also experience allergic reactions to soy.

How do you manage an allergy?

Avoiding the foods that cause the body to overreact is the best way to avoid an allergic reaction. The jury is still out on what causes allergies — the tendency toward allergies, but not specific allergies, is most likely inherited — but some physicians feel that the later potentially harmful foods are introduced, the less likely your child is to develop a reaction to them.

Luckily, more people are learning about food allergies and food producers are hopping on the bandwagon too. You can now find many substitutes for common food *allergens,* those foods that cause an allergy. Wheat-free breads, pastas, and baking products are available; you can buy egg substitute for baking; and cow's milk can be easily replaced by soy or rice milk. Many day care centers, kindergartens, and schools have banned nuts and nut products from the premises in a move to ensure the safety of children with nut allergies.

It can be hard to work out whether your child is in fact allergic to certain foods. Talk to your pediatrician — you may be able to have your child tested for the most common allergies, if he has common symptoms.

If your child is allergic to certain foods, you'll have to be more vigilant about reading labels on food packaging, and to make other parents and caregivers aware of your child's allergy so that at day care, on play dates, or at birthday parties, your child isn't given food that may cause a reaction.

Some people think that just having a small amount of an allergen is okay, but this has been shown to be very dangerous. Small amounts or even being in the same room as an allergen is enough to make some children seriously ill. For severe cases of allergies, children may have to carry an EpiPen, which administers medicine in the event of an allergic reaction. Talk to your doctor about allergies and discuss ways of managing your child's allergy, including EpiPens. It may also be helpful to speak with a dietitian who can help manage the allergy and teach you and your child what you need to do to avoid allergic reactions.

WARNING

Smooth peanut butter can be given to children from eight to nine months of age, but watch them closely for any signs of a reaction. If your family has a strong history of nut allergies, wait until your child is 3 before trying nuts. If your child has any breathing difficulties, call 911 immediately.

TIP

Being informed about what you're dealing with when your child has a food allergy helps you stay on top of it. See this site for tips on managing your child's allergy and contacting support networks: acaai.org/allergies/who-has-allergies/children-allergies.

Vegetarian children

A vegetarian diet is becoming a lifestyle choice for more and more parents, be it to save the planet or on moral grounds. If you want to bring up your child on a vegetarian diet, you have to pay a bit more attention to where he gets his iron and protein, especially because children have higher iron needs than adults. Good sources of iron include the following:

>> Most dark green (leafy) vegetables such as broccoli, spinach, Swiss chard, and kale

>> Dried fruit such as prunes and raisins

>> Lentils, chickpeas, and dried peas

>> Whole-grain cereal and bread

>> Egg yolks (if you follow an ovo-lacto vegetarian diet)

TIP

Vitamin C helps the body absorb iron, so make having fruit such as citrus or kiwifruit with a meal part of your routine.

You can help your child get plenty of protein by feeding him

>> Dairy products

>> Eggs

>> Grains like brown rice, oatmeal, buckwheat, and millet

>> Hummus, chickpeas, and most legumes, such as soy beans and lentils

>> Peanut butter and nuts (for children age 3 and older)

>> Tofu and tempeh

>> Vegetables like eggplant, zucchini, beets, and cabbage

TIP

A great way of getting protein into your child is adding puffed-up grains to muesli or cereal. Puffed-up grains include millet, rye, or quinoa (they're all healthy alternatives to wheat).

A vegetarian diet can be bulkier and more filling than a nonvegetarian diet, so your child may feel fuller with less food. Offer smaller meals more frequently throughout the day to ensure he gets enough energy and nutrients to get through his day.

Excellent Exercise

We've talked a lot about how being active from birth helps to develop your child's brain. And, this may not be earth-shattering news — exercise is quite good for her body too!

Getting your child (and yourself) into exercise

An amazing fact of human biology is that, just by being active with our bodies, we grow our brains. So keeping active and exercising can help your child develop her mental powers!

But the balancing act of life at work, home, and getting time for yourself may mean exercise falls to the bottom of the priority list, never to be seen again. When it comes to your body, you either use it or lose it.

Yes, you've grown a gut and your partner may be teasing you about potential man boobs. Retaliating by pointing out her saggy boobs and stretch marks may boost your ego (temporarily) but won't do anything to help you get fit now — and may have you sleeping on the couch. So time once more to man up to a big task and get on with it.

Try the following:

>> Check out gyms that offer child care and take the whole family.

>> Get off the bus a few stops early and walk the rest of the way home. Park your car farther away from work, or walk or cycle to work. Skip the elevator and walk up and down the stairs.

>> Involve your child in your exercise program. Stroller jogs; swimming lessons at the local pool; or exercising at home using your child as a weight, sitting on you while you do sit-ups or push-ups, are all great ways to incorporate her into your exercise program.

>> Schedule some time into your week for exercise. Make exercise a priority, a promise to yourself that you can't break. Take turns with your partner; one day she goes for a run, the next day you do.

>> Team up with a few friends and get a personal trainer. There's nothing like peer pressure and professional advice from a coach to get you in shape.

You are your child's role model, so by making exercise and activity normal and a high priority in your own life, you're making exercise normal and a high priority in her life.

Exercise with your child by

>> Clambering over the monkey bars and climbing walls at your local playground with her — if you're physically up to the task.

>> Doing chores around the house. Vacuuming, mowing the lawn, and washing the car can help you work up a sweat. Get your child to help — a good foundation for the day he can mow the yard himself.

>> Getting a trampoline for the backyard. Jumping around for 15 minutes gets your pulse up. Don't get too tricky with your jumps; a trip to the ER won't add to your overall fitness.

>> Going for walks (short ones at the beginning). Encourage your child to walk by himself rather than be carried.

>> Having a pillow fight or a bit of rough-housing to get all the muscles working!

>> Showing her how to climb trees; again, know your limitations.

>> Signing up to coach a sport at your local school and having your child come along to play too.

Workout routines

Can you imagine your toddler or preschooler doing aerobics, or being able to follow what a weightlifting class instructor is saying? Not likely. Working out with your child should be fun, not a stream of complicated instructions to follow. You can use the activities listed earlier as your workout routines, or try more traditional exercises with weights (for you, teddy bears for your child) and set moves. Here are some tips to make working out work out smoothly:

>> Don't eat just before exercise and especially not before swimming.

>> Explain how important it is to warm up, stretch, and drink water.

>> Give lots of praise and encouragement. If he can't master an exercise yet, show him how and encourage him to do it himself. Helping his body through an exercise shows him he can do it.

>> Make doing exercise together a regular activity — say, after day care or before dinner — so that your child looks forward to exercise and it becomes part of his routine.

>> Start off slowly. A quarter of an hour of exercise is a good way to start.

Practicing yoga and meditation

Yoga is an ancient method of not only strengthening the body and maintaining physical well-being but also maintaining mental well-being. The practice consists of moving into *poses* by using breath and movement. Yoga encourages flexibility, stamina, and relaxation for general good health, including stress relief.

And what better time to start practicing yoga than when you have a frisky toddler or preschooler to entertain? Though a young child's attention span may not cater to long sessions of yoga or deep meditation, there are a lot of poses you and your tyke can do at home, or you may want to enroll her in a class specializing in children's yoga.

Many yoga poses are named after animals or things found in nature. Children often enjoy imagining they really are a dolphin when doing the dolphin pose or have the roots of a thousand-year-old oak when practicing the tree pose.

The best way to get started is by enrolling in a yoga-for-children course. And don't think for a minute that yoga for children is too easy for you. You can do lots of poses along with your child, and they are just as challenging for you to do. In fact your child will probably do many poses better than you, which is a great source of motivation. Keep up with your toddler so he doesn't call you "old man" (just yet).

Coping with Common Health Problems

There's no more scary time than when your little one comes down with something and you're not sure what's happening. Before your child can speak and tell you what the matter is, you have only your innate dad-sense to tell you what the trouble is. So we've made it a little easier by laying out for you some basic health issues you'll probably have to delve into sometime or another.

Childhood illnesses

At times it may seem that every couple of weeks your child is struck down with a cold — or worse, an ear or chest infection. As your child's immunity is still developing and he spends more time in the company of other children, he's going to pick up a lot of nasty illnesses. The list in this chapter covers the "usual suspects" of childhood illnesses. Chapter 17 examines what to do when you find out your child may have a serious or rare illness.

Following are some of the most common childhood illnesses to watch out for and what you can do about them.

Bronchiolitis

An acute (usually viral) chest infection, bronchiolitis usually comes after a cold, ear infection, or tonsillitis. It affects the small airways in the lungs called *bronchioles*.

- **» Symptoms:** A hacking cough, difficulty breathing, and wheezing. Sometimes a child's lips or tongue turn blue, a dangerous sign that he's not getting enough oxygen. Some children vomit. Children can be ill for seven to ten days.

- **» Treatment:** Keep your child well hydrated. Because bronchiolitis is viral, in mild cases there is no drug treatment. Severe cases may require hospitalization. See your doctor if you're concerned.

- **» Precautions:** Watch for secondary bacterial infections, which can be treated with antibiotics. If the bronchiolitis symptoms don't go away as quickly as predicted by your pediatrician, or new symptoms, such as flu symptoms, appear, go back to your doctor or hospital. They may diagnose a secondary infection. If your child turns blue or is struggling to breathe, call 911 immediately!

Chickenpox

Chickenpox usually affects children and is a viral illness that can be transmitted through coughing and sneezing, or from touching one of the fluid blisters that appear on the skin of a patient. Having chickenpox usually provides long-lasting immunity to the disease, and only rarely have people had chickenpox twice. In adults, chickenpox can result in complications such as shingles.

- **» Symptoms:** Cold and flu-like symptoms — runny nose, cough, tiredness and fever. A rash of small round lumps appears, which a few days later are replaced by itchy, fluid-filled blisters. The blisters tend to appear more on the torso, stomach, and back, but they can also form on the extremities, the inside of the mouth, the scalp, and the face.

- **» Treatment:** Applying topical lotions to the blisters can help with the itch, but bed rest, acetaminophen for pain and fever, and not scratching are recommended.

- **» Precautions:** Let your day care or preschool, friends, and family know that your child has chickenpox, because it's contagious for about five days before the first symptoms appear.

You can now get your child immunized against chickenpox. Looking after a child with chickenpox is horrendous and quite a nasty experience for her too, so consider having her immunized, even if you have to pay for it.

You may have heard of the concepts of a "chickenpox party." The idea behind chickenpox parties is to purposefully expose children to another child who has chickenpox to get the inevitable infection out of the way. We don't believe this is a fantastic idea as chickenpox can be very severe — and in a few cases, life-threatening — so it should not be treated lightheartedly. Immunization may be a better alternative.

Common cold

A cold is a viral infection, mainly affecting the nose and throat and lasting from two to three days to a week.

>> **Symptoms:** Runny nose, nasal congestion, weepy eyes, sore throat, tiredness, cough, sneezing, and fever.

>> **Treatment:** Bed rest and fluids, along with a cool-mist vaporizer. Acetaminophen can be used for pain and fever. Ask your doctor before using chest rubs or any other over-the-counter medications to alleviate coughing.

>> **Precautions:** If your child doesn't get better over three to four days, see your pediatrician. There may be a secondary infection like an ear infection or worse on the way. If your child has a fever of 100.4 degrees Fahrenheit or higher, a strange cry, or a very sore throat, call the pediatrician.

Conjunctivitis

Also known as pink eye, conjunctivitis is an inflammation of the tissue that lines the eyes. A range of things cause conjunctivitis — allergens in the air, a bacterial or viral infection, food allergies, or a blocked tear duct. If your child's case of conjunctivitis is caused by an infection, it can be very contagious, so wash your hands after touching your child so you don't come down with it as well! Keep your child away from day care and tell staff about the infection.

>> **Symptoms:** Red, sore eyes and possibly green or yellow mucus at the corners.

>> **Treatment:** Wash your child's eyes with a disposable cotton ball dipped in clean water. Wash and dry your hands after doing this to curb infection spreading to you. A doctor can prescribe eye drops or ointment.

>> **Precautions:** Wash bedding, clothing, towels, and washcloths in hot water with some disinfectant to curb further infection or reinfection.

Ear infection

Children under 7 years old are particularly prone to ear infections, which occur when germs get into the middle ear. Pus and fluid can build up in the eardrum, making your little one pretty miserable.

Deal with ear infections promptly because fluid can remain in the ear, which can make it hard for your child to hear, and therefore listen and learn.

>> **Symptoms:** Ear infections are pretty distressing for young ones. Your child will be cranky, rub his ears, and not want to lie down for sleep or diaper changes. Ear infections can coincide with colds, the flu, and chest infections. Older children will tell you the ear feels full, and in severe cases the eardrum can burst. Don't waste time — see your pediatrician because you need to get confirmation of an ear infection from a healthcare professional.

>> **Treatment:** Pain relief like ibuprofen and acetaminophen can help. Antibiotics can help when the infection is caused by bacteria, but not with viral ear infections, so see your pediatrician. Raising the head of the bed slightly can help too. Your child won't be able to hear well, so keep background noise down so he can hear you.

>> **Precautions:** Recurring ear infections may mean more drastic action needs to be taken. Doctors can put ear tubes — small tubes inserted in the eardrum to allow airflow and drainage between the inner and outer ear — in children's ears to prevent fluid build-up.

Gastroenteritis

Bacteria and viruses can attack the gut, causing a tummy bug. Gastroenteritis can happen because of a range of causes, from not washing hands properly after using the toilet or changing a diaper to food poisoning.

>> **Symptoms:** Vomiting, diarrhea, stomach cramps, body pains, fever, nausea, and in extreme cases, diarrhea with blood or mucus.

>> **Treatment:** Losing fluids through vomiting and diarrhea means you have to be careful that dehydration doesn't occur, so make sure your child is drinking plenty of fluids.

>> **Precautions:** Refusing to eat is less of a worry (in medical terms) than dehydration. However, refusing to eat is an indicator that something may not be right. Monitoring your child's temperature and ensuring she has plenty of fluid intake when she's ill is always the priority. If you see blood in your child's stool, call your pediatrician immediately.

WARNING

See your doctor right away if your child becomes very weak, is overly sleepy, has difficulty breathing, vomits, develops a high fever, has very dry skin or sunken eyes, doesn't want to eat her favorite food, or stops passing urine.

Meningitis

Meningitis is a very serious disease in which the *meninges,* or protective membranes of the brain and spinal cord, become infected and inflamed (swollen). Meningitis often comes on very fast and can be fatal or cause severe disability if not treated. There are different kinds of meningitis, but the most well-known is caused by the meningococcal bacteria. Meningitis is passed through coughing, sharing eating utensils or cups and glasses, or being in close contact with a carrier. Many people carry the meningococcal bacteria but don't develop symptoms. Familiarize yourself with the symptoms of meningitis. You need to constantly be on the watch for these symptoms because the disease develops so quickly and is potentially fatal.

>> **Symptoms:** Severe headache, neck stiffness, sensitivity to light and loud noises, frequent crying with a high-pitched cry, refusing food or feedings, vomiting, fever, or a rash with blotchy skin or red and purple spots. The onset of symptoms can be very fast. Your child may have an unusual cry or be very sleepy.

>> **Treatment:** See your doctor immediately if you suspect meningitis. Call an ambulance if you can't see your doctor immediately. Your child can become seriously ill very quickly, so don't second-guess yourself — get to the doctor or hospital!

>> **Precautions:** Vaccines can help prevent some types of bacterial meningitis. Check out www.cdc.gov/meningitis/index.html.

Pneumonia

Pneumonia is a disease in which the air sacs of the lungs become infected.

>> **Symptoms:** A wheezy or rattling cough, rapid breathing, making a noise when breathing, or having a hard time breathing. Your child may be very tired and look really unwell. Viral pneumonia starts out like a cold, while bacterial pneumonia can cause a fever as well.

>> **Treatment:** Go to your pediatrician. Keep your child hydrated with fluids.

>> **Precautions:** Pneumonia makes it hard for people suffering from the disease to get oxygen, so your child may look very pale, even a little blue, and be very sleepy. If this happens, see your doctor immediately, because your child needs more oxygen urgently.

Tonsillitis

Tonsillitis is an inflammation of the tonsils, which are two lit-tle slits at the back of the throat, one on each side. Tonsils can become extremely sore and covered in pus. Symptoms can go on for four to six days. Tonsillitis can be caused by the streptococcus bacteria and can be highly contagious.

>> **Symptoms:** Tonsils become red, sore, and swollen, and sometimes secrete pus. Your child may also have flu symptoms like tiredness, fever, muscle aches, and swollen glands in the neck.

>> **Treatment:** Visit your pediatrician. Antibiotics can sort out a case of strep-caused tonsillitis. However, if the disease is viral, bed rest, fluids, and ibuprofen or acetaminophen for pain relief are your best bet. Because your child's throat will be very sore, eating cold, soft foods like gelatin is best. Gargling with warm salt water can clear any pus build-up.

>> **Precautions:** Some children have recurring bouts of tonsillitis, which may result in having their tonsils removed surgically.

Whooping cough

Also known as pertussis, whooping cough is easily preventable because vaccines have been available in most communities for years. Whooping cough has three stages and can last many weeks, even up to three months. The defining characteristic of whooping cough is the cough with a "whoop" at the end, but it's no whooping matter — the cough is nasty and will make your child pretty miserable for the duration of the illness.

>> **Symptoms:** The first stage, which lasts about a week, includes a hacking cough at night, loss of appetite, sneezing, and possibly a slight fever. The second stage lasts about another week and is characterized by the horrendous coughing spells ending with the loud "whoop." Your child may cough up lots of mucus, which may make her vomit. Sometimes children can stop breathing during these spells, so keep them close to you for monitoring. The third stage is usually when things are on the mend, though watch for secondary infections like ear and chest infections.

>> **Treatment:** Go to the pediatrician. Some children need to be hospitalized. Small meals and lots of fluids are important, as is lots of love for your little one while she gets through the

illness. Antibiotics may be prescribed. Steam and humidifiers can be used, but talk to your doctor.

>> **Precautions:** Keep your child at home for three weeks from the start of the illness, or for five days after starting antibiotics to prevent infecting other children.

Infants too young to have been vaccinated against whooping cough may become very ill, so if your child or someone else in your family has whooping cough, stay away from infants.

If your child is treated at home, take turns with family and friends to stay up at night to monitor your child because the cough is often worse at night.

Recurring health problems: Where to go from here?

Children under 5 have an average of six to eight respiratory tract infections (or colds) a year. The range in the number of infections children have is huge, though; while some children can get away with no infections at all, other children can have many.

Kids get sick so often because they

>> Catch bugs from other children, and their immune system is still developing and getting up to speed trying to fight all the bugs around

>> Could have an overactive or an underactive immune system

>> May have problems with the way they are put together anatomically, such as circulation problems, broken skin, and obstructions in the ears and lungs

You can't influence some of the factors cited previously, but you can do your bit to help your little one stay healthy. For example:

>> Check that your child is adequately dressed for the weather when playing outside. For example, in windy weather make sure she wears a hat. Take an extra set of clothes so you can

change them quickly if they get wet or put on an extra layer if the temperature drops suddenly.

>> Ensure room temperatures at home (and in her bedroom) are close to the World Health Organization (WHO) recommendation — 66 degrees Fahrenheit. Go easy on air conditioning near children and avoid drafts.

>> Keep up general hygiene standards such as washing hands after going to the toilet or petting animals, especially before touching food or eating. Teach your child not to pick up things from the floor and put them in her mouth.

REMEMBER

If you think the number of times your child is ill, or the severity of your child's recurring illness, is unusual or excessive, talk to your pediatrician. There may be an anatomical or immune issue here that you can treat.

Alternative medicines and remedies

Some dads seeking help with their children's illnesses sometimes turn to the less beaten track by checking out alternative medicine. Many of these treatments look at preventing or curing illness through examining the whole person rather than just the disease. Types of alternative care include

>> **Acupuncture:** An ancient Chinese technique where special needles are inserted at pressure points in the body

>> **Essential oils:** Using plant oils to promote general well-being and help with illnesses

>> **Homeopathy:** Using plant extracts to treat illness and promote well-being

>> **Massage:** Using touch to relax muscles and stimulate blood flow around the body

>> **Naturopathy:** An alternative medical system that uses the body's ability to heal itself

>> **Osteopathy or chiropractic:** Treating the body with manipulation of the musculoskeletal system

Many of these techniques may be beneficial for your child. However, they're generally not designed to replace primary care, so a trip to your pediatrician is still a good idea even if you swear by the benefits of the various alternative approaches. There are also some things to be aware of when turning to alternative medicine to treat your child:

>> Check the use of alternative medicine beforehand with your pediatrician or hospital. Many alternative therapies are unproven and unregulated, and some could cause harm.

>> Some herbal remedies may contain allergens. Read labels carefully. Some can cause high blood pressure and liver damage. Check with your pediatrician if in doubt.

WARNING

We have listed the preceding techniques and remedies for the sake of completeness and because some of them are very common. The effectiveness of alternative medicines and remedies in many cases has not been scientifically proven.

Child obesity

Obesity is a serious problem in the United States, affecting 17 percent of children and adolescents between the ages of 2 and 19. Around one in three children is either overweight or obese. Obese children are prone to many of the same health problems as obese adults, including type 2 diabetes, high cholesterol levels, high blood pressure, sleep apnea, liver abnormalities, and joint problems. Obese children are also more likely to have low self-esteem, to be teased at school, and to suffer from depression — things that no parent wants his child to have to deal with.

Obese parents are more likely to have obese children. Both genetic and environmental factors play a part in this. Although you can't control your child's genetic background, you can control his environment — and your own weight. Limiting non-nutritious snacks and encouraging exercise will help your whole family maintain a normal weight and better health.

Your child's pediatrician can tell you whether your child's weight is rising above a healthy limit. Take weight issues seriously, ignore your great-grandma when she tells you that a fat child is a healthy child, and start building a healthy lifestyle when your child is young. He'll thank you for it later.

A word on health insurance

Healthcare insurance generally covers well visits for young children as well as immunizations. Government programs can help with child health expenses if your income falls below a certain level. If you have medical insurance for yourself already, talk to your insurer about adding your child to your policy as soon as he's born.

If your child is seriously ill and you need to take time off work to look after him, find information about the Family and Medical Leave Act, commonly known as FMLA. Check out www.dol.gov/whd/fmla/ for more information on what is and isn't covered under FMLA.

Chapter 15

Getting an Education

School is a major part of your child's life for the next 12 years — or more. Into adulthood, her school days shape her decisions, her values, and her way of thinking, not just the qualifications she earns or the things she knows. As a dad, you obviously want to get the best schooling for your children. This may mean a focus on academic achievement, on a holistic view of the child as a well-rounded individual, or on spiritual and religious elements important to your culture or ethnic background.

Your child's school should also be somewhere you feel comfortable so that you can stay connected to your child and involved in her school life as much as possible. Research shows that the better the student's family support and involvement, the better she performs at school.

In this chapter we lay out all the options you have in navigating the education landscape, from private and pricy prep schools to public or religious schools, and give you some tools to help decide which is best for your child.

Exploring Education Philosophies

When you were a kid, wasn't school just a place that you went to down the road? These days we know a lot more about how a good education determines the path your life will take, and therefore there's a lot more pressure on parents, and in some cases on dads, to get it right.

Understanding education choices

Lots of choices in schools are available, and trying to pick the best school for your child can be baffling. Here's a look at what there is to choose from.

In the United States, you have a choice of

>> **Alternative schools:** Schools such as Montessori or Waldorf, which stress creativity and more independent learning than most public schools.

>> **Public schools:** Publicly funded schools in your local area. In most cases, your child will go to an assigned school, usually but not always the school nearest you.

>> **Private schools:** Schools where you pay fees for your child's tuition. The majority are Catholic schools or other religiously based schools.

>> **Preparatory schools:** Schools where you pay fees for your child's tuition and where your child has to make the cut to go there. Many have a religious affiliation, usually Protestant.

>> **Single-sex schools:** Some schools admit only boys or girls. These schools aren't common in the United States, but they do exist, more often in private than public schools.

To help you make your decision about which school your child should go to, it may help to ask yourself these questions:

>> Besides getting good grades, what else is important at this school? Are there sports teams, language classes, or music

facilities that you would like to encourage your child to get involved with?

>> Can you afford to send your child to a private school? Private schools cost anywhere from a few thousand dollars a year to more than $10,000 per year.

>> Do you feel happy and confident about coming in to talk to teachers and the principal? Do you like the vibe when you walk into the school?

>> How practical is it to get your child to the school and back? Are long journeys by car, bus, or train involved? Is the school en route to work or a long way out of your work travel route?

>> What are the school's values and teaching philosophies? Do they match your values and philosophies?

TIP

Spend some time at the school if you can. Ask yourself if you like the atmosphere, the way the teachers and children respond to each other, and the children there. Are the children precocious, spoiled, respectful, or meek? Ask teachers why they became a teacher. Is teaching their "calling," or is it simply a job they ended up in because other career options didn't work out?

Alternative education philosophies

If public school philosophies, with their emphasis on reading, writing, and 'rithmetic, aren't your thing, you do have alternatives. Both Montessori and Waldorf methods aim to educate children in a holistic way, shaping the child to be a good person with strong values and a sense of self.

Montessori

Developed by Dr. Maria Montessori in 1907, this approach involves observing and following the child's interests and encouraging him to explore and learn at his own pace. Here are the basics:

>> Children are separated into age groups 0–3, 3–6, 6–9, 9–12, and 12–14 years.

>> Learning environments are designed so children can explore and have lots of specially designed materials to encourage skills and development that are easily manipulated by children. Classrooms are very calm, ordered places, where children learn to respect the space and needs of their classmates. Children are taught to put things back where they belong so others can use them.

>> Montessori believed that with the right environment and freedom to explore, children develop a love of work, order, and silence, and grow to become independent, self-disciplined adults who are true to their natures.

>> Older children are encouraged to be role models and support younger children.

Check the website www.montessori-namta.org/School-Directory for a list of Montessori schools to see if there's one near you.

TIP

Waldorf/Rudolf Steiner

Rudolf Steiner was an Austrian philosopher who founded the school of thought called *anthroposophy*. Without getting too technical here, Steiner's schools (sometimes called Waldorf because that was the name of the first school) use the concept of imagination and creative thinking to develop children into free-thinking adults. Steiner schools regard the child's inner life as important as learning to read, write, and do math. Here are the basics:

>> Childhood is divided into three parts: early childhood, where emphasis is put on learning through experience; elementary age, where emphasis is put on the child's spirit; and adolescence, where emphasis is on developing analytical and abstract thinking skills.

>> Foreign languages and crafts like knitting, art, and artistic movement are used to teach staple subjects like reading, math, and science.

>> The first lesson of the day is called *main lesson* and it lasts for about two hours. During main lesson, a particular curriculum area is taught using art, stories, recitation, or physical movement. Main lesson has a theme, which continues for about a month.

>> The same teacher stays with children as they progress through school for the first six years.

TIP

Waldorf schools are not as common in the United States as they are in other parts of the world. Check the Waldorf Education website, `https://waldorfeducation.org/`, for a list of schools.

Private versus public

For some fathers, whether you send your child to private or public school comes down to finances — you can either afford the fees, or you can't.

Many factors affect a child's performance at school. The most important factor is the child's background — the place he comes from and the support he receives from family and the community. More children from well-off backgrounds go to private schools, and those schools may perform better than some public schools. Private schools may send more children to college, although this doesn't always hold true. When considering which school to send your child to, ask yourself these questions:

>> Do I want my child to be educated in a religious setting? If yes, private schools of your denomination are for you.

>> Do I want my child to have access to a large range of extracurricular activities? If yes, check out the programs offered at the public and private schools around you. Private schools have scholarships for young people who excel in sports.

>> What value do I place on cultural diversity? Private schools may have fewer children of minority backgrounds.

TIP

Talk to other parents and students at the school you're looking at. They are the best gauge of a school.

TIP

Take a look at your potential school's results on the website `www.greatschools.org`.

Same-sex versus co-ed

Girls and boys learn in different ways. Boys learn better when they stand up and are active; girls learn well in a structured/formal setting. So the idea of separating boys and girls to have a more effective learning experience seems pretty straightforward.

That said, experts are divided on the effectiveness of single-sex schools. Principals at single-sex schools claim that without the distraction of the opposite sex around, students get on with learning and girls are more likely to come out of their shells a bit. Those who champion co-educational schools say that there are social advantages in having the opposite sex around on a daily basis.

But that doesn't help you dads, does it? Perhaps this is something you'd like to talk about with your child. She may have a preference, and you can always check with parents whose children attend single-sex or co-ed schools. Ask yourself the same questions we suggest for checking out schools in general: Does this school reflect your family values? How comfortable are you about this school?

Starting School

Welcome to a whole new world — the world of school! Going to school is a big milestone in any child's life. Be sure to take lots of pictures and enjoy seeing your child in his new environment. As his role model, if you enjoy school and being there with him, he'll love it too.

In the United States, the school year runs from late August or early September to May or June, and the academic year is generally divided into two semesters, although this may vary, depending on where you live. There are short breaks between semesters, with a longer break of roughly 10 weeks over the summer.

Preparing for school

If your child has been to day care or preschool, he has some experience with being around lots of other children and teachers without you, and the transition to school may be quite straightforward. On the other hand, going to school is also a new environment. Bigger kids will be there, he may be riding the school bus for the first time, and he may be quite scared about all the changes in his life right now. There's also the fact that this is school, which is such a big milestone in his life that you'll undoubtedly be feeling all sorts of emotions — your little person is growing up!

Day care centers and preschools take part in getting your child prepared for school, emotionally and educationally. Just like when you were settling your child into day care or preschool, taking your child to school and staying with him for visits will help him adjust and become familiar with his new surroundings. Talking together about what happens at school, what playtime is, what happens during the day, and where his bag goes will also help him be less overwhelmed by the change in his life.

TIP

Tell your little one what it was like for you when you were in school (hopefully you still remember some details!). Show him photos if you have some and get him excited about school by telling a few tall tales of your own school days.

Most schools have an orientation day for new students before your child starts school. As well as helping your child, the orientation day also helps you be more at home in his new school, which is important. Studies show that fathers who are comfortable at a school are more likely to be actively involved in their child's education.

REMEMBER

School vacations come around quickly, and you need a plan for when your child doesn't have to go to school for a while. Plan well ahead by arranging with your partner or family who will look after junior during the holidays or on the inevitable sick days.

Things kids need to know about school

Imagine you're starting a new job. You turn up at your new office and are shown your desk and a stack of work to do. And that's it. You don't know where the bathrooms are, where to make a cup of coffee, what time lunch is, where meetings are held, or what time you call it a day. You'd be feeling pretty out to sea if this happened to you, and your child will feel the same. She may find going to school and settling into a new environment overwhelming if she doesn't get a heads-up from you about what's going to happen, so here are a few things you may have overlooked that your child needs to know:

>> Let her know that asking questions if she's not sure of anything is okay. There are always teachers and teacher aides around who can help.

>> Explain the school rules — no hitting, no running with scissors, no stealing, and other good rules.

>> Give your child a rough guide to the day's structure: There'll be a playtime and lunchtime, if your school has all-day kindergarten.

>> Explain that only the people she knows well, such as Dad, Mom, and special relatives and friends, should take her home from school. Most schools today have very strict rules about who can pick up children.

>> Tell her that school is on every day except weekends.

>> Make sure she knows that looking after her bag, clothing, and lunch box is her responsibility. Dad won't be able to run around finding stuff for her at going-home time, especially if she takes a bus home.

>> Show her how to go to the toilet and wash her hands by herself.

>> Be sure she understands that the teacher is in charge of the class. If she needs something, she should ask the teacher.

You can help the transition to school by saying hello to the teacher every morning and stopping to talk to any children or parents that you know. Goodbyes should be short, however. Say "goodbye" and "I love you," give a quick kiss, and let the teacher — a trained professional in these matters — take over.

REMEMBER

Your child will be really tired from school in the first few weeks, so let her have some time to herself and a snack after school before making her do any chores. Show lots of interest, though, and be prepared to listen when your growing little one is ready to tell you about her exciting day at school.

Just as when you leave your child with a babysitter or when you've taken her to day care or kindergarten, your child may be a bit clingy when you leave her at school on the first day. To get around this "return of separation anxiety," make sure your child is with an adult, such as a teacher or teacher aide, or an older child like a cousin or friend when you leave. Give her a big kiss and a hug, and tell her you love her. Say something like "I'll be back after school" or "see you later" and walk away. Don't draw out the goodbye. Your child is in good hands in school, and she'll be just fine starting her journey to becoming an independent adult. Be there for your child when she needs you — walk her into class and be there to pick her up.

Homework with dad

Along with schoolwork comes homework, where the day's learning is reinforced. You may be surprised that homework starts as early as kindergarten. Just like when your child was a baby and you repeated things over and over for him to learn, your child needs a second try at what he learned that day to make it stick in his head. But finding a child who likes doing his homework is as rare as hens' teeth, so here are some ways to make homework less of a battle and more conducive to learning:

>> If he's using the Internet to do research for a project, monitor where he's getting his information. There are a lot of unreliable sites out there.

>> Let your child do his homework independently, but let him know you're there to help should he need it. If reading books is part of the homework, read them with him to help him with new words.

>> Let your child have some down time after school and before homework starts. Go outside and kick a ball around or water the garden together. Then get into the homework.

>> Make a set time for homework. Homework isn't finished until he has it in his bag, ready to go to school tomorrow.

>> Set aside a quiet space where your child can do his homework. Turn off the TV or music — they are distractions.

You remember what doing homework was like, so don't be too hard on your child. If you see him struggling with something, spend some extra time with him. You don't need to do the homework for him (and in fact that would be detrimental to the learning objectives), but inspire him by looking at different approaches to overcoming an obstacle he may be facing. Doing homework with your child is really no different than coaching — help him do a good job himself without doing the job for him.

Special dads for special needs

The term "special needs" covers a wide range of issues that some children face, from physical difficulties such as disease or disability, to mental, behavioral, and emotional issues that affect the way they learn. Just as all children are unique, so are the problems they may face, and there is no one-size-fits-all approach when it comes to children with special needs.

Some examples of disorders and disabilities that may require special education include:

>> Children who are hearing or visually impaired, who are wheelchair bound, or who have chronic illnesses like cystic fibrosis

>> Children with autism, attention deficit disorder, fetal alcohol syndrome, developmental delay, Down Syndrome, or Tourette Syndrome

For some fathers, it's obvious that their children need special help with their education. For others, it may just be a feeling that something isn't quite right. As always, talk to your child's healthcare provider or teachers.

Recognizing that your child needs special help with her education doesn't mean she'll be packed off to a Dickensian school where she'll be left to languish. In some instances, children can attend mainstream school with the help of a teacher aide, while others may flourish at a special needs school.

Fathers must be strong advocates for their children — be informed and willing to go the extra distance to get your child the educational opportunities she deserves.

TIP

If you're concerned about your child's education and feel she may need access to special education services, here are some places to start. The U.S. Department of Education's website at www2.ed.gov/ about/offices/list/osers/osep/index.html can provide information on different types of programs. Your state government education website can provide more detailed information on what programs are mandated by your state.

When schools don't meet your expectations

If you have any concerns about the education your child is receiving, there are issues with how your child is settling in, or you have any concerns at all with your child's school, make an appointment to see his teacher or principal. Talking it through may bring to light some issues you weren't aware of that you can address, or vice versa for the school.

If issues such as bullying or questionable standards of teaching continue and you still aren't happy with the school, it may be time to look at what other schooling options are out there that may be a better fit for your child.

REMEMBER

Wherever your child goes to school, your attitude and role modeling are most important as a father. Keep reading to your child and encouraging him to do his homework, talk about his day, and become a part of your child's education. You're still the most important part of his learning.

Choosing Extracurricular Activities

Many people had a whole lot of extracurricular activities going on when they were growing up. Today there are more and more classes and courses that your child can do to complement the learning she does at school.

The best time to start on subjects like language and music is now. As they get older and don't have the absorbent brains they used to have, many adults have regretted not learning an extra skill, such as music, in their youth. But before you enroll junior in every class under the sun, ask her what she would like to do and follow whatever her interests are, rather than your own.

Learning languages

Languages other than English form part of the school curriculum depending on where you live. But the languages taught at your school may not be what your child wants to learn, or you may have a passion for a particular place and will be visiting there a lot, making learning that language important.

Depending on where you live, private tutors are available to teach your child a language other than English. Word-of-mouth is often the best source for finding a language teacher, although putting the language you want your child to learn into your search engine can also help you find someone who works with children. Many schools also teach foreign language, starting in the lower grades, but your child will have to learn the same language as everyone else.

Making music

Starting-school age is a great time to start learning to play an instrument. Your local paper or community noticeboard may have listings for local teachers.

TIP

Your local music store may offer certain types of music lessons or may maintain a list of local teachers. Word-of-mouth can be a good way to find music teachers who work well with young children.

Start small. Don't expect your child to be able to handle a full drum kit or stand-up double bass just yet. Piano, guitar, violin, or wind instruments may be up your child's alley. See what he would like to play. A great way to inspire junior is to go into a music store and show him the various instruments. Get the sales assistant to put on a show so he gets to see them in action.

Many schools provide music education, usually starting with singing in the lower grades and moving up to simple instruments, such as recorders, played as a group, before starting individual instruments.

Playing sports

Getting your child involved in the sport of his choice is a great way to keep him active, give him goals, and show him how to play with others. Your child should decide which sport he wants to get involved with, because the main thing at this age is to enjoy the sport. If he's not sure or can't decide, watch some games, research the sport on the Internet, or if you happen to know how, show him how the sport's played.

Sports can be organized through schools or clubs in your town. Traveling teams made up of kids from several districts are available for many sports, but your child will have to try out and make the cut.

Getting your child involved means more than just dropping him off at practices and games. Be ready to stay and watch — or even help coach. It's a good way to get involved with other parents in your community.

Remember, though, that games are for the kids — not for adults who criticize the other team, yell at their own child every time he misses a play, or display generally bad sportsmanship. Bad sports run the risk of being tossed out of the viewing area, so practice holding your tongue during games and work on yelling only when you're praising your team members — or even the other team, when they make a good play.

TIP

Many schools send home information on available local sports programs. If yours doesn't, check with your township or city's recreation department, which should be able to provide you with a list.

Religious education

If your child's not going to a school associated with a particular religious denomination, you may want him to have religious education outside the school environment. These classes are generally organized by local churches or places of worship, so they should be your first port of call.

5

What Happens When

Chapter 16

Being a Stay-at-Home Dad

You and your partner have made a decision — and it's pretty radical. You're going to stay home with the baby while your partner heads back to work or school. You'll be the number-one caregiver, taking care of your baby's needs for the majority of the time. You're about to board a new, scary roller coaster and, as any stay-at-home mom will tell you, a really rewarding one.

Stay-at-home dads (SAHDs) have yet to get much respect. Millions of years of moms being primary caregivers means some people may still find it a little weird for dads to stay home and look after a baby. But the times, they are a-changin', and just as women pursue careers and take on formerly male-dominated roles, men can make a change to what was once firmly female territory.

In this chapter we give you a list of the reasons why dads make great primary caregivers — you may want to carry it around with you to shoot down any naysayers — and give you some food for thought on balancing your new full-time job with a little paid work on the side. We also give you the low-down on making the transition into your new role as smooth a ride as possible.

Daddy's in Da House

According to the Pew Research Center, in 1989, 10 percent of males said that their main activity was "child-care/home duties." By 2012, this proportion had risen to 16 percent. Of these dads, 23 percent were at home because they couldn't find work, while 21 percent of SAHDs were staying at home specifically to take over child-rearing duties. Another 35 percent were home because they were ill or disabled, and 17 percent were students or retired. Those numbers are still relatively low, but they show that the phenomenon of the SAHD is on the increase.

Debunking some myths about guys as primary caregivers

Stay-at-home dads are a recent phenomenon, and lots of people don't really understand what "stay-at-home dad" means. They'll make judgments about you and your family, which can be hard to swallow sometimes. Here are some of the myths you may encounter:

» Fathers can't parent as well as mothers until their child is older.

» Fathers can't breastfeed babies, so the baby will miss out on breast milk.

» Fathers can't handle looking after a baby without causing chaos in the house and leaving a mess wherever they go.

» Fathers won't be able to handle being a SAHD at all.

» Fathers will forget practical things like food, diaper changes, and appropriate clothing.

» Fathers don't have a "mother's intuition" and won't be able to tell if their child is unwell.

We say this is rubbish. Although fathers parent differently from mothers, it doesn't mean dad's way is wrong. To the skeptics, we say this:

>> Showing love and wanting the best for their kids makes fathers just as qualified to look after their little ones as their mothers.

>> Mothers can express breast milk for dads to give to their babies, or dads can feed formula if appropriate.

>> Fathers can do everything moms can do, such as looking after the household in addition to looking after baby, even if they haven't been doing it for as long as moms.

>> Dads make fantastic parents. Active father involvement has been linked to improved performance at school and fewer problems during teen years such as teen pregnancy or binge drinking.

>> Fathers aren't dense. We can remember diaper changes and to do the washing. Figuring out our own way of doing things may take some work, but we get there.

>> Fathers who spend time with their babies learn everything there is to know about their little ones, and are able to use their common sense and the tips they discover in this book to tell when baby is ill.

>> Guys are very practical and often good at things that moms struggle with (and vice versa, of course). So dads have lots of useful skills they can transfer to raising their offspring from an early age.

Coping with your new career

As dads in the 21st century, chances are you were brought up to be the breadwinner and to provide financially for your children. This gender role goes right back to the days of the caveman — men went out to bring home the mammoth. Going from a full-time career to staying home with a baby is a big change — ask any first-time mom how she coped with it! And guys don't have the physical changes of pregnancy to prepare for how weird the whole parenthood thing is. But that could also be a blessing, of course!

Having a support system in place helps when it comes to your new career. Family, friends who have children, and other men who can remind you it's not all about diapers, bottles, and crying can all provide support.

Being out of the politics of your office, without a demanding boss or several people to report to, can be nice. You don't have any deadlines for reports or projects to manage. But on the other hand, the small new boss is a pretty demanding one, and if you don't get the work done right — if you don't burp that gas out, if you let her get overtired, or if you don't have enough formula on hand — you're going to be rapped on the knuckles pretty quickly. There is no clocking out at five o'clock, no one to take over the late shift, and hardest of all, no sick leave. When you're the primary caregiver, the buck stops with you.

So how do you go from being a career man to being the main man at home? Remember that what you're doing is a privilege and doing so will bring you much closer to your little person than you could ever have imagined. Why would you ever want to go back to work? The time that your child is small is so short, and he'll never be this age again. Looking after a baby or toddler is tough work, and your career may have been important to you; however, there aren't many men out there who have the same opportunity to be this close to their children. Enjoy it!

You're never alone. Set up your own group of fathers and create a network of people you can call on. See our tips later in this chapter for networking as a SAHD.

Getting organized

Being organized when you have a child is essential. Having systems and routines in place that save you time and effort make life a lot easier, giving you time for the things you like to do rather than have to do.

Use your cellphone to keep track of baby supplies, to-do lists, appointments, and other jobs around the house. Most phones come with all the tools you need, or you can download specific applications to keep track. Nothing like a gadget to keep you focused!

Checking every night at bedtime to be sure you have the essentials for the next day will prevent you from finding you've run out of something really important.

Here's a quick run-down on the essentials that you may want to have on hand:

>> Clean diapers

>> Food, whether it be expressed breast milk or formula for babies under six months, or solids and finger food for older babies

>> Wipes or cloths for diaper changing

>> Diaper cream

>> Any medicine or ointments your child needs

>> At least two changes of clothes

If you get out and about a lot, which we recommend, keep the diaper bag stocked at all times so loading up the stroller and going out isn't a big deal.

Always take your diaper bag with you everywhere. Even a short trip to do the grocery shopping may require a diaper change, or circumstances may mean you're away longer than you planned.

In the first few weeks of life, your baby may have a very busy appointment book — checkups with your midwife or doctor, vaccinations, or trips to a specialist. Keep a list or calendar of appointments in the early weeks so you don't forget. You'll be too tired to remember your own name, let alone when an appointment is coming up.

Some SAHDs plan out their weeks well in advance with activities such as swimming, playgroup, and story time at the local library. Use technology, such as your computer, laptop, or phone, to plan your activities. Mom will be very impressed when you show her the schedule on your cellphone!

All that organization may sound boring right now, but children keep things interesting and generally respond well to a change of plans. Even if you're adhering to a strict routine or schedule, children like to mix things up a bit. So what if you miss a swimming lesson or don't make it to music class? If something else turns up, that means you'll have to change plans. It's not worth panicking over.

My Daddy Just Cares for Me

If you're the primary caregiver, the buck stops with you. Being the primary caregiver is like being the head of a major corporation, only you have one very demanding, unforgiving, but utterly cute client who pays you in smiles and love.

Figuring out what your baby wants

Trying to figure out what your baby is saying to you when he arches his back or screws up his face in a certain way is daunting. It can be baffling when he's grumpy and cranky and nothing seems to settle him. You're not a bad father; you just don't have the skills to deal with each stage of your child's life yet. By the way, stay-at-home moms face the same challenges.

Figuring out what your baby is trying to communicate is a matter of finding out what you don't yet know. Fortunately, this is relatively easy these days! Parenting classes are available to help you decipher your baby's many cues and help you act on them. Parenting classes can also be an invaluable support network. You'll meet other dads, hear what they've been experiencing, and get tips on how to deal with any issues you have with your fatherhood experience.

Healthy bodies and active minds

Just as your child needs food to grow her body, active movement and experiences feed her mind. When she was first born, her brain was about 15 percent developed, but by 3 years of age, her brain is well on its way to being fully developed. The first three years in particular shape your child's life like no other period. By making a great connection with your child, giving her lots of opportunities to explore and learn, and lots of physical encouragement, you're doing the best job a dad can do.

All those little things children do when they play — feeling textures, judging distances, figuring out what's hot and cold, pouring water from one cup to another, and making those raucous noises and squeals — is all about practicing skills that we adults have (almost) perfected. By offering lots of things to touch and play with, you're giving your child lots of opportunities to get some practice in for the real deal — growing up and adulthood. See our other chapters on specific age groups for ways to get active with kids.

REMEMBER

To ensure your child's body stays as healthy as it can be, give your child lots of healthy and nutritious foods. You may also need to improve your cooking and baking skills in case you're not a natural-born chef. Remember the basics — avoid fatty, sugary foods; establish a feeding and eating routine; avoid distractions during eating; and ensure your child gets lots of rest and good sleep. For more on nutrition, see Chapter 14.

Keeping mom in the loop

In a busy household, where you're at home with your child and your partner is out at work, it's easy to fall into a trap where you're so absorbed by the hectic lives you lead that you have no time for each other. You're tired from chasing your little one all day and can't wait to hand her over to your partner, who's exhausted from meetings and deadlines. You may fall into a trap of thinking that spending time with your child is a chore.

Remembering that the three of you need to spend time together as a family and enjoy each other's company is really important.

If your partner is away at the office and your child does something that would be of interest to her, let her know — send a text message or an image of your child to her. Have the video camera around to capture any new words or milestones your child reaches when your partner isn't there. And when she comes home, rather than plopping your child on her lap the instant she walks through the door, have a family meal or a general catch-up on what the three of you have been doing all day.

TIP

As your child gets older, encourage him to do something special for his mom when she gets home, such as bringing her slippers or showing her a drawing he has made.

Working from home

You may decide to be a SAHD who works from home. If you're used to working with a lot of people or in a busy environment, suddenly finding yourself at home with a child and a laptop to work with can be strange, lonely, and a little boring. You may be tempted to make yourself a cup of coffee every ten minutes, or feel unmotivated because you don't have a work environment around you to keep that energy going. If you're not self-disciplined or motivated, chances are working from home is not going to be easy for you.

You can do things to stop yourself from going crazy or being so lonely that you invite the meter reader in for coffee:

>> Have a routine for you and your child, so you can slot work in around when she sleeps. Having a structured routine allows you to more easily make appointments, schedule phone calls, or take part in online meetings. If possible, be flexible to allow for those days when your child's unsettled.

>> Don't be too ambitious with what you can achieve. You'll have days when you can't get any work done and other days when your princess is a dream who sleeps for hours at a time. Overcommitting yourself to your boss will just stress you out and make your fathering life more difficult.

>> Give yourself a few hours each day to get out and about — go for a walk or attend a planned activity like playgroup or

swimming lessons. Most of all, use that time to see other people!

>> If you have face-to-face meetings to attend, check ahead of time to see whether you can take your child, or arrange for a sitter, friend, or relative to cover for you.

>> Be enthusiastic about the work you're doing. Otherwise, you have to ask yourself whether it's worth the stress of trying to do your job *and* be a SAHD (which is also a full-time job).

>> Make a work space in your house that's just for your work. By having your own work space, you don't have to set up your gear every time you want to work. You're more likely to settle into productive work if you don't have to clear the breakfast dishes away from the dining table to work at it while baby is sleeping. When your child gets older, explain to him that this is daddy's office and not an indoor playground.

The Brotherhood of Dads

There's a reason why men in the armed services tend to call themselves bands of brothers — they look after one another as if they were blood relatives. The same can be kind of said about SAHDs — we're on the front line of parenting, taking the hits (dirty diapers), outwitting the enemy (playing chase), fighting the good fight (rough–housing), and going the extra mile (in the stroller, when junior won't go to sleep). The Brotherhood of Dads is all about camaraderie between fathers and ensuring that dads gather together and get through any good and bad times they may be experiencing.

Being at home means that you may become slightly isolated, but you can call on your brothers. See the following sections for the various ways you can get in touch with the brotherhood.

Networking as a SAHD

So how do you find these mythical brothers who are going to be your rocks when you need them? SAHDs are more common than they used to be, but they're still a rare beast, so keep your eyes peeled at the local library, music sessions, playgroups, and coffee groups, or just stroll up to other guys pushing strollers — you don't need an excuse to start a conversation. You can also ask your healthcare provider if she has other SAHDs on her books or knows of any dad groups in the area.

Basically, just do what the moms do (but in a man kind of way). Get together with other SAHDs at a local coffee shop, go to child-friendly movie sessions, or take turns meeting at each other's homes. Moms do this all the time, and they are pretty good at it — no reason why dads can't network too.

Being the only guy in the room

Because most primary caregivers are women, most of the activities that you take your child to, especially in his first year of life, are bound to be full of moms and babies. Being the only guy in the room can be a bit weird. Then again . . . it can be really cool because you'll get lots of attention, and in our experience, most moms love the fact that there is a SAHD in the group to add some variety and dad-perspective. You may even be overrun with moms keen to find out about the male approach to parenting. Single moms may be especially grateful for exposure to male parenting. So enjoy the attention and show you can keep up with the best of the moms!

Chapter 17

Serious Illness and Losing Your Baby

I n an ideal world, we wouldn't be writing this chapter and you wouldn't be reading it. Your child should always be well, happy, and carefree. But unfortunately, life's not that simple. Children do get ill, they get hurt, and sometimes they die.

When a person close to you dies, it's heartbreaking. But it just doesn't seem right that children should die before their parents — it's not the natural order of things. In our culture, we tend to measure the impact of a tragedy against others — thinking, for example, that a sudden death is worse than a gradual one or that a miscarriage is less painful than losing a child at birth. In reality, that child's loss will be felt greatly by his parents, no matter what the age or how it happens.

Sometimes illness is unavoidable; sometimes it isn't. In this chapter, we show you ways to minimize the risk of illness, starting with pregnancy, and how to cope should serious illness strike. Lastly, we discuss terminal illness and getting through the unthinkable — when a child dies.

TIP

It may be hard to find the right words if someone close to you experiences the loss of a child. Take a look at americanpregnancy.org/pregnancy-loss/supporting-others/.

Avoiding Health Problems

What you put in your body plays a big part in your health. Making your home a smoke-free environment and eating nutritious meals go a long way toward staying healthy (see Chapter 3 for more about healthy eating during pregnancy).

Protecting against diseases

Having your child immunized against diseases like whooping cough, meningitis, and diphtheria protects her from these illnesses that can cause death or serious, long-term harm to a child. Talk to your child's pediatrician about the right ages to have her vaccinated.

Providing a violence-free home

Shaking your baby or hitting your young child may cause serious physical harm or death in extreme cases. The message is simple — never, ever shake your baby, and consider discipline that doesn't include hitting your child.

Beyond the physical harm shaking and hitting can cause, in the first years of your child's life he's learning to form a safe and secure attachment to you, his father, and this attachment plays a big part in how well he'll act and form relationships as an adult.

If you're violent toward him, chances are he'll be a violent person himself.

If you're at the end of your rope and just feel like making your baby or child shut up, take a deep breath and count to ten, or leave him in a safe place and get some air for a minute. Stress is the distance between the situation in front of you and how well you think you can deal with that situation. Tell yourself you can do it and see how much better you'll feel.

If you're often angry at your child, your partner, or the situations you're in, it may be time to get help dealing with your emotions.

Many therapists specialize in helping people with anger management issues control their temper and express feelings without violence. Check the Internet for resources by typing in "Anger Management Therapists" for someone near you.

Keeping accidents at bay

Keeping your child physically safe around your home, in the street, and in your car is also really important. See Chapter 7 on childproofing your home and Chapter 4 for car seat safety.

Keep your child safe around roads by teaching her to hold your hand crossing the road at designated crosswalks and when you're near driveways, and to never go in the road without an adult.

Giving your baby a healthy start to life

Doesn't every child deserve the best start in life you can possibly give him? Keeping mom tanked up with healthy food, lots of fresh air, and gentle exercise from when you first know you're going to be a dad goes a long way toward keeping your baby healthy in the long run.

Risks during pregnancy

Creating a whole new person is an enormous task, and pregnancy can make a woman's body vulnerable to infection and conditions such as high blood pressure. It's also important to consider the effects of what your partner eats and is exposed to on the developing baby.

If your partner has any chronic health issues, such as diabetes or asthma, make sure both of you are happy with the way that your health provider is monitoring the progress of the pregnancy. If not, find a health provider you *are* happy with.

These are some of the things your partner should be aware of during her pregnancy:

>> **Smoking:** Pregnancy is a great time to take the plunge and quit smoking. Poisons from the smoke are passed to the baby through the placenta. Babies born to mothers who smoke are at risk of developing breathing problems and having a lower birth weight, and are twice as likely to die from SIDS (Sudden Infant Death Syndrome). However, quitting smoking is tough and not made much easier by having a preachy dad-to-be around or one who continues to smoke himself. Instead, give your partner your wholehearted support and contact a helpline in your area, not just for your partner, but for both of you to quit smoking.

If you want to give up smoking, check out these sites for help and advice:

- **American Cancer Society:** www.cancer.org/healthy/ stayawayfromtobacco/guidetoquittingsmoking/

- **American Lung Association:** www.lung.org/ stop-smoking

>> **Alcohol:** Experts are unsure of what a "safe" level of alcohol is for pregnant women, so it's best to avoid all alcohol. *Fetal alcohol syndrome* is caused by alcohol crossing the placenta and affecting the baby's developing brain. Children with fetal alcohol syndrome can have problems with learning, concentration, hyperactivity, and speech.

>> **Chickenpox:** When we're kids, chickenpox (also called *varicella*) is much like any other illness, and the only long-lasting effect of the disease may be a few pock scars. But in

adults, chickenpox is a serious illness. If your partner gets chickenpox when she's pregnant, it can be transmitted to your growing baby. Though rare, the baby's development can be affected, causing limb deformities, mental retardation, or even miscarriage or stillbirth. If you haven't had chickenpox, consider being vaccinated now.

>> **Listeriosis:** Pregnant women are much more vulnerable to an infection from bacteria living in certain foods, called *listeria.* The infection, *listeriosis,* can be caused by eating deli meats, soft cheeses, unpasteurized milk, unwashed fruit and vegetables, raw meat, pâté, ready-made salads, smoked seafood, and smoked shellfish. It's best to avoid these foods while pregnant. Listeriosis can cause miscarriage and stillbirth.

>> **Rubella (German measles):** If a pregnant woman contracts rubella, it can seriously harm the developing baby, including severe mental retardation and blindness. Most women are vaccinated against rubella as teenagers, but if your partner hasn't been vaccinated and you're planning to get pregnant, talk to your healthcare provider about being vaccinated now.

WARNING

Being vaccinated against rubella doesn't always guarantee a lifetime immunity against the virus. Women planning pregnancy should have their immunity status checked.

>> **Toxoplasmosis:** This is an infection that can be caused by a bacteria living in the guts of animals. It can be carried in raw meat and in cat poop, so pregnant women should avoid dealing with kitty litter boxes and take care when gardening, as cats may have used the soil for a toilet. Cook all meat thoroughly.

Breastfeeding

Encouraging and supporting breastfeeding in the first months of life boosts your baby's immunity and gives her the very best nutrition she needs to grow and thrive. Breastfeeding's difficult in the beginning, and your partner may be pretty exhausted and frustrated at times, so give her all the help you can.

MISCARRIAGE

A miscarriage is the death of a baby before 20 weeks gestation. Many women don't even know they're pregnant when they miscarry, but many others lose much-wanted and cherished babies. In the past, people have had the attitude that miscarriages are something to be gotten over, that everything will be fixed by trying for another baby. Fathers in particular, who can often seem withdrawn or uncaring about the loss because men can be more private about the way they deal with grief, are encouraged to "just get over it." But for parents who lose babies, it can often be devastating. You also feel you have to be strong for your partner, and in a sense you do — you need to advocate for your partner at a time when she's confused, angry, vulnerable, and grieving. But you also need to be empathetic and caring, and one way to do that is to talk openly about your feelings with your partner. You also need to acknowledge your feelings of loss and sadness, rather than pretend to keep a stiff upper lip.

Having a ceremony or funeral for your lost baby may be comforting and give you a chance to express your grief and let others support you. The ceremony can be anything from a few people lighting a candle to a funeral with a minister. Just do what comes naturally to you and your partner. Naming your baby can also help you heal — acknowledging your baby as a real person, not a "loss" or an "it," can really help.

If you need to talk to someone outside your family and friends, support is available. You just have to ask for it. One site that can offer advice and additional support sources is http://miscarriage support.com/.

Safely getting through pregnancy and delivery

Approximately one percent of babies die between 20 weeks gestation and up to 28 days after birth. This is referred to as a *perinatal* death. Most of these babies die because they're born too early and their bodies aren't developed enough for life outside the womb. Others die from congenital abnormalities, and in some cases, there is no known reason. Completely normal, healthy pregnancies can end in stillbirths.

Women in the United States are at very low risk of dying during pregnancy or childbirth, with approximately 2 in 5,000 pregnant women affected. According to the Centers for Disease Control, 600 women die each year during pregnancy or childbirth. Access to good healthcare facilities, skilled maternity healthcare providers, and plenty of nutritious food for pregnant women and their growing babies help keep the numbers low.

To reduce the risk of complications during pregnancy and childbirth, find a healthcare provider you trust, whether it be an obstetrician, general practitioner, or midwife, and attend regular checkups with them. Your healthcare provider will monitor for conditions such as preeclampsia, gestational diabetes, and other factors that may cause complications during pregnancy and childbirth. If you're not familiar with these terms, check Appendix B and read up on them.

Home birth

You may be wondering whether having your baby at home is riskier than having your baby in a hospital. While being nearer to medical facilities should something go wrong during your child's birth may help, babies can still die in hospitals with experienced healthcare providers, even after mom-to-be took great care of her health during pregnancy and excellent healthcare was provided to her during her pregnancy. We don't mean to put you off or frighten you, but there's no absolutely certain way to eliminate all risks.

Home birth is a contentious issue in the United States. Fewer than 1 percent of American women deliver at home, according to the American Congress of Obstetricians and Gynecologists (ACOG). Home birth may pose an increased risk for your newborn, ACOG cautions. Talk with your healthcare provider about your birthing options.

Women with high-risk pregnancies — who are at risk of preterm labor or have preeclampsia, gestational diabetes, or any other medical complication during pregnancy — are not advised to have a planned home birth.

Cesarean birth

You may think that avoiding a vaginal birth and the stress on baby and the mother's body may be the way to go, but there are risks associated with elective caesareans too. After all, a cesarean is major surgery, and the mother may experience hemorrhaging and infection.

Babies born by cesarean can have breathing difficulties because fluid in the lungs is not squeezed out as it is in a vaginal birth. Emergency cesareans are performed when the condition of the baby or mother is deteriorating, such as *cord prolapse,* when the umbilical cord comes out of the uterus before the baby, blocking off his lifeline. In those cases you often don't have a choice about having an emergency cesarean, because the life of the mother or child is at risk.

REMEMBER

If your partner has had a textbook pregnancy, we suggest *not* worrying about the risks of fatality. Concentrate instead on creating a peaceful and calm environment for your baby to be born into, with lots of support for your partner. Relax and enjoy this momentous time in your life.

Reducing the risk of SUDI and SIDS

SUDI stands for Sudden Unexplained Death of Infants. In some cases, death is caused by smothering or some other known cause. SIDS is a type of SUDI and stands for Sudden Infant Death Syndrome, where the baby, for reasons unknown, stops breathing. It's thought that babies who have been around cigarette smoke are more at risk. SIDS used to be commonly known as *crib death.*

There are some simple ways you can reduce your baby's risk of SUDI/SIDS:

>> Keep your baby's environment smoke-free. If you both gave up smoking when your partner was pregnant, your home will be smoke-free.

>> Put your baby to sleep on her back, not on her side or front. The number of SIDS death decreased by 50 percent after the American Academy of Pediatrics initiated the Back to Sleep campaign.

>> Keep your baby's crib or bassinet free from bumpers, blankets, covers, cuddly toys, and sheepskins that could smother her.

>> If you share your bed with your baby (known as co-sleeping), do so only when neither you nor your partner has been drinking or is excessively tired, to avoid the risk of rolling onto your baby. Use a firm mattress and keep all bedding, including covers and pillows, far away from your baby. Co-sleeping is also safe only if you haven't been smoking, because exposure to smoke puts your baby at risk. A bassinet that attaches to the side of your bed is a much safer option.

TIP

If you're worried about your baby's risk of SUDI or SIDS, consider buying an advanced baby monitor that constantly checks the baby's heartbeat and breathing. Check your local baby supply store for these monitors.

TIP

The following sites have more about SUDI and SIDS:

>> **American Sudden Infant Death Syndrome Institute:** http://sids.org/

>> **American Academy of Pediatrics:** www.aap.org/en-us/ about-the-aap/aap-press-room/pages/aap-expands- guidelines-for-infant-sleep-safety-and-sids-risk- reduction.aspx

Calling all dads: Creating a healthy and safe home

Keeping up to date with household chores while looking after a small child can sometimes seem like taking one step forward, two steps back. You wash and clean all the diapers, only to have junior need changing twice as often. Or he's suddenly power-spewing all over the place. You may have your hands full just tending to baby. But washing your hands after diaper changes, cleaning up spit-up, or dealing with laundry is absolutely essential and will help cut down the risk of bacterial infection from diapers and stomach bugs. You can also

» Have a bottle of hand sterilizer in your diaper bag.

» Empty garbage cans with disposable diapers and wipes in them regularly — at least once a day.

» Wash toys regularly. Most plastic toys can be scrubbed in a basin, while soft toys can go in the washing machine.

» Air your rooms regularly to reduce the risk of respiratory infections caused by damp, dusty houses.

» Keep baby's room at a temperature between 65 and 70 degrees Fahrenheit, and avoid any drafts.

» Avoid tummy bugs by not reheating food for your child that has been in the fridge more than 24 hours. Cook fresh food or food that has been safely frozen and thawed. If you need to keep food in the fridge, make sure it's covered (for example, with cling wrap).

» Check the childproofing you've made in your house (see Chapter 7 for more).

Coping with Illness and Injury

Having a sick or injured baby or child is no fun. As well as feeling pretty darn terrible, your child may have trouble understanding what's wrong with him, not be able to communicate well with you about what's wrong, and be scared of the treatments he's receiving.

Spotting injury

When your child is constantly getting bumps and bruises, it can be hard to tell when something is going on that can't just be fixed with a bandage and a hug. So how do you figure it out? And what do you do if it's more serious than you first thought?

First of all, stay calm. Reach for the first-aid kit and let us show you the way:

- **Broken bones:** Your child will let you know he's broken something because he'll be in a lot of pain — much more than usual. You may even be able to see how the limb is broken. The area may swell or bruise immediately. Keep your child as still as possible and support the broken limb. Weight on the limb will make it more painful. Get to the emergency department of your local hospital as soon as you can. If your child can't move, or you think he shouldn't be moved, such as in the case of a spine or neck fracture, call an ambulance.

- **Burns and scalds:** Run cold water on a simple, small burn for 20 minutes. If your child has scalded himself with hot liquid, take his wet clothes off as the heat in the liquid will continue to burn his skin. If material is sticking to the skin, don't try to take it off. If the burn is serious and you see redness and blistering, get someone to call an ambulance while you take care of your child. After you've finished pouring cold water over the area, cover it with a clean cloth or tea towel and see your doctor. Your child will probably be very cold from the cold water, so make sure he's dressed warmly.

- **Concussion:** A bump to the head can result in more than just a lump and bruise. Concussion is a temporary loss of brain function, from the brain banging against the skull. Your child may have hit his head so hard he lost consciousness, or he may have a headache, seem disoriented, and vomit repeatedly. Being irritable and sensitive to light can also be a sign of concussion. Take your child to the hospital immediately.

REMEMBER

If you're in doubt about anything to do with your child's health, it's better to be safe than sorry, so visit your pediatrician. For any of the following injuries, get yourself to the hospital quickly:

- Anaphylactic shock from food or a bee sting, where the face or mouth swells and your child has trouble breathing.

- Bite from a snake, spider, or another animal.

- Car accident.

- Convulsions, also called seizures, especially those that last five minutes or more. Some children under age 5 have febrile seizures whenever they run a fever; if this happens regularly, follow your pediatrician's instructions on whether or not your child needs hospital care every time.

>> Eye injuries.

>> Electric shocks.

>> Swallowing of poisons, toxic material, or prescription medicines that were not prescribed for your child.

Having emergency phone numbers on hand

In the United States, 911 is the emergency number in every state.

The number for Poison Control is 1-800-222-1222.

Putting together a first-aid kit

Keep a well-stocked first-aid kit to deal with injuries. If you don't have a first-aid kit, see Chapter 4, where we give you a run-down on first-aid essentials.

REMEMBER

If you haven't done so, consider taking an infant and child first-aid and CPR course. It can literally save the life of your child or the lives of others. If you haven't done a general CPR course for a while, getting a refresher by attending an infant and baby CPR course may also be a good idea.

Diagnosing a serious illness

All some children have to deal with healthwise are colds, the odd ear infection, or a tummy bug. But some unfortunate children have to cope with much worse. As an involved dad you'll probably spot the first signs of a serious illness, because you know your child inside out and can tell when something's not right.

It takes a doctor's diagnosis to confirm when your child has a *chronic* illness, such as asthma, diabetes, a genetic disorder, or a disease such as cancer. Seeing your little child being admitted to a hospital is stressful and heartbreaking, but fortunately lots of support is available.

Your child may be very frightened or blame herself for the chaos her illness is causing in your lives. Try to be as open and honest with her as you can about her health and how you feel, and be available to answer any questions she puts to you.

TIP

The following organizations can help you in the event of your child being diagnosed with a serious illness. Don't be afraid to ask for help if you need it — think of the good it might do your child:

» **American Academy of Allergy, Asthma and Immunology:**
   www.aaaai.org/conditions-and-treatments/asthma

» **American Cancer Society:** www.cancer.org/cancer/
   cancerinchildren/detailedguide/
   cancer-in-children-types-of-childhood-cancers

» **American Diabetes Association:** www.diabetes.org/
   living-with-diabetes/parents-and-kids/

» **Cystic Fibrosis Foundation:** www.cff.org/What-is-CF/
   About-Cystic-Fibrosis/

Preparing for the End

To find out that your precious child has a life-limiting illness is possibly the toughest thing you may have to go through in your life. Anger, confusion, denial, helplessness, despair — you may experience every negative emotion you can imagine. Staying strong for your child when you feel like falling apart will be hard, but with little steps you *can* do it. Take things one day at a time.

Taking care until the end

Some may think it's a good idea not to frighten a child with a terminal illness with the knowledge that he's going to die. But *palliative care* professionals — those who care for people at the end of their lives — say communicating with your child honestly and openly helps allay some of his fears rather than cause them.

Your child may be very confused about what's going on, and talking honestly and planning for the future can help put his mind at rest. He may be concerned about why you and your partner are so sad, may blame himself for your sadness, or may be worried about his pets or schoolwork. Reassure him that it's not his fault that you're upset and be open to answering any questions he may have.

REMEMBER

Talk to your healthcare team about palliative care options for your child. Care can be provided at home, with or without the help of hospice, or in the hospital. These health professionals can help you talk to your child about what he's facing in an age-appropriate manner.

These ideas may also help you get through this seemingly impossible time:

>> Enlist the support of family and friends to help with tasks like laundry, food preparation, feeding pets, and so on. They can also babysit your other children, if you have them, when you need to be at the hospital or hospice.

>> Look after yourself, rest, and eat well when you can.

>> Talk to counselors or chaplains at your hospital. Your care team can put you in touch with them. Involve your partner and other children if you like.

>> Find out if there are any special activities your child would like to do. Perhaps you can take a trip to the beach together as a family, or visit a special place together.

>> Write in a journal, take photographs, and revisit old photographs with your child. Make memories.

>> Cry, shout, stamp your feet. It's okay to be angry, to need time to yourself, and to grieve.

>> Don't let anyone hurry you into making any decisions about anything. Take your time and do things at your own pace.

Where to care for your little one

Palliative care is specialized care for people who have a terminal or life-limiting illness. Palliative care professionals take into account not only the stages that the body goes through as it shuts down, but also how the patient and her family are coping and dealing with this most traumatic event. For adults, most palliative care takes place in a hospital or hospice, which is a special facility for palliative care.

Of course, you can also consider caring for your child at home, with assistance from palliative care workers, depending on the type of illness or injury your child has and which services are available to you.

REMEMBER

You may be overwhelmed by having to make a decision about where your child will spend her last days. Take your time. Talk it through with your partner. Don't hurry into a decision.

Letting family and friends know

Dealing with the devastating news that your child has a life-limiting illness is hard enough without having to tell friends and family. Ultimately this is something only you'll know how to do and when the time is right to tell others.

After you have told them, people will usually be only too happy to help out with any errands that need to be done, cooking, laundry, and the like, which may be in the too-hard basket for you right now.

REMEMBER

If it's just too hard to tell people, perhaps you could tell someone in your immediate family who can do this for you. Don't force yourself to do anything you don't want to do right now. Just getting through each moment is challenging enough.

You may have to break the news to your other children or nieces and nephews, and here we give you some pointers:

>> Be honest. Tell your children only what you believe to be true.

>> Be somewhere safe, with the cellphone off and the phone off the hook, and with the children's full attention.

>> Anticipate that there will be tough questions to answer, but answer them as honestly as you can. Trying to soften the blow may mean your children are upset even more when things get messy.

>> Give small pieces of information that the children can chew on. They don't need to know all the ins and outs of cancer treatment or anything too detailed.

>> It may take a while for the information to get through. Give the children time to digest what they've heard, and be available to answer any other questions they may have in the coming days and weeks.

>> Give lots of hugs, and let your children know it's okay to be upset.

>> Reassure your children that it's not their fault that this is happening to their sibling or cousin.

Seeking help

You'll have a lot of questions and be feeling all over the place. Knowing there's someone there who can guide you and your partner through your grief helps. While everyone grieves in a different way, it can help to talk it through with people who can share their knowledge and help you on your journey.

These organizations can help:

>> **Bereaved Parents of the USA:** bereavedparentsusa.org/

>> **Daily Strength:** www.dailystrength.org/c/Stillbirth/forum

>> **First Candle (stillbirth):** www.firstcandle.org/grieving-families/stillbirth/

>> **Healing Hearts for Bereaved Parents:** www.healingheart.net/

>> **Online Grief Support, Help for Coping with Loss/Beyond Indigo Forums:** forums.grieving.com/index.php?/forum/14-loss-of-a-child/

>> **The Compassionate Friends:** www.compassionatefriends.org/home.aspx

Dealing with the Unthinkable

When a child dies, we lose more than a person we loved — we lose the promise that person brought with him. It can threaten our identity as fathers. We blame ourselves, because as fathers we're supposed to protect our children and look after them, ensuring they're well. The death of a child cannot be approached rationally. You can only acknowledge your feelings and thoughts, many of which may not make any sense.

What to do, what not to do

Men grieve differently from women, so while our partners may find it easy to go to friends or family for support, it may not be so easy for you (or vice versa). It may take a little longer for some dads to really process feelings. Some may not know how life is supposed to carry on without their child. Here are some suggestions for getting through this difficult time:

» Talk to your partner — even if it's just to say you don't want to talk. Let her know you need some space, or a hug, or to just sit together.

» Being physical can help. Go for a long walk, ride a bike, or play some sport. Being outdoors close to nature can be restorative and help you process your feelings too.

» Try not to let yourself become isolated. Sure, you want space, but shutting everyone out is not going to help you in the long run. Let people know you need space for a bit.

» Keeping busy really works for some guys who are grieving. Creating a memorial or starting a project can distract you from the all-encompassing nature of grief.

» Try to look after yourself. Eat, sleep, and shower. Though they may make you feel good in the short term, avoid drugs and alcohol.

Saying goodbye

Take time with your baby to say goodbye, to hold him, and to let other members of your family see and hold him too. You can ask your funeral director to arrange to have photographs of your baby taken by a tasteful, sensitive photographer. You'll probably feel a bit hesitant about this, but it can be a healing experience for you to look back and remember holding your child.

There's a good reason most cultures have a funeral tradition — the ritual of saying goodbye to a loved one who has died is a very powerful and healing process. Funerals encourage us to confront our grief and to express how we feel about our loved one. A funeral also marks that child's place among her family.

When a baby is stillborn (dies *in utero* after 20 weeks gestation) or dies shortly after birth, states require that the baby be buried in a cemetery or cremated. For your baby's funeral, consider music to be played, songs, readings, and poems to be read. You can have your baby's funeral at home and can transport your baby from the hospital or home to the cemetery.

REMEMBER

There's no hurry to do anything. Don't feel forced into doing anything you don't want to do. Take your time and decide when you feel you're ready.

Is there such a thing as "moving on"?

Each parent and person grieves differently for the child they've lost. The term "moving on" implies that the intensity of feeling you had for the child you've lost fades and the significance of that child also fades. Organizations helping parents grieve report that no parent ever forgets the loss of a child.

Some parents report that they haven't moved on, but the way they feel is different. The child they've lost, whether he was at 12 weeks of gestation, stillborn, or a teenager when he died, is still a big part of his parents' lives and a part of their family, and they celebrate the impact he had on their hearts.

Chapter 18

Disabilities, Disorders, and Special Conditions

E very father wants his child to be happy and healthy. Fathers want their children to experience everything, to have every opportunity, and to be able to do anything they want to do. But for some children, that world of possibilities is limited by illness, injury, or an inherited disorder or condition.

Although medical science and technology can help improve the mobility, hearing, and sight of a disabled child and our more enlightened society can give children with disabilities the same rights and advantages that nondisabled children have, it's still a hard road for many dads.

But where to start? How do you discover your child has a disability? Once you have a diagnosis, what do you do then? In this chapter, we offer some suggestions along the way — with tips for finding help and knowing your speech pathologist from your occupational therapist — and give you a heads-up on how having a child with a disability may change your lifestyle.

What Is a Disability, Anyway?

A *disability* is a condition, disorder, or disease that disables the person from taking part in one or more life activities. The disability stops the person from doing what other people can do, whether it be walking, listening, grasping ideas, or talking. Disabilities can be physical or mental. Children with disabilities are sometimes called *special needs* children.

Knowing when something is wrong with your baby

Some children are born with a noticeable disability. Congenital abnormalities (also known as *birth defects*) or genetic disorders that manifest themselves physically, such as Down Syndrome, are pretty obvious when the child is born. These problems may have been discovered during the pregnancy.

But other disabilities aren't so obvious, and it may be a while before they make themselves known. Disabilities such as visual and hearing impairment, learning disabilities, and autism aren't apparent for months, sometimes years.

Sometimes you can just tell when something's not right. Perhaps your baby doesn't recognize toys or shapes, or perhaps he doesn't seem to hear or respond to your voice the way other babies respond to their dads. Perhaps he doesn't try to crawl or move when other kids his age are already running. Or perhaps it's just a feeling you get, your intuition telling you things aren't quite right.

Your first port of call should be your pediatrician. If necessary, get a referral to a specialist or psychologist to pinpoint what the problem may be. If your doctor tries to placate you with an "I think he looks fine" and you're sure he's not, stand your ground. Your child isn't able to stick up for himself the way you are. Your job is to advocate for your child and get him the help you feel he needs. If you don't trust and have confidence in your pediatrician to take your concerns seriously, try another doctor until you find one you feel comfortable with.

It may pay to track your child's progress before going to see your healthcare provider, so you have something concrete to show him when you have your appointment. Keep doing this until you've spoken to a specialist and have decided on a course of action or had a diagnosis made.

Waiting for a diagnosis can be a long and incredibly stressful process, but try to stay positive for your little one. Don't blame yourself or your partner for any perceived problems — neither of you is at fault.

After a diagnosis is made, you and your specialist can decide on a course of action and get your child started on medication or treatment if required.

Physical disabilities

A physical disability is a permanent disability that restricts body movement or mobility in some way. Some physical disabilities are caused by genetic disorders, a *congenital abnormality* or birth defect that has developed while growing in the womb, an illness such as meningitis, or as the result of an injury to the spine, brain, or limbs.

The main forms of physical disability include

>> **Brain and spinal injuries:** These injuries are mainly caused by an accident that breaks or damages the spinal cord or causes damage to the brain. Brain and spinal injuries can cause paralysis or mental impairment.

>> **Cerebral palsy:** This is a condition where parts of the brain are damaged either during pregnancy, during birth, or as the result of a lack of oxygen.

>> **Disabilities of the senses:** Children can be born with visual or hearing impairments because of a congenital abnormality or a genetic disorder. These senses can also be affected by disease after birth.

>> **Muscular dystrophy:** This is a genetic disorder in which muscle strength and function deteriorate over time. Most commonly seen in babies and young boys, some forms aren't diagnosed until early adulthood. *Duchenne muscular dystrophy* is the most common form, and it affects mainly boys (Duchenne muscular dystrophy is rare in girls). About one-third of those affected also have some sort of learning difficulty. Not only are muscles in the limbs affected, but also heart muscles, which eventually affects life expectancy.

>> **Spina bifida:** A congenital abnormality, which means it happens while the baby is growing in the womb, spina bifida literally means "split spine" and happens in the early weeks of pregnancy. As the spine develops, vertebrae grow and close around the spinal cord, protecting it. In the case of spina bifida, the vertebrae don't close completely, and in some types of spina bifida, the spinal cord and *meninges* (a system of membranes that envelop the central nervous system) protrude from the back. As a result, the spinal cord can be damaged and messages sent to and from the brain get confused. Paralysis, incontinence, loss of sensation, and a build-up of fluid on the brain called *hydrocephalus* can occur.

TIP

To find out more about any of these physical disabilities, see these websites:

>> **American Foundation for the Blind:** www.afb.org/default.aspx

>> **Muscular Dystrophy Association:** www.mda.org/

>> **National Association of the Deaf:** https://nad.org/

>> **United Cerebral Palsy:** http://ucp.org/

REMEMBER

Most states also have associations that you can find on the Internet using a search engine.

Intellectual disabilities

Just as congenital abnormalities and genetic disorders can affect a child's body, so they can also affect a child's intellectual abilities — the ability to think, reason, communicate, control emotions, and grasp ideas. Increasingly, people with intellectual disabilities are being integrated into mainstream society, where they're appreciated for their individual attributes rather than judged by their disability.

Some intellectual disabilities can be diagnosed at birth or even before. Others aren't obvious until your child is a few years old or at school.

Some of the most common syndromes and disorders that can cause intellectual disability include the following:

>> **Autism:** Autism is also known as *autism spectrum disorder* because the range of severity differs from person to person. A person with autism may have trouble making sense of the world and find it difficult to communicate, cope in social situations, or control his emotions. Autism affects as many as one in 45 children in the United States, with boys affected over four times more frequently than girls. The causes of autism are unknown.

>> **Down Syndrome:** Down Syndrome is caused by an extra bit of chromosome being replicated in cell division very early on after the mother's ovum has been fertilized, meaning that a child with Down Syndrome has an extra chromosome in his body. Children with Down Syndrome have varying degrees of mental and sometimes physical disability.

Intellectual disability can also be caused by drinking, drug abuse, or illness during pregnancy; an infection like meningitis; head injuries; or a lack of oxygen during birth or during an accident, like a near-drowning. There are also other rare genetic conditions, such as Prader-Willi Syndrome, that cause intellectual disability.

With a very small child, doctors and health professionals often use the term *developmental delay* rather than labeling the child as intellectually disabled.

For more about specific intellectual disabilities, see these websites:

>> **Autism Speaks:** www.autismspeaks.org

>> **Brain Injury Association of America:** www.biausa.org/
brain-injury-children.htm

>> **National Center for Learning Disabilities:** www.ncld.org/

>> **National Down Syndrome Society:** www.ndss.org/

Multiple disabilities

Most disorders, illnesses, or injuries are rarely limited to only one part of the body, so in most cases a child with a particular problem has more than one disability. For example, Down Syndrome affects cognitive abilities as well as physical growth. Children with Down Syndrome also have a higher risk of having congenital heart defects, recurrent ear infections, and thyroid dysfunctions as well as other conditions.

Getting formal confirmation

In some cases, the specialist you've been referred to will be able to tell you whether your child has a specific disability or a range of disabilities and may be able to tell you how the disabilities were caused.

In other cases, a diagnosis isn't clear, and your child may continue to undergo tests, which can be a fairly traumatic time.

After you have confirmation about a disability, it's time to put a plan in place to manage the condition through medication, physical treatment, or getting any equipment you may need, such as a wheelchair. In some situations you'll be given a caseworker to help you.

Support groups and organizations for almost every condition, illness, and disability that exists are available. Contact the organizations listed in this chapter or consult your specialist or healthcare provider. Having support from people who've been through what you're going through now, who may be able to share information and strategies or help you get access to specialist services, is invaluable. Sometimes even just knowing that you are not alone with a condition and discussing what it was like for other parents can be a huge help.

What comes next?

You're in for yet another journey as part of your fatherhood experience. Treatment, therapy, and learning about the fathering your special needs child will probably require takes some extra effort. This is also a huge opportunity for your own personal growth and development to become an amazing father.

We've come across a number of inspiring stories from fathers with disabled children. They generally all say that looking after a disabled baby and child in many ways is no different from looking after a nondisabled child. Babies and children with disabilities all cry, laugh, eat, soil their diapers, and want to be loved. When dealing with the limiting factors of their child's condition, these dads have often challenged doctors or therapists about their expectations of what children with a particular disability may or may not be able to do. Often parents have managed to achieve amazing results with their children by finding alternative ways around barriers, allowing their children to participate in what life has to offer just like any other child would.

Here are some general tips on living with a child with a disability for both you and your family:

>> Work with your child's strengths and likes. What does your child like doing? You can incorporate dancing, art, and foot and water play into your child's therapy or treatment plan. Does she like to be hands-on? Or does your child need a strict routine to give her security? Being aware of the way your child learns best and the routines she needs is a key dad-skill to develop.

>> Involve your child whenever you can with simple tasks like food preparation, vacuuming, or making the bed. Break instructions down into simple, bite-sized pieces and give heaps of praise for her efforts.

» Get support. There are a lot of support organizations out there that can put you in touch with other fathers and guide you to find funding, treatments, and even respite care.

» Give lots of praise for your child when she accomplishes a new skill or takes on a new challenge.

» Focus on the things your child can do rather than what she can't.

» Learn as much as you can about your child's disability. Knowledge is power.

» Have realistic expectations about your child's development, but challenge any preconceived limitations people place on your child about what she can and can't do. Perhaps there's a way she can accomplish a task — after all, you know your child best.

Being on a New Journey When Your Child Is Disabled

You've had confirmation that your child is disabled. This can bring out all sorts of frustrations and disappointments, and you may keep these emotions pretty tightly under wraps for the moment. That's fine, but it may also feel good to let it all out with someone who has been in a similar situation.

Imagining the hard road ahead of you can be devastating, and you may even blame yourself for whatever the problem is. But another way to look at your child's disability is as a way to motivate yourself to help your child develop to her full potential.

Adjusting your expectations

When you first find out you're going to be a father, thinking of your child as a way to fix all the things that went wrong in your own life, or wanting your child to have more opportunities or career options than you did, is tempting. Perhaps you imagined your child becoming an astronaut, a concert pianist, or anything that she may dream of being.

So it takes a bit of getting used to the idea that your blind child will never see the world, your face, or his own children (unless there are amazing leaps forward in technology). But then again, would Stevie Wonder have become the amazing artist he is if he weren't blind? You never know what's in store for your offspring, which is really no different from the experience all other parents have.

DISABLED IN ONE WAY — VERY ABLE IN OTHERS

Disabled is a misleading term. For one thing, it defines a person by what he's not able to do.

What do we most remember about Beethoven, Louis Braille, or Stephen Hawking? They've all achieved incredible things, far beyond what many able-bodied folk have done!

- The great composer Beethoven gradually went deaf, but was still able to create incredible music without any sense of hearing.

- Louis Braille was blinded by an accident as a young child and went on to create a way for the blind to read with their fingers.

- Stephen Hawking has a form of motor neuron disease called *amyotrophic lateral sclerosis* and was given only a few years to live when his condition was diagnosed in his early twenties (he's now in his seventies). Hawking is wheelchair bound and needs a computer to communicate. Despite these limitations, he has produced groundbreaking work in the field of theoretical physics. Hawking writes about his experience of disability on his website at www.hawking.org.uk.

Other famous people who have shown disability is no barrier to success include actress Marlee Matlin, who went deaf from a childhood illness; Helen Keller, who proved being deaf, blind, and mute couldn't stop her from getting a university degree; and Franklin Roosevelt, who became president of the United States despite the fact that his legs were paralyzed from polio.

Going into fatherhood, we also expect that our children will grow up and one day leave home. It may not be possible for children with a severe intellectual disability who need one-on-one care 24 hours a day to live an independent life. This can take quite a while to sink in, so cut yourself some slack and allow emotions and frustration to come and go.

But there are incredible things to be said for accomplishing things that are relevant to your child's world. The triumph of an autistic child — who, with time, patience, and the right support, is able to communicate her needs and ideas to a range of people — feels like a huge achievement, on par with any other milestone parents see their children accomplish.

And who's to say that your child won't be able to do what most experts think he can't do? You may find that your little one completely shatters your ideas of what it means to have a disability and achieves much more than you ever imagined.

Finding help, assistance, and resources

Knowing where to go to find assistance — both monetary and emotional — is a minefield. Start with your caseworker, your healthcare provider, and the support organizations listed earlier in this chapter, and check out the following resources for information about funding, schooling, and your child's rights. Local and state organizations can also point you in the right direction. Most parents of special needs kids become very savvy about getting the help their child requires:

>> **Early Intervention:** www2.ed.gov/programs/osepeip/index.html

>> **Supplemental Security Income for Children:** www.socialsecurity.gov/ssi/text-child-ussi.htm

>> **U.S. Department of Education:** www2.ed.gov/parents/needs/speced/edpicks.jhtml

Access for People with Disabilities

After you know what you're dealing with, it's time to get into solution mode — something dads are great at! You can shine as your disabled child's dad in numerous ways, such as by making a little ramp for the wheelchair or coming up with a computer program that assists your child's communication. No doubt you have many skills you can readily use to create a better experience for your child.

Your special baby

You're bringing your baby home from the hospital for the first time. It should be a time of great excitement, but you're probably overwhelmed with the challenges of not only looking after a new, small human being, but a new, small human being with special needs. These tips may help you get through this time:

» While you may still experience an emotional roller coaster, try not to forget that you have a small child who needs all the love and nurturing you can give him as he becomes aware of his world. As for any newborn child, this time is fleeting, so take some time to admire those little fingers and those chubby little legs, and enjoy the new addition to your lives.

» Get family or close friends to support you by perhaps fending off unwanted visitors, organizing appointments with health workers, or just doing your laundry. Let someone look after you for a while, just as you need to look after your baby.

» Ask for help if you need it. There's no point in struggling on bravely because you can't ask for a hand. Plenty of people are around to help you.

» Keep records of health visits and your baby's daily progress, or any notes you need, in one central place so you can grab them the next time you need to talk to your healthcare workers. Because so much paperwork is associated with the care of a disabled child, staying organized is essential.

Working with health professionals

Some of the health professionals you may meet when caring for your special needs child include

>> An *audiologist,* who assesses your child's hearing and can recommend treatment or hearing aids.

>> A *dietitian,* who can be very helpful if your child's illness involves following a certain diet or certain dietary restrictions are tried.

>> An *occupational therapist,* or OT, who assesses how well your child is able to perform day-to-day tasks, like dressing or brushing his teeth. She may also assess how you'll manage getting from place to place if transport is a bit more complicated with your little one. The aim of an OT is to help your child become involved in all aspects of day-to-day life, and increase his independence and well-being.

>> A *physical therapist,* who will work on your child's physical delays.

>> A *psychologist,* who assesses your child's mental health and cognitive skills. Psychologists may help with strategies for managing emotional and behavioral problems.

>> *Speech therapists* and *speech pathologists,* who assess how well your child can communicate with others and either figure out ways to improve his speech or find alternative ways of communicating, such as electronic devices or sign language.

Living with a disability

It doesn't matter what condition, illness, injury, or syndrome your child has; finding out that your child is not the child you had hoped he would be can be devastating. On top of managing your own feelings and frustration, you may also be sensitive to other people's reactions when they see your child. As with all feelings, give yourself time to work through them (rather than ignore or suppress them) and seek help if you need to. Most importantly, keep communicating with your partner, who's likely to be feeling the same thing.

TIP

Be aware of what triggers negative feelings, such as going to doctors' appointments or seeing friends' children. Then you can prepare yourself and work out strategies for coping with any negative emotions.

Living with a disabled child is often a bit more involved than living with an able-bodied child, but there are things you can do to make it easier:

>> Do your own research. Knowledge is power. These days, practically everyone has access to an amazing information resource — the Internet. Find out whether there are any devices, techniques, or therapies that could help your child (or you) become more independent or make life easier.

>> Set small, achievable goals for your child, as you would for any child. Pushing him too hard will only leave both of you frustrated.

>> If your child is going to day care or school, talk to teachers and administrative staff well in advance so they can build ramps, obtain resources, and apply for any special teacher aide staff that may be required. Find out what rights your child has in regards to education in your state.

>> Keep in touch with teaching staff about your child's progress. This helps you, your child, and the teachers, who can personalize a program for your child.

Changing your lifestyle

Having a child with a disability will probably mean you have to adjust your lifestyle to suit his needs:

>> Depending on the level of care your child needs, you or your partner may have to give up working outside the home.

>> If your child uses a wheelchair, you'll need to renovate your home to make doors wide enough to get the wheelchair

through, install ramps rather than steps, and fit equipment for lifting the chair in and out of vehicles.

» With one less income and more expenses, your family may be under extra financial pressure, so seek out any subsidies or allowances you can from government agencies. See the section "Finding help, assistance, and resources" earlier in this chapter for links.

» You may need to go to more doctors' appointments and make more trips to the hospital. If you live far from a hospital, it may mean you need to move to be closer to medical facilities.

» Some children need 24-hour, seven-days-a-week care, which is hard work. You may need a dedicated healthcare provider or full-time nursing assistance to organize care in your home. In many cases, insurance covers this cost.

REMEMBER

If your child is disabled and needs a lot of care, you must take some time to take care of yourself and your partner. Talk to your health workers about respite care or get support from family and friends so you have a little time off every now and then.

Sharing the love

REMEMBER

If there's one word we've used over and over again in this book, it's *support*. Nothing beats having people to help share not only your problems, but also the love. When your child is disabled, small victories are to be had along the way. With other parents in similar situations, you have a whole lot more people to share those successes with.

Chapter 19

Separation and Divorce

Having a relationship these days is hard. You're expected to be all things to all people — your partners, families, friends, employers, and children. This puts a lot of strain on you and your relationships. As a result some marriages and relationships don't survive the stresses of parenting, financial worry, the frenetic pace of life, and the need for your own space.

A relationship failure is devastating, even more so when children are involved. As a father in this situation, life can feel pretty rough and frustrating. But being a great father doesn't end with your relationship.

You're the adult here, the dad, and where you have control and the power to make decisions for your family, your children don't. They may be confused, blaming themselves and frightened about what the future brings for them. They may be hoping you and their mother can patch things up. It's important to tread carefully, for their sakes.

In this chapter, we offer some ways to help save an ailing marriage or relationship and avoid the devastation a breakup causes. But if your relationship's beyond help and it's time to call it a day, we guide you through the separation and divorce process in terms of how it impacts you as a dad. And we give you some advice on surviving your new life as a single dad, whether you're the primary caregiver or not.

Taking Action if Your Marriage Is on the Rocks

Every relationship goes through difficult times, but knowing what you can do about it can mean the difference between calling it quits or building a better relationship than you and your partner had before.

What you can do

If your marriage or relationship is going through a rough patch, you need to take a close look at yourself and your part in the difficulties the two of you are experiencing. It's true that it takes two to tango and two to make a relationship work, but here we need to focus on the part you as an individual play in it. You need to be able to take full responsibility for your actions in the relationship. Ultimately you have full control only over your own actions. You can't make someone else do what you want. So to avoid further frustration, start looking at the man in the mirror to see what he can change before pointing the finger at your partner.

To be able to look at your role in the relationship objectively, let go of negative emotions like anger and blame. Being righteously indignant or holding on to the feeling that you've been wronged doesn't help you fix whatever the problem is. If you're feeling guilty or ashamed, try to let it go. Clear your head, and sit down and make a list of what you really want from your relationship. It can help to put some thought into what your partner wants from the relationship and whether you're able to provide that for her. Ideally, ask your partner if she wants to do the same exercise as well.

Look at what you've written and keep it in mind as an inspirational goal for your relationship. When you're clear about what you want, discuss your list (and her list) with your partner. Remember that you and your partner are on the same side of the mediation table and the "problem" in your relationship is on the other side. The process of getting your relationship back on track is much more productive if you work together rather than get wound up in a blame game.

TIP

Asking others for some feedback may also help. This can be pretty tough, but a close friend will tell you straight up how he sees things. Keeping a clear head and seeing things objectively when your relationship is in a tailspin can be tricky. A third-party perspective may give you a more unbiased view of yourself and your relationship.

REMEMBER

Repairing a marriage takes time. Try to be patient and realize things aren't going to magically happen overnight. Be conscious of, and patient about, how things are changing as a result of your efforts.

WARNING

You're an adult and a dad who is in the process of bringing up a child or children to be responsible, able to deal with their emotions, and have self-control. It therefore makes sense to demonstrate those qualities in yourself and not fight or bad-mouth your partner in front of your children. It places a lot of stress on a child and forces her to take sides, which clearly isn't fair. If you need to let off some steam, find a place where you can be alone and do whatever helps you release some tension (in a safe way). Ideally, do something that's physically exhausting.

What you can both do

You can only change yourself — but if you get your partner working with you, the two of you can agree on ways to rebuild your relationship. Both of you have to be willing and able to make changes. Here are some ideas:

>> Talk openly about what is and isn't working in your relationship. Rather than blaming the other person for what's wrong,

try to explain things in terms of how you feel or think. If talking between yourselves about the relationship gets you nowhere, consider involving a relationship coach or counselor.

>> As a couple, come up with a strategy for making things better. Write down your strategy. Assess how well you're sticking to it and figure out whether you need to make some adjustments.

>> Make it a rule to say three to five positive things for each negative thing you say about each other.

>> Eat together at night, so you have a chance to talk about your day and catch up a little bit. Maybe go out for lunch or dinner every now and then.

>> Listen without interrupting your partner, even if you strongly disagree with what she's saying. Ask your partner to do the same when you've got something you want to express.

>> If financial stress is an issue, sit down with a calculator and work on remedying your financial problems once and for all. Money is one of the biggest stresses a relationship faces. If you feel lost, get a money coach or financial adviser.

>> Don't get complacent. Your relationship isn't going to fix itself without a little work from both of you. You both need to work on your relationship and keep at it.

TIP

You can find relationship counselors through these sources:

>> Licensed therapists in private practice (some may be certified through the American Association for Marriage and Family Therapy)

>> Therapists who work through state or county mental health organizations

>> A pastor or other spiritual adviser

Where to go if all fails

Sometimes, despite all the efforts you've made to hold onto your relationship, it still fails.

The best-case scenario when a relationship comes to an end is that your relationship is amicable and you're both a daily feature of your children's lives, with that same loving bond with them.

However, if the relationship has ended badly, or you've been kicked out or had to leave the family home, it can be very easy to slide into despair. Sure, you're not going to be the life of the party right now, and feeling rotten is normal, but if you have trouble getting out of that dark place and feel hopeless, you need to get help climbing back out. Feeling depressed and frustrated only holds you back from moving on and being a great dad. Your kids will be feeling confused and anxious, and if they're still young, they may be blaming themselves for what has happened. They need you right now, and your job is to be there for them.

REMEMBER

Your role as a lover and partner is over, and it may hurt and be embarrassing, but you're still the father of your children, and this will always be the case. Your fatherhood journey doesn't end here, although you may have to take a different route.

These are some places you can look to for support and advice when your relationship has gone south:

>> **Counselor:** Get help dealing with the grief and emotions you have about the end of your relationship or marriage.

>> **Lawyer or legal aid:** Find out where you stand legally with regard to seeing your children, and what rights and obligations you have.

>> **Mediator:** Talk to someone who can assist with family group counseling sessions.

Splitting Up

Your relationship, sad as it is, is beyond help. You and your partner can't see a way to stay together and have decided to split up. Whether it's amicable or not, the end of a relationship means the start of a whole new world for you, your former partner, and your children.

Waiting for the dust to settle

You may find your relationship has taken a turn for the worse and you're out the door with next to nothing. Or, as many men experience, you end up haggling over shared assets, personal possessions, and of course, the tricky question of how best to manage your children's care.

REMEMBER

Sorting out child-care arrangements and the distribution of assets is best done when the dust has settled a bit — not in the heat of the moment — and you and your estranged partner are able to talk without antagonizing each other or ending the discussion in tears.

Understanding the divorce process

When you are separated, you may be thinking about getting divorced or dissolving your civil union, which puts a permanent end to your legal relationship. Every state sets its own rules for how divorce is handled. There are residency requirements, and different courts handle divorce in each state. To make things even more complicated, child custody may be handled in a different court than divorce. Finding a lawyer well versed in divorce proceedings in your state should be your first step.

If you have friends or family members who have gone through a divorce, ask them whether they found their lawyer helpful, but keep in mind that the lawyer your friend loved may not be right for you. Personality is important, because you'll be working closely together. Cost and the lawyer's proximity can also play a part in finding the right person. Some lawyers offer one free consultation, which can help you find the right person.

TIP

If you have friends who are lawyers, they can give you the lowdown on other lawyers who practice in your area.

TIP

The American Academy of Matrimonial Lawyers maintains a list of lawyers who specialize in this area; check its website at www. aaml.org. Some states offer certification in family law, which requires additional continuing education in this field.

Making separation easier on your children

A separation can be quite tough as you struggle with all your feelings about the relationship ending, but your kids also need you. Try to offer them support and continue to nurture that loving relationship you've worked so hard at all this time.

Children react to separation and divorce in different ways. Some act out and go "off the rails." Others are clingy and need reassurance that you're not abandoning them. Some children blame themselves for what's happening. Others hide how they really feel and appear to be coping well.

However your child reacts to the news that you and your partner aren't together any more, these tips will help get them through this traumatic time:

>> **Fighting in front of your children is not okay.** Fighting in front of your kids is stressful for them, puts them in the middle of your fight, and can dent their trust in you. Leave your kids out of any conflict you have with their mom — don't ask them which parent they'd like to live with, don't ask them to lock her out, and don't ask them for information about what she's doing.

>> **Don't lie to your children.** When you tell your children about what's going on, use neutral language rather than blaming their mom or getting angry. Take the emotion out of what you're saying. Be honest and genuine with your children.

>> **Let your children know that you're there for them.** You may be living away from home right now, but make it clear you're always able to talk to them. Be open and honest with any questions they may have and remember to take the emotion — anger, frustration, animosity — out of what you're saying, so you leave your children out of the conflict you're experiencing.

Counseling and therapy aren't just for adults going through a difficult time. Children may also benefit from talking to a child therapist, who can help them work through the process. Look for therapists who specialize in treating children and whose treatment will involve play therapy and other ways to express feelings they may not be able to verbalize.

While the Internet is a good place to start your search for a child therapist, ask friends, family, and your child's healthcare provider for recommendations as well. Psychiatrists, psychologists, social workers, and family counselors can all specialize as child therapists, and one isn't necessarily better than the other. As with divorce lawyers, personality, proximity, and cost will play a part in your choice, but the therapist you choose should be certified or licensed in this area.

You're not just another statistic

Marriage breakdown is, sadly, extremely common. Around 50 percent of all marriages in the United States end in divorce.

With these high rates of divorce, you're clearly on a well-trodden path, but that doesn't mean it hurts any less or that your kids aren't going to be hurt by it too. It may even help you to know that many people are going about their ordinary day having gotten over a divorce and having found great solutions to what was once a very messy situation for them.

On the other hand, even though separation and divorce aren't uncommon, every relationship breakdown, just like every relationship itself, is unique. The way you cope with, and help your kids cope with, this tricky time in your lives is unique to your family.

You may be able to find a support group near you. However, it's important that the group is a positive influence and not just a group of bitter, angry people interested only in bashing their ex. As tempting as it may be to rant and see yourself as a victim, it generally does nothing toward being a successful role model for your children. Separation and divorce are yet another opportunity for you to be the bigger man and for your own personal growth.

Finding good support

It's essential that you find someone to support you through this time — a kind of "breakup buddy." You're probably getting all sorts of advice from all sorts of people, but they don't necessarily know what's best for you or your kids. You need someone who

>> Can be honest with you, perhaps even a bit blunt at times

>> Is 100 percent there for you when you need it

>> Isn't vindictive toward your ex

>> Knows how important it is for you to remain a strong role model and loving father to your children

REMEMBER

You can also turn to a counselor, a men's group, or a group for divorced and separated men and women for advice and support. If you can't find a group in your area, try joining an online group. (Some groups, such as Divorce Care [www.divorcecare.org], may have a religious bent.)

WARNING

Avoid any group or professional who makes you feel like you're not being heard. Try to avoid groups that foster negative action toward any or particular organization, such as the family court.

When you find great support, hang onto it. The process of separation and divorce can take several years or more to get through, and you'll need ongoing support to keep you focused and moving forward.

TIP

Online forums can give you a place to vent and a sense that you're not the only one going through this. Some sites that include single dad forums include

>> **Daily Strength:** www.dailystrength.org/c/Single-Dads/support-group

>> **Single Dads Support Group:** single-dads.support groups.com

>> **Single Parents Network:** singleparentsnetwork.com

Separating being a husband from being a father

Though the relationship with your partner is over, your relationship with your kids continues and will last for as long as you live. For many years to come, there may be frustrations and difficulties when dealing with your ex, but it helps no one if you voice these feelings to your kids, who still have a loving relationship and bond with their mom, even if you don't.

At the same time, it's not helpful to lie to your children. They deserve to know what's going on between the two most important people in their lives, but try not to couch the conflict in terms of who's at fault or what one person did to another.

Instead, try to explain the situation to your kids by taking out the emotion. It's easier said than done and takes some practice. The trick is in choosing your words carefully. You may find it helpful to think about or even write down what you want to say before you talk to your children. Try hard to describe the situation in neutral terms.

This leaves your children to make up their own minds about what is happening, and it fosters a safe and stress-free environment for them to share their own concerns. They'll be more likely to feel comfortable asking questions and voicing how they feel about the situation.

Are You Still Dad?

With your family split in half, you may be asking yourself how you can continue to be the stellar father you've been so far. Now you're either living away from your kids, which is the most common post-breakup situation, or their mother is away from the family home. What new responsibilities and roles do you have?

Who'll look after the kids?

When you and your partner are no longer living together, you'll need to work out who the children will live with as their primary caregiver and how the day-to-day care of your children will be managed.

You need to think about these issues:

>> Who will your children live with most of the time?

>> How will your children get to and from school and other activities? Who will pick up a younger child from day care or school?

>> How often will the other parent be able to see the children?

>> Who will look after the children on weekends, school vacations, and holidays?

Custody can be shared between the two of you, with time spent at both houses equally, or mainly at one parent's house with visits to the other's house. (We discuss custody arrangements in more detail later in this chapter.)

If you can agree with your former partner amicably about custody and time spent with the other parent, then you don't need to go to court; you can work it out between you. You can write a non-binding *parenting plan* or *parenting agreement,* so both of you are singing from the same song sheet and your children know what's going on too. The court will also be satisfied as you go through the legal process of divorce that your children are in good hands.

But if you can't agree about day-to-day care and the contact that the other parent has with the children, you'll need to get legal advice and take the matter to court to get a *parenting order* or *court order.* This is an order made by the court deciding who will take care of the children on a day-to-day basis, and when other people, which may include you, can see your kids. Even if you and your former partner have agreed amicably about the care of your children with a parenting agreement or parenting plan, you can take it one step further and have it formalized by the court with a parenting order.

Being a remote or part-time father

An unfortunate consequence of separation and divorce is that a large number of fathers are separated from their children.

Separation should be no barrier to continuing to be a great dad and role model for your child or children.

There's very little difference between the responsibilities of a nonresident father and a living-at-home father.

REMEMBER

You don't have to be going through separation to be regarded as a remote father. Fathers who are away overseas on military service, fathers who are in prison, and dads who are very busy or travel often can also be considered remote fathers.

Here are some tips for continuing to be a great dad, even though you can't be there for every bedtime:

» Be punctual. If you're expected at noon, be there at 12 p.m. sharp. Waiting around for you can be very hard on a young child, especially one who doesn't understand why you don't live at home anymore.

» Don't slack off on all those fatherly duties you may have had when you were still living with your kids, such as discipline and encouraging their development. Be consistent with your rules and boundaries. As difficult as it may be, you also need to work hard to agree to some basic principles for disciplining your children with your ex. And of course, keep going with the principles of parenting — provide your child with love and warmth, a secure and safe environment, and lots of time spent listening to and talking with him.

» Foster a good working relationship with your child's mother. Your child will pick up on when things aren't going well between you two, so work hard at putting the anger, bitterness, or frustrations behind you.

» Keep your promises. If you told your child that you'd be there on Thursday to pick him up after school, then do it.

» Take care of yourself, mentally and physically. Being positive and happy is rough after separation and divorce, but it makes you a positive role model for your kids. Neglecting your basic needs (eating decent food, showering every day, getting some exercise, and keeping your place tidy) or turning your place into a new bachelor pad is not a great situation for your children to spend time with you.

>> Try to avoid falling into the trap of buying your kids special presents or taking them on special outings all the time in an attempt to be the favorite parent or to ensure they love you. They love you unconditionally, and the best things you can give them are your time, respect, and unconditional love.

>> When you drop off your child at his mother's house, try not to draw out the goodbyes like you're about to go to the moon for a month. Normalize the situation by telling him good night, that you love him, and that you'll see him very soon.

REMEMBER

Your child may be feeling abandoned, resentful that you've left, or just plain confused about when he'll see you again. Being on time and a man of your word means your little one can trust in you and believe in what you say. Remind him that even though you don't live at his home anymore, you'll always be there for him.

Understanding custody arrangements

When you're not granted day-to-day care of your child or children, or it just works out better for your family situation that your children live with their mother, you'll still have time with your kids.

Custody arrangements range from shared 50/50 (though you're not listed as the primary caregiver) to strict supervised access with time restraints in an enclosed area if the children are believed to be at risk.

At first it can be tough to accept that you need to put special time aside to see your kids when you used to be around them all the time. Work hard to make the most of the time you have with your little ones.

Here are some tips to make custody arrangements work smoothly for both parents and children:

>> Communicate with anyone you need to about how the contact arrangements are working out. If they're not working, talk to your ex or lawyer about changing them.

>> Don't complain to your children about the time or circumstances around your custody arrangements. They can't do anything about the arrangements, and your complaining will just make them feel bad.

>> If the time you have together is limited, plan what you're going to do well in advance by asking your children what they would like to do a few days beforehand.

>> If you're going to be late or there's a change of plans, let people affected know as soon as you can.

>> Keep a good working relationship with their mom. Your kids will pick up on any tensions between you and your ex, and those feelings will dampen their excitement.

>> Keep your word. Don't let your kids down by not showing up or by promising something you can't commit to, like a weekend at the beach or a special gift.

>> Try not to ask your kids to spy on their mother for you. She's getting on with her life, and so are you! Asking them to spy puts your kids in the middle of your conflict, which isn't fair for such little people to cope with. Your children love both of you — don't ask them to choose.

>> Try not to bad-mouth your former partner, even if you find out your partner does this about you — again, be the bigger man. Your children still love their mom. Blaming your ex may eventually make your children defend your ex's actions.

>> When making special arrangements for yourself or your child, remember to notify your ex-partner and any persons or organization involved in the access arrangements of your intentions. Give them plenty of notice.

REMEMBER

The most important thing, whether you're in charge of day-to-day care or have limited contact with your children, is that you enjoy the time you have together.

TIP

For the nitty gritty about parenting orders, parenting plans, and guardianship of a child or children, the website family.findlaw. com/child-custody/the-various-types-of-child-custody. html defines different types of custody arrangements and how they work.

Paying child support

Though you and your former partner have split up, both of you still have to pay for your children's food, clothes, housing, school fees, and all those other expenses like pocket money and sports fees. It usually falls on the shoulders of the guardian or custodian — that's whoever manages the children's day-to-day care — but between the two of you, you can work out a mechanism so both of you pay your way.

If you're the guardian or custodian of your child or children, ask yourself these things when making a child support agreement with your former partner:

» What costs are involved in bringing up children? What special expenses do your children incur, like extracurricular activities, medical expenses, or special dietary requirements?

» Have you captured all costs accurately and fairly, such as by keeping receipts, so you can explain how you got to a total figure?

» Are you on any benefits that may affect the amount of child support you are entitled to? How will child support payments affect your eligibility for benefits?

In some cases, where there's been a nasty split or reaching an agreement without resorting to other means isn't possible, the guardian parent can get child support from the ex-partner with the help of government agencies.

Seeking guardianship of your children

The care of your child used to be called custody, but it is now called day-to-day care of your child or children. If you and your former partner can't agree who'll be the main caregiver for your child and you're determined that it should be you, you'll have to seek custody through whichever court in your state handles child custody cases. Your lawyer can help guide you through this process. If you're successful, you'll be named the guardian or custodian of your child.

Applying for a parenting order can be a very challenging, emotional, and stressful endeavor, as well as being very time-consuming and expensive. The process of applying for a parenting order depends on your expectations and your former partner's expectations, and the ability to make an agreement that serves the best interests of the children involved. You'll need to get a lawyer who specializes in family law.

When you set out to gain guardianship of your children, ask yourself whether what you're doing is in the best interests of the kids or yourself. Be honest about your motivation. As tempting as it may seem, try hard not to use guardianship of your child as a way of getting back at your ex. Guardianship and contact arrangements are always done for the maximum benefits of the children, not either of the parents.

Before you start the process to claim guardianship, check the following. Are you

>> Able to commit to being in charge of your children by yourself? Bear in mind that at times you'll be sick, have a stressful period at work, or start seeing another person. Are you sure you're up for having the day-to-day care of your children?

>> Concerned about your children's safety if they stay in your former partner's care? Then you're totally justified in attempting to get a parenting order.

>> Trying to have the children with you because you don't want your ex to have them? This is not a good reason for trying to get a parenting order.

REMEMBER

Gaining guardianship of children should only be about what is best for the children and never about personal gain and pride. Be honest and real about your expectations and try never to lose your cool and get angry during the process.

Also ask yourself these questions:

>> Have you worked out what child support you may be eligible for? Are you financially able to take care of your children by yourself if child support isn't forthcoming?

>> How practical is it for you to be guardian? What help do you need from your former partner to pick up your kids from school or day care?

>> Would your children be happy living with you? Are you living near their friends, other relations, and familiar haunts?

The following may help you on your path to guardianship:

>> Ensure you're well set-up to look after your child or children, with a clean and child-friendly home close to their school.

>> Dress well when going to any appointments or hearings with family court judges.

>> Always keep in mind that you're seeking day-to-day care of your children because it's in the best interests of your kids. That will help you stay motivated when things get rough.

>> Keep a record of the time you spend with your kids at the moment, with receipts and notes on interactions with your former partner.

If you really think about it and decide that being your children's guardian isn't in their best interests after all, don't be afraid to stand up and say so. Be upfront with your lawyer and your former partner. It's better to find out now than when your children come to live with you. Perhaps after admitting it, you'll be able to reach an amicable voluntary agreement with your former partner about shared arrangements or contact time.

REMEMBER

At all times act with dignity and integrity. Think of how your children will remember you during these trying times when they've grown up and have families of their own.

Getting advice

You probably know from when your child was a newborn baby that every man and his dog like to give you advice. Sometimes the advice is helpful; sometimes it's not. Ultimately you have to make the decisions. Do what you can to avoid poor choices because you got carried away.

The advice that will be truly useful and beneficial to you is anything that gets you through this time and on to happier, greener pastures, even if the advice is hard to hear, such as being told to get off the couch, stop wallowing in misery, and shave. Sometimes that's just what you need to hear to move you forward. Anyone who allows (or encourages) you to keep resenting and blaming your former partner for everything is not doing you any favors.

Counseling and support

REMEMBER

If you're struggling to deal with day-to-day tasks or feel hopeless about your future, get some professional help quickly! It's easy — look on the Internet and then pick up the phone to call a counselor, therapist, your doctor, or your pastor (or other spiritual adviser) for help. Don't try to bulldoze your way through without help; you can find yourself in a much deeper mental hole very quickly.

Hiring a lawyer

Navigating the legal system is tricky, but a good lawyer can help you negotiate your way through parenting orders, contact agreements, and your divorce. They know the legal system and have experience in dealing with these matters. Many specialize in family matters like parenting orders and divorce.

When looking for a lawyer, ask yourself these things:

>> Does he explain proceedings and your part in them adequately?

>> Does he advise you what to do rather than tell you?

>> Are you bamboozled by what he says, or do you feel fully informed?

REMEMBER

This is about the future of your family, and you should feel comfortable that your lawyer is representing *you* skillfully in a way you're comfortable with.

TIP

Finding a private lawyer who specializes in divorce and/or custody issues is simple. Finding the right lawyer may not be. Many offer one free consultation, which is a good way to find someone you're comfortable working with. If you can't afford legal fees (which can reach stratospheric heights), your local Legal Aid office can help.

Becoming the Primary Caregiver

You have either been granted a parenting order by the courts or negotiated with your former partner to be the primary caregiver. It's more unusual for dads to be primary caregivers than it is for moms, so take pride that you're blazing a trail for dads everywhere! As the primary caregiver, you're in charge of your kids. Whenever you have to make a decision about your family, keep in mind that the kids come first.

Coming to terms with being a primary caregiver

Having day-to-day care of your children on your own can be both exciting and terrifying. Being primary caregiver is a huge responsibility, and you need to take a lot into consideration:

» How do you look after yourself in all this?

» How will you handle contact arrangements with your former partner? How often will your children see your former partner's family?

» Where will you find the money for mortgage payments or rent, food, clothes and school uniforms, school fees, doctor's visits, transport, school supplies, extracurricular activities, and sports fees? Will you work, or receive welfare or child support payments?

» How much time will you have for paid employment? How will you juggle your children's school and sports schedules?

» How are you going to sort out life with your children if you have a new partner?

At times it may seem daunting to be a single dad, but plenty of single moms are out there looking after children and doing a bang-up job. As we've always maintained, a dad can do just as good a job as a mom! It helps to have a routine and make sure your kids know what's happening. Enlisting family (both yours and, if practical, your former partner's) to give you some space or help with pick-ups or babysitting from time to time also helps.

See Chapter 16 about stay-at-home dads, a good place to start for more information about all the things you need to know/do/remember when being the primary caregiver.

REMEMBER

Being the primary caregiver for your children is a great thing, as well as a big responsibility. But just think — your daughter will learn what sort of man she may want in her life, and your son will learn what sort of man he wants to be from the examples you provide as you bring them up. How cool is that?

Supporting your children's mother

Even though you're not partners in a romantic sense, you and your children's mother are still partners in a parenting sense. Whatever happened during the marriage or partnership that caused the breakdown and separation, it's time to let go of the negative feelings — the hurt, the resentment, the anger — and get on with raising your children as best as you can.

Your children need their mother around. Although she doesn't live with your children anymore, she can see them all the time and have a close, loving bond with them.

What can you do to support the relationship between your kids and their mom? Here are some ideas:

>> Just like bedtime and dinnertime, you might like to make mom time a daily ritual. Mom could call at the same time each night to say good night or read a bedtime story on the phone. If she lives nearby, she could come over for half an hour at the same time each night to tuck the children in.

>> Keep your children's mother up to date with your children's progress at school, any special events that are coming up, or parent–teacher evenings she should attend.

>> Keep your negative comments about your kids' mom to yourself — bad-mouthing her to your children is not okay. They love their mother and have trust in her, and eroding those feelings helps no one.

>> Realize your former partner may be feeling inadequate or irresponsible as a mother. Appreciate that this arrangement is probably quite tough for her.

>> Share pictures, stories, artwork, and school successes with your former partner so she still feels a part of what the children are up to when she's not there.

>> Try not to be too rigid with contact arrangements. Go easy on your ex-partner if she's a little late. At the beginning she may be a bit nervous or unsure of how her relationship with her kids is going to work out. Make sure the kids are ready to go when she arrives and pack their bags so she's not caught out without diapers or sippy cups.

Seeking help and assistance

As the primary caregiver of the children, you may require some (or loads) of help and assistance. You shouldn't hold back from making use of what is available. This book, for example, is written with the idea that dads are just as good parents as moms and can do everything moms can do (except breastfeed and be pregnant, of course). No part of this book relies on mom to do anything — you can do it all!

Parenting courses

In some cases, courts can require you to complete online parenting courses during the divorce process. Websites such as positiveparenting.com can provide you with a list of acceptable courses. The government website at www.fatherhood.gov/for-dads/connect-with-programs can help you find local programs in your state as well as provide other sources of information that can help you be the best parent possible.

Financial help

Contact the appropriate government department to see whether you're eligible for any benefits or tax credits. The website at www.irs.gov/uac/Ten-Facts-about-the-Child-Tax-Credit can give you information on whether or not you qualify, based on your income and other factors.

Getting out and about

Just knowing you're part of a wider network of dads raising their kids alone and well is invaluable. It's also really healthy for your kids to know they're not the only ones dealing with mom and dad being apart. If parents' groups or dads' groups are close to where you are, join in so you can network with other parents.

Personal help

The end of a relationship can bring up some personal issues. You may realize you need help with anger management, self-esteem, or managing stress. Don't procrastinate — if you feel you could benefit from a coach, therapist, or other specialist, pick up the phone or search the Internet. Your kids need you to be the best dad you can be, so if that means getting a bit of help, just do it. See "Finding good support" and "Getting advice" earlier in this chapter.

Having fun

Despite everything that has happened, spending time with your children is still generally great fun. But you may encounter some times when it isn't so much fun. When you've had a rough day in the office and come home to bills in the mail and children who turn up their noses at their dinner, just stop for a moment and clear your head. Take a look at your children's faces. Remember how much you love them and how they make you smile and laugh. Your children are worth every bit of extra effort in the end.

Your children will bring you more joy than frustration if you're open to it.

REMEMBER

Play and interact with your children as much as you can. Read books together, give them lots of hugs, and let yourself be a bit silly with them. Children can learn so much from an involved and caring father.

If you're an older dad, constant playing can take a toll on you, so get other family members involved, set up play dates, and share the fun, while you spend time with adults watching the children have fun. Actually, you don't need to be an older parent to do this — it's highly recommended for parents of all ages!

Introducing a Stepmom

Wanting to find another partner, or at least have a romantic relationship with someone new, is natural. Your life doesn't have to be all about being a father and working to support your family. But beware — you're not the carefree single man you used to be. You now come with extras.

When you go on dates or meet someone you'd like to be more than friends with, be honest from the outset that you have children. With the high rate of relationship breakups, it's no longer unusual to be single with kids, so you needn't feel self-conscious about it. By letting this person know you have kids from the outset, you're letting her know how important your children are to you. Some women may not want to get involved with a man who has children — that's okay, their loss.

Talking about a new partner to your children

The idea of a new special person in your life after all the mess and trauma of their parents' breakup may be tough for your children to deal with at first. Initially your children may be confused when they think of how you used to be with their mom and now they're seeing you with another woman. When you start dating or have met someone special, talk to your children about why you want to date and what it means for your family. Take things slowly and don't rush your children into anything they're not comfortable with.

Thinking this new person is going to replace their mother may be very painful for your children. The reality is that children are likely to think of their birth mom as "mom," but over time they can get used to the idea of having two moms.

Give your children lots of time and let them know they can ask you lots of questions about your new partner. Be aware that your children may be resistant to the idea of your new partner. If possible, get their ideas for the first meeting and involve them somehow. It may be easier for your children to deal with the situation if they feel they have some sort of say over what happens.

REMEMBER

Your children may be secretly hoping that you and their mom are going to get back together. The idea of a new romance in your life will mean that's not going to happen and can be tough for your kids to deal with.

Surviving the meet and greet

When you have found the right person, she'll one day need to meet your children, and your children will want to meet her. The meeting doesn't have to be stressful; it can be as simple as having any of your friends over to visit. You may want to choose this first meeting to happen in a neutral area, like a park, playground, or café. Keep it short, sweet, and casual, and don't push your kids into liking this new person.

After a few visits, chances are your children will get used to having your new girlfriend around. Again, never push them into liking her. It can take years for children to accept that a new person is around and that she's going to become part of the family.

TIP

Make it clear to your kids that your new partner or girlfriend isn't replacing their mother, but is an addition to the family. Continue to support the relationship between your kids and former partner, and make her a priority in your kids' lives. Ask her to do the same if she gets involved with another partner as well.

This situation is probably pretty intense for your new partner too. Listen to the concerns she may have. Just as in any good relationship, you should foster an environment of open communication, where all of you can talk openly about anything, including feelings.

Getting remarried

If the time comes that you and your new partner decide to get married, get your kids involved with the whole shebang. Ask them what they would like to do. Tell them that this is a very special day for you, and it would be even more special if they helped. Cut them some slack if they're not hugely enthusiastic about you getting remarried. After all, they may still be clinging to the way things used to be with you and their mom being married.

Make sure you don't get so wrapped up in the event on the day that you don't notice your children looking lost and feeling sidelined. It can be helpful to have family dedicated to looking out for them and to give them loads of hugs and kisses, because the wedding's a big day for them too. They now have a stepmom!

The Part of Tens

IN THIS PART . . .

Enhance the pregnancy experience (for both you and your partner).

Check out pointers for bonding with your newborn.

Share quality dad time with your toddler.

Chapter 20

Ten Ways to Improve Your Partner's Pregnancy Experience

Pregnancy looks easy when it's happening to someone else. As a man, you don't have to endure what's going on in a pregnant woman's body 24/7 — and there's a lot going on. Media depictions of pregnancy have led us to believe that a woman demurely throws up a few times, and then swells elegantly into a glowing, radiant, Venus figure, à la Angelina Jolie. Finally, birth is quick with a few screams, and voilà, a beautiful baby is here.

Not so. Turn to Chapter 3 for what really happens when your partner is pregnant, and then help her get through it by trying a few of these tips.

Take Care of Your Partner

Growing a baby is hard work and takes quite a physical toll on a woman's body. Sure, some women climb mountains and run marathons up to the day they give birth, but those are exceptions rather than your average woman's pregnancy experience. For starters, morning sickness can be debilitating, and for some women the morning sickness never eases until the pregnancy is over.

The tiredness and carrying around all that blood, fluid, and an extra person puts all sorts of strains on the female body. Look after your partner 24/7 if need be, especially if she's having a difficult pregnancy, and do all you can to make life easier for her. It may mean looking after the household for nine months all by yourself, and for sure you'll get sick of it. But let's face it — would you prefer to squeeze a baby out of your body? So, man up and do whatever needs doing in the house. You can take it one step further and really pamper your mom-to-be by painting her toenails, giving her a foot rub, or helping her rub oil onto her belly.

Get on the Wagon

Your partner has to stay off alcohol, drugs, cigarettes, blue cheese, seafood, and a whole lot of other stuff to keep that baby in there safe and sound. Seeing you downing a pint of beer and enough salami to sink a small ship could be enough to send her over the edge. Staying off alcohol and cigarettes, not to mention anything heavier you may be into, and eating what she can eat is not only better for you, but it sets up a precedent for how you intend to live as a father.

Give Your Partner Some "Me" Time Every Now and Then

The prospect of becoming a mother, while really exciting for your partner, is also a daunting one, both mentally and physically. For most mothers, the first few months after birth end up being a 24-hour, seven-days-a-week job. Even though they traded in their old life of meetings, schedules, work commitments, and deadlines that they may have no sentimental attachment to, for the care of a tiny, helpless baby whom they love, the role can be overwhelming.

During pregnancy, your partner is bound to have some trepidation about her new responsibility and how she'll cope. Over the next few years — perhaps until your child has left home — your partner's always going to have one eye on what she's doing and one eye on your child. So in the months before this all kicks off, let her have some time that's just for her.

Be There for the Medical Stuff

Go along to all the medical appointments, scans, and meetings with your midwife or obstetrician. Your partner will want you to be there to share in it. The first time you hear your baby's heartbeat through the Doppler or see the faint shadows of your baby moving and bouncing around in your partner's belly during an ultrasound scan, you'll be glad you came along.

REMEMBER

Although you're not carrying the baby right now, that tiny growing thing in there is your child too. Your place is to know about how well he's developing, any potential health issues, and what options you as a couple have for welcoming your child into the world.

Going to appointments also supports your partner because, in the event of any unwelcome news, you'll be there to help her.

Get with the Program

Start getting some hands-on practice with essential baby knowledge and skills. Moms-to-be love to see their partners getting excited about their new life as parents, and what better way to show it than to throw yourself into the preparations? There's so much to learn about looking after a newborn baby and the months after that, so why not find out all you can about it?

Ask your midwife or obstetrician about prenatal classes in your area and discuss which one you think would suit you and your partner best. Make it a priority to never miss a class, even if there's work to be done at the office or you've been invited to drinks after work. Let's face it; the office and your work will be there for a long time. Preparing for your first child happens only once in your life.

Go on a Babymoon

As a couple, now is the perfect time to take a relaxing and indulgent holiday somewhere. We're not talking about backpacking through India or somewhere hot, with wild animals and tons of people, but somewhere low-key. Someplace where lounge chairs and swimming pools are more common than office buildings, with great restaurants and shops to browse. Somewhere the two of you can just hang out, sleep late, read books, and do whatever you want when you want.

REMEMBER

Check with your healthcare provider before heading off to parts unknown. She may suggest not traveling for a certain number of weeks before your partner's due date or to certain parts of the world.

Be Excited about Becoming a Dad

Finding out you're going to be a dad is a little scary. You may have some reservations because of your own childhood, your financial situation, or the responsibility you're going to have. Your partner may also share some of those worries and concerns, but burying your head in the sand and pretending the baby's not going to arrive won't help.

REMEMBER

Even if the impending change of lifestyle takes a while to sink in, you can definitely make the pregnancy experience more enjoyable for your partner if you show a bit of excitement about becoming a dad. Showing your partner that you're excited will get her excited and happy about becoming a mom. You want her to be happy and excited.

A lot of parenting is about attitude. The anecdote about dealing with picky eaters really sums this up. One father complains that his daughter is a terrible eater and won't eat anything unless it has cheese on it. He's really stressed out about it and is pulling his hair out thinking of a solution. On the other hand, another father happily tells the first guy that his son is a terrific eater because as long as it has cheese on it, he'll eat anything. It's all about attitude.

Celebrate!

In a few months when the baby is born, you'll be celebrating a new person's presence in your life. Not just any new person, but the person who is on this Earth because of you. That's pretty special! But it does come with a price — temporary sleep deprivation and a restricted social life.

So make the most of your quiet nights and unlimited access to the outside world now! Take your partner out for a posh dinner somewhere fancy, visit a special place together — do whatever spins your wheels as a couple.

One dad-to-be surprised his partner with a picnic lunch at the local zoo in the weeks before their baby was born. He'd even packed sparkling grape juice to toast their health and a pillow for his partner to sit on. She spent most of her time waddling back and forth from the restroom, but the gesture was most appreciated.

Record That Beautiful Belly

In our great-grandmothers' and grandmothers' days, having a whole litter of children was common, and the pregnant belly was hidden away as if it were some kind of obscenity. These days, though, it's rare to have more than five or six children, and more usual for a woman to have one to three children in her lifetime.

Celebrating the physical changes that take place during pregnancy (not the heartburn and hemorrhoids, mind you), such as the voluptuous new shape of a pregnant belly and those plus-sized breasts that you gotta love, is now more usual. Most pregnant women, while despising the weight they put on, love their bellies, so get out your camera from week one and get snapping. You'll laugh when you look back and see how your baby grew even before you got to meet your little one. Even better, hire a professional photographer to take some shots of your partner's gorgeous shape. Professional photos will help her feel sexy and beautiful and boost her confidence.

Keep Telling Your Partner How Beautiful She Is

For many women, the hardest part of pregnancy is near the due date. Your partner may be having a difficult time getting comfortable at night and suffering from heartburn, hemorrhoids, and various aches and pains. She may have stretch marks, and her legs and feet may be sausage-shaped. Your partner's tired all the time but can't sleep. She wants her body back but is frightened about how she's going to handle giving birth.

REMEMBER

You, as your partner's great ally, her support, and her rock, will earn mega brownie points and endear yourself to her always if you keep telling her how beautiful she is. She wants to know that you still find her attractive and that she's still, despite everything going on in her body, the hot woman you fell in love with — not just because of the way she looks, but because of who she is and the fact that she's going to make a wonderful mother.

Chapter 21

Ten Ways to Bond with Your Newborn Baby

Bonding and forming an attachment to his caregivers allows your child to feel secure so he can focus on growth and development to become independent and self-confident in the world at large. He's half your DNA, so shouldn't bonding happen by default? Yes and no. Bonding is a process that needs to be worked at, but it's not hard, and because you're the adult, you'll have to lead the way at the beginning. In this chapter, we give you our favorite ways to get to know your baby and let him get to know you.

Be 100 Percent Committed

Make a point of totally committing yourself mentally to looking after your little one, not just on a day-to-day basis, but for life. Becoming a father is like getting married — you're in this thing for better or worse, in sickness and in health. But there's one big difference — if things don't work out, there's no divorce. Your child will be your child forever. And because this is your child's one shot at life, give your little one the best shot you can.

It's a little bit like the Dr. Seuss book *Horton Hatches the Egg*, which you'll probably come across in the course of your fathering duties. The story tells of a lazy bird that sits on her egg but gets bored and wants a vacation. So she asks Horton, an elephant, to sit on the egg for her. Horton sits on the nest and endures snowstorms, being hunted, and the ridicule of his friends because he said he'd be 100 percent dedicated to sitting on the egg. When the egg hatches, it's Horton the baby bird feels connected to and wants to be with, not the lazy bird who wasn't there for her.

Be at the Birth

The first time you lay eyes on your long-awaited baby is indescribable. Some fathers say the world changed in an instant, and the instinct to protect their vulnerable new child was overwhelming. Others say it took them a few weeks to truly feel special about their child. Either way, seeing your baby for the first time is a once-in-a-lifetime event that's not to be missed. It's an exclusive gig that's happening for three people, and you've got a backstage pass, so use it!

If you're at the birth, you not only get to see the amazing process of birth itself, but you also get to take part! You get to hold your baby (often even before your partner), you get to mop up your partner's blood (just kidding), and you can cut the umbilical cord (if you can muster the courage).

And while mom is getting a bit of a rest and some attention from the medical staff, you'll have a chance to check out your precious new little parcel in detail. Don't forget to take lots of photos!

Get Up Close and Personal

Newborn babies have spent their entire lives inside a person, so it makes sense that your little one will still want to be close to the people who love him — that's first and foremost, you and your partner. And what better way to be close than skin-to-skin? Your newborn will love snuggling into your chest, be it thick with hair or not, so whip off that shirt and cuddle. *Kangaroo care,* as skin-to-skin contact is sometimes known, is a technique used in the care of premature babies to facilitate better breastfeeding, temperature control, bonding, and attachment. But your baby doesn't have to be premature to benefit. He'll learn your smell and your sound, and love listening to the gentle thud of your heartbeat putting him to sleep.

Another way to get some close contact with your baby is to take a bath or shower with him. Wait until the belly button is fully healed. You may feel a bit clumsy with a wobbly, tiny baby, but after a few attempts you'll feel more confident. Let your baby rest on your chest in the tub. Have mom nearby to hand you the baby when you're settled in the bath, and give her a call to take the baby out when you're finished. Be careful that the water isn't too hot, or the room too chilly, as your baby doesn't have good control over his temperature yet. Some newborns will object loudly to having to take a bath, but by taking your baby in the bath with you, you can make it much easier for him. After your little one gets the hang of bathing with you, he'll love bath time even more because it means he gets to hang out with dad.

Ready, Set . . . Read!

Your newborn baby loves lots of things. She especially loves spending time with you and everything she can find out about you, such as your smell, the sound of your voice, the shape of your face, and the color of your eyes. Reading to your baby from day one not only encourages closeness, but it also gives her a chance to see colors and shapes and listen to your voice. Your little tyke can't tell whether you're speaking Spanish or Swahili, but she adores the sound of your voice, your smell, and being close to you. As your baby grows up and becomes more aware of her surroundings, she'll learn that books are just a normal, everyday part of life that have always been there.

Being read to also helps with language development, which starts happening on day one. Before she can speak, she'll be learning through you about the colors, shapes, animals, and emotions that she sees on the pages in front of her.

Engage in Tummy Time

Tummy time is an important technique in kick-starting your child's development. Simply lay your baby on his tummy (he'll have his knees curled under him to start with) and encourage him to lift his head. This is important because it gets him to use his neck and upper body muscles, and encourages him to look ahead and focus on objects. As he gets older, tummy time helps him develop cross-line movement, which is the action a baby does when he crawls.

Start with just a few minutes a day and build up from there. Most newborns aren't that fond of tummy time. Tummy time is hard work for them, so expect a bit of resistance at first. But keep at it because tummy time helps your baby develop on many levels.

Be Hands-On — Literally

Baby massage is a technique that every dad should have in his repertoire. Baby massage is easy to learn, and both you and your newborn will love it. Start by bathing your baby; then dry her on her change table or a similar flat surface. Make sure the room you're in is warm, just like when you go for a massage. Get some natural oil, like calendula, or a commercial product made especially for babies and start massaging. Use gentle strokes up and down your baby's limbs, and gently roll her over to rub her back. Use your thumbs to gently knead her legs and feet.

TIP

If you want to get more technical about baby massage, a variety of instructional videos and booklets are available.

Be the Paparazzi

In the first year of his life, your baby will change so much that you may not recognize pictures taken on the day he was born when you look at them on his first birthday! He'll grow out of his newborn face into a smiley, chubby-cheeked cutie pie, his hair will fall out and grow back again, and his eyes will begin to change into their true color.

The first year is also populated by so many firsts that your head will spin: first smile, first bath, first outing, first swimming lesson, first bump or bruise, and (possibly) first steps. So take lots of photos in lots of different settings. Before too long, you'll be looking at the photos and getting all nostalgic.

Put the photos on your phone, on your work computer, on your desk, and in your wallet. Immerse yourself in the world of your little one. If you work outside the home, photos can be a great way to remember during the day that you're a dad now, and it means you'll look forward to going home to check on your little one. If you're a stay-at-home dad, taking photos can help you remember the good days when you're having some bad ones and will help keep mom in the loop about what you've been up to with your baby during the day.

Get Creative

Remember that beloved toy truck your granddad carved for you, the one that's gathering dust in your spare room? Or the quilt that an aunt made for you when you were a baby? Things that are handmade by people who love you not only show you how much they care for you, but they can also become precious heirlooms passed down from generation to generation.

Make a future heirloom now by making a mobile, some wooden toys, or decorations like murals for your baby's room. You'll get untold pleasure from seeing your child use and enjoy whatever you make or fall in love with a painting you've made for her.

Take a Walk

You never would have seen a man pushing a stroller when we were kids, but now pushing the stroller — or running with the jogger — is totally the "in" thing. And who doesn't want to show off their stroller with all the adjustable this, that, and the other things strollers come with these days? As you take junior for a stroll, you can check out what models other dads have.

TIP

In the early weeks, have your child facing toward you, so that she can make out your familiar face and feel comforted by your presence. The more your newborn sees you, the more she'll realize that you're her dad. Some experts believe that all strollers should face toward the parent to encourage the two of you to talk and interact more.

Get Your Hands Dirty

Yep. You're gonna have to change some diapers. Most dads don't exactly relish the idea of dealing with urine and poop several times a day. Neither do moms. Changing diapers is a dirty job, but someone's gotta do it. We strongly believe that real men change diapers. If you can't handle a simple diaper change, you may have to hand in your man card for real!

But there are also fringe benefits to being a diaper changer. The distance between you and your little tyke when you change a diaper is just perfect for singing and talking together. Many a new dad has seen his baby's first smile while changing a diaper.

Your baby's tiny little feet and gorgeous little tummy are at just the right distance for a little raspberry kiss too (after you've cleaned him and put a fresh diaper on!).

REMEMBER

It's the day-to-day care of your baby that tells him you care and can look after him when he needs it. That builds trust, a connection and an attachment your child needs to grow up feeling loved and secure.

Chapter 22

Ten Ways to Engage with a Toddler

Toddlers are funny little creatures. They're curious and cute, interested yet impulsive, and are like little learning sponges soaking up everything they see, hear, and do. Playing with toddlers is really fun, and interacting is great for both of you. One of nature's best tricks is that playing with you is a way of learning and developing for your child. In this chapter we give you lots of great ideas for having fun with your little one.

Building an Obstacle Course

Our top pick for busting boredom on a rainy day, or just for fun and everything in between, is to set up an obstacle course. Use chairs with a sheet draped over the top, coffee tables to crawl under, big cardboard boxes to crawl through, toys or suitcases to maneuver around, and bean bags to shimmy over. Of course getting through the obstacle course is all the more fun for having to avoid the dad'o'saurus who threatens to tickle the hide off any toddler who doesn't avoid him in time!

Getting Handy

Hand games like "Itsy Bitsy Spider" and "Twinkle Twinkle Little Star" are more than just a good time; they encourage the development of hand–eye coordination, gross motor skills, language, and memory.

Playing Chase and Tag

Have you noticed that your little one loves it when you run after him and will encourage you to do so by taking off in the middle of a crowded street or near a busy road? Near a highway isn't the best place to play tag or chase, but your backyard or home is. Chasing your toddler into another room and then having him hide when you come looking for him is an advanced form of peek-a-boo — it never fails to delight toddlers.

And what's wrong with a little running around the house anyway? Running's good for the heart and lungs and ensures your toddler sleeps well that night. And hey — it may even help you burn a few extra calories!

Putting Together Puzzles

Fitting shapes into a jigsaw puzzle is pretty easy for dads, but it wasn't always. A lot is going on in your brain when you do a jigsaw. You need to identify colors and patterns and visualize the piece in a bigger picture, as well as have the motor skills necessary to make that piece fit. Doing a jigsaw puzzle is almost like rocket science for toddlers.

REMEMBER

Best of all, jigsaws help your toddler develop his patience. What many parents don't realize is that patience is a skill that needs to be learned, just like riding a bike or learning to swim. Patience is not something that some people have and others don't — it needs to be learned and practiced regularly. Doing puzzles with your little one is the perfect way to practice patience.

Blowing Up Balloons

When was the last time you bought a bag of balloons and blew them up? Back in the 1980s at the "99 Red Balloons" party? Well, that's about to change. Though your toddler may not understand how to blow up balloons, there's nothing to stop you from doing it and letting them go so they whiz around the room in a crazy freefall. Toddlers love to look at balloons, play with balloons, have air come out of balloons in their faces, and watch balloons float into the sky. Balloons should be part of every great dad's kit. Same goes for bubbles.

WARNING

Balloons can present a choking hazard, so cleaning up all the deflated and/or broken balloons when you're finished playing with them is also part of being a great dad.

Tossing Around a Ball

Like balloons, balls are an endless source of fascination for toddlers. The unpredictability of where a ball is going to bounce, roll, or fall can keep a toddler engaged for whole . . . well, minutes anyway. Show your toddler how to throw a ball and watch how excited she becomes. Then try throwing the ball gently to her. She probably won't catch it but will try again and again. And that's how skills are learned — by repetition. At the beginning you can start engaging with your child by rolling a ball to her and getting her to roll it back to you. As your child gets older you can do trickier stuff with balls, until finally you can teach her (or learn with her) the art of juggling.

Don't let your child play with balls small enough to fit into her mouth; she could choke on them.

Playing Water Games

Who would have thought that an old bucket, some empty drink bottles, and a little watering can could be a great investment for engaging with your child? Most children are fascinated by water play — the simple acts of pouring, splashing, and swishing develop their motor skills and their spatial awareness. Have a water "play set" ready to go on warm days, and show your child how to water the garden or the balcony plants.

You may want to take this a step further and enroll your toddler in swimming lessons. Swimming lessons for toddlers usually entail just playing in the water and building up confidence in the pool.

A small child can drown in a puddle of water. Stay vigilant and never leave your child alone — not even for a minute — when playing with or around water.

Creating Art

Every culture in the world has a concept of art as a way of expressing itself. Children do too. Get messy with finger paints, crayons, pencils, and felt pens. This lets your children explore *schema* — repetitive patterns and shapes that develop a child's brain. He'll also get the hang of the idea of writing and holding a pen in a certain way, and you'll begin to see more recognizable shapes and themes as he grows up.

Encouraging a Love of Reading

You can't read enough to your child. As time passes, you'll find story time before bed, whether you're perched in bed together or sitting in a favorite armchair, one of the highlights of your day. Many a father knows *Goodnight Moon, The Very Hungry Caterpillar,* or *The Cat in the Hat* by heart from his many story times with his children.

REMEMBER

Reading together isn't just about the words on the page, just as eating together isn't just about food. Reading together is about spending time together, exploring a new world together, and providing a safe, secure place for your child to be.

Children learn by repetition and often want you to read to them the same story over and over again. So go with it, and soon your little one will be reciting *Goodnight Moon* back to you. Don't forget to stop at each page and see which things your child can point out or name as you go.

Stacking Blocks and Building

Most toddlers are fascinated by textures, colors, and stacking things. Sit down with your child on a rainy day with a bucket of blocks, and you may not get up again for an hour or so. Not only will you get a kick out of making the perfect Lego spaceship, but you may also discover that your child has just built the Eiffel Tower.

You can build all sorts of things from basic wooden blocks — garages for toy cars to be parked in, tunnels for trains to rumble through, houses for cuddly toys to sleep in. You're limited only by your imagination.

7

Appendixes

IN THIS PART . . .

Read through a handy list of resources for dads.

Check the glossary for new terms and acronyms.

Appendix A
Resources for Dads

This appendix lists helpful resources and contact details of organizations set up to provide general support for dads (parents) or offer assistance for parents in particular circumstances.

Child Care and Education

GreatSchools: School Ratings
1999 Harrison St., Suite 1100
Oakland, CA 94612
Website www.greatschools.org

Music Teachers National Association
1 W. 4th St., Suite 1550
Cincinnati, OH 45202
Phone 513-421-1420
Website www.mtna.org

National Association for the Education of Young Children
1313 L St. NW, Suite 500
Washington, DC 20005
Phone 800-424-2460 or 202-232-8777
Fax 202-328-1846
Website www.naeyc.org

North American Montessori Teachers' Association
13693 Butternut Rd.
Burton, OH 44021
Phone 440-834-4011
Fax 440-834-4016
Email staff@montessori-namta.org
Website www.montessori-namta.org

Waldorf (Steiner) Schools: Association of Waldorf Schools of North America
Phone 612-870-8310
Email awsna@awsna.org
Website waldorfeducation.org

Child Development

American Academy of Pediatrics
141 Northwest Point Blvd.
Elk Grove Village, IL 60007-1098
Phone 847-434-4000
Fax 847-434-8000
Website www.healthychildren.org/English/ages-stages/Pages/default.aspx

Centers for Disease Control and Prevention: Child Development
1600 Clifton Rd.
Atlanta, GA 30329-4027
Phone 800-232-4636
Website www.cdc.gov/ncbddd/childdevelopment

Child Safety

Consumer Product Safety Commission
4330 East West Highway
Bethesda, MD 20814
Phone 301-504-7923
Fax 301-504-0124 or 301-504-0025
Website www.cpsc.gov/en/Safety-Education/Safety-Guides/Kids-and-Babies

Safe Kids Worldwide
1301 Pennsylvania Ave. NW, Suite 1000
Washington, DC 20004-1707
Phone 202-662-0600
Website www.safekids.org

Disability, Illnesses, and Conditions

American Academy of Child and Adolescent Psychiatry
3615 Wisconsin Ave., NW
Washington, DC 20016-3007
Phone 202-966-7300
Fax 202-464-0131
Website www.aacap.org/AACAP/Families_and_Youth/Facts_for_Families/FFF-Guide/Services-In-School-For-Children-With-Special-Needs-What-Parents-Need-To-Know-083.aspx

American Cancer Society
250 Williams St. NW
Atlanta, GA 30303
Phone 800-227-2345
Website www.cancer.org

American Council of the Blind
1703 N. Beauregard St., Suite 420
Alexandria, VA 22311
Phone 800-424-8666 or 202-467-5081
Fax 703-465-5085
Email info@acb.org
Website: www.acb.org/node/392

American Diabetes Association
1701 N. Beauregard St.
Alexandria, VA 22311
Phone 800-342-2383
Website www.diabetes.org/living-with-diabetes/parents-and-kids

American Society for Deaf Children
800 Florida Ave. NE, #2047
Washington, DC 20002-3695
Phone 800-942-2732
Fax 410-795-0965
Website deafchildren.org

Autism Speaks
Phone 888-288-4762
Website www.autismspeaks.org

Children with Diabetes
Website www.childrenwithdiabetes.com/

Cystic Fibrosis Foundation
6931Arlington Rd., 2nd floor
Bethesda, MD 20814
Phone 800-344-4823 or 301-951-4422
Email info@cff.org
Website www.cff.org

Muscular Dystrophy Association
222 S. Riverside Plaza, Suite 1500
Chicago, Illinois 60606
Phone 800-572-1717
Website www.mda.org

National Down Syndrome Society
666 Broadway, 8th Floor
New York, NY 10012
Phone 800-221-4602
Email info@ndss.org
Website www.ndss.org

National Federation of the Blind
200 E. Wells St.
Baltimore, MD 21230
Phone 410-659-9314
Fax 410-685-5653
Website nfb.org

National Institute of Neurological Disorders and Stroke: Autism Spectrum Disorder Fact Sheet
Website www.ninds.nih.gov/
disorders/autism/detail_autism.
htm

National Institute on Deafness and Other Communication Disorders
31 Center Dr., MSC 2320
Bethesda, MD 20892-2320
Phone 800-241-1044 or
TTY 800-241-1055
Email nidcdinfo@nidcd.nih.gov
Website www.nidcd.nih.gov/health/
communication-considerations-
parents-deaf-and-hard-hearing-
children

Reflux Support
Website www.infantreflux.org

Special Education: U.S. Department of Education
400 Maryland Ave., SW
Washington, DC 20202
Phone 800-872-5327
Website www2.ed.gov/parents/
needs/speced/edpicks.jhtml

Supplemental Security Income for Children
1100 W. High Rise
6401 Security Blvd.
Baltimore, MD 21235
Phone 800-772-1213 or
TTY 800-325-0778
Website: www.ssa.gov/ssi/text-
child-ussi.htm

United Cerebral Palsy
1825 K St. NW, Suite 600
Washington, DC 20006
Phone 800-872-5827 or 202-776-0406
Website ucp.org/

Divorce and Separation

Divorce Care (religious)
P.O. Box 1739
Wake Forest, NC 27588-1739
Phone 800-489-7778
Fax 919-562-2112
Email info@divorcecare.org
Website www.divorcecare.org

DivorceSupport
1600 Lehigh Parkway East, Suite 1K
Allentown, PA 18103
Phone 610-820-8120
Fax 610-770-9342
Email divorce@divorcesupport.com
Website www.divorcesupport.com

Men's Divorce Forum
Website forum.mensdivorce.com/
viewforum.php?f=12

National Stepfamily
Website www.stepfamilies.info/
support-groups.php

General Fatherhood

National Center for Fathering
1600 W. Sunset Ave., Suite B
Springdale, AR 72762
Phone 800-593-3237
Email dads@fathers.com
Website www.fathers.com

Grief and Baby Loss

Bereaved Parents of the USA
P.O. Box 622
St. Peters, MO 63376
Phone 501-920-4852
Website bereavedparentsusa.org

Grieving Dads: To the Brink and Back
Phone 630-561-5989
Email GrievingDads@gmail.com
Website grievingdads.com

The Compassionate Friends
P.O. Box 3696
Oak Brook, IL 60522
Phone 877-969-0010 or 630-990-0010
Fax 630-990-0246
Website www.compassionatefriends.org

Health

American Academy of Allergy, Asthma, and Immunology
555 E. Wells St., Suite 1100
Milwaukee, WI 53202-3823
Phone 414-272-6071
Website www.aaaai.org

American Association of Poison Control Centers
Phone 1-800-222-1222
Website www.aapcc.org

Centers for Disease Control and Prevention: Vaccines & Immunizations
1600 Clifton Rd.
Atlanta, GA 30333
Phone 800-232-4636 or
TTY 888-232-6348
Website www.cdc.gov/vaccines

Multiple Births

Multiples of America
2000 Mallory Lane, Suite 130-600
Franklin, TN 37067-8231
Phone 248-231-4480
Email info@multiplesofamerica.org
Website www.multiplesofamerica.org

Palliative Care

National Hospice and Palliative Care Organization
1731 King St.
Alexandria, VA 22314
Phone 703-837-1500
Fax 703-837-1233
Website www.nhpco.org/pediatric

Ronald McDonald House Charities
One Kroc Drive
Oak Brook, IL 60523
Phone 630-623-7048
Fax 630-623-7488
Email info@rmhc.org
Website www.rmhc.org

Postpartum Depression

National Institute of Mental Health
6001 Executive Blvd., Room 6200,
MSC 9663
Bethesda, MD 20892-9663
Phone 866-615-6464 or 301-443-4513;
TTY 866-415-8051 or 301-443-8431
Fax 301-443-4279
Email nimhinfo@nih.gov
Website www.nimh.nih.gov/health/publications/postpartum-depression-facts/index.shtml

WebMD Postpartum Depression Health Center
Website www.webmd.com/depression/postpartum-depression

Pregnancy and Birth

American Academy of Husband-Coached Childbirth
P.O. Box 5224
Sherman Oaks, CA 91413-5224
Phone 1-800-4-A-BIRTH or 818-788-6662
Website www.bradleybirth.com

American College of Obstetricians and Gynecologists
Website www.acog.org/-/media/For-Patients/faq032.pdf

Lamaze International
2025 M Street NW, Suite 800
Washington, DC 20036-3309
Phone 800-368-4404 or 202-367-1128
Fax 202-367-2128
Email info@lamaze.org
Website www.lamazeinternational.org

The International Childbirth Education Association
2501 Aerial Center Parkway, Suite 103
Morrisville, NC 27560
Phone 919-674-4183 or 800-624-4934
Fax 919-459-2075
Email info@icea.org
Website www.icea.org

SIDS and SUDI

CJ Foundation for SIDS
30 Prospect Ave.
Hackensack, NJ 07601
Phone 551-996-5111 or 888-825-7437
Fax 551-996-5326
Email info@cjsids.org
Website www.cjsids.org/about-us/contact-us.html

The Sudden Unexplained Death in Childhood Foundation
549 Pompton Ave., Suite 197
Cedar Grove, NJ 07009
Phone 800-620-7832 or 973-239-4849
Fax 973-559-6191
Email info@sudc.org
Website sudc.org

Appendix B
Glossary

To help you understand the medical mumbo jumbo you may be exposed to during pregnancy or when visiting a pediatrician, we've compiled a list of the most commonly used terms.

active movement: Developing your child's fine and gross motor skills, cognitive skills, and senses by doing things like rolling on the floor, crawling, playing finger games, and climbing.

active phase: A phase of the first stage of labor, in which contractions are increasingly painful as the cervix is nearly completely dilated and getting ready to start pushing your baby out.

acute illness: A short-term illness.

allergens: Substances or materials that cause an allergic reaction or allergy. Examples include certain foods, grass, and animals. See also *anaphylaxis.*

allergy: When the body has an overactive immune system and reacts to particular substances, such as certain foods, grass, and animals, which are called *allergens.*

amniocentesis: A test to check for genetic birth defects like Down Syndrome. The test involves inserting a long, thin needle into the amniotic sac and drawing some amniotic fluid for testing. Amniocentesis is usually done around 16–20 weeks into the pregnancy. See also *Down Syndrome.*

amniotic fluid: Also called *liquor amnii,* this is the fluid that your baby floats around in, in the amniotic sac in the womb. When your partner's "water breaks," amniotic fluid is what comes out.

amniotic sac: The thin membrane that holds the amniotic fluid. When your partner's "water breaks," it's the amniotic sac that leaks fluid.

anaphylaxis: A life-threatening reaction to an allergen, in which parts of the face and body swell up and block airways. See also *allergens.*

Apgar score: A score from one to ten given to a newborn baby at one and five minutes after birth to determine his health and well-being.

assisted reproductive technologies: Using technologies such as IVF and IUI to get pregnant.

attachment parenting: A style of parenting in which close contact with the child is maintained at all times. Attachment parents co-sleep with their baby, breastfeed, and carry their baby in a sling or carrier rather than a stroller.

Attention Deficit/Hyperactivity Disorder (ADHD): A condition in which children have trouble concentrating and are easily distracted, hyperactive, and impulsive.

authoritarian parenting: A style of parenting in which children are told what to do, parents are to be obeyed, and rules must be observed.

authoritative parenting: A style of parenting in which children and parents have a give-and-take relationship. Parents have high expectations of children, and children have an open and honest relationship with parents.

autism: Also known as *autism spectrum disorder* because the range of severity differs from person to person. A person with autism may have trouble making sense of the world and find it difficult to communicate, cope in social situations, or control his emotions.

baby carrier: A back or front pack in which you carry a baby or small child on the body. Slings are another form of baby carrier.

bassinet: A basket on wheels for newborns to sleep in.

birth canal: A term used to describe your partner's vagina during childbirth and labor.

birth plan: A document in which you and your partner make clear how you intend the birth of your child to go in the best-case scenario. A birth plan should also include which forms of pain relief your partner is open to or would like available, whether or not you want to cut the umbilical cord, who you want to have in the room with you, and which kinds of intervention you're open to, if any.

birthing center: A specialized birthing unit run by midwives. Some birthing centers are attached to a hospital; others aren't. Birthing centers aren't available in all areas.

bodysuit: A T-shirt that snaps at the crotch, making changing babies and young children simpler. This item is often called a *onesie.*

Braxton-Hicks contractions: The false contractions that many women experience in the weeks, days, or hours leading up to real labor starting.

breech: When your baby is "upside down," meaning his feet rather than his head are pointing down, ready for birth.

bronchiolitis: An inflammation of the lungs' airways. Your child will develop a nasty cough and may have trouble breathing. Go to your pediatrician.

burp: The process of getting your baby to bring up gas by rubbing or patting her back.

cerebral palsy: A condition where parts of the brain are damaged during pregnancy or birth, or as the result of a lack of oxygen.

cervix: The opening between the uterus and vagina. The cervix is sealed shut during pregnancy and must widen far enough to let the baby through during labor.

cesarean section: A baby born by cesarean section is removed from the uterus through an incision in your partner's belly. Cesareans are performed when labor has been going on too long, when there is some condition in which the baby must be born immediately, or when vaginal birth is too dangerous.

chickenpox: An infection that starts with a fever and cold symptoms. After a day or two, your child starts getting red, itchy blisters on her skin. You can calm the itch with calamine lotion from your pharmacy and give your child lots of soothing baths.

chloasma: Darkish patches that appear on a pregnant woman's face, also known as the *mask of pregnancy.*

chronic illness: A long-term illness, such as asthma or diabetes.

cognitive skills: Thinking skills and the ability to grasp concepts.

colic: Persistent crying at certain times of the day, usually the early evening, for babies under three months. The cause of colic is unknown.

conjunctivitis: A highly contagious eye infection in which the linings of the eye are inflamed.

conscious fathering: Actively developing parenting skills and researching information to understand why babies and children behave the way they do. Respond to your children by using these skills and knowledge, rather than with a reaction picked up from your parents or others.

controlled crying: A technique in which a crying baby is comforted at regular intervals in an effort to help her learn to fall asleep on her own.

cord prolapse: A rare event in which the umbilical cord blocks the baby from being born.

cradle cap: A type of dermatitis that causes flakes on the scalp in young babies, similar to dandruff in adults.

croup: A viral infection that starts out as a cold but becomes a pretty nasty and wheezy cough that comes on suddenly. Go to your pediatrician.

crowning: A term used to describe the baby's head showing in the birth canal, meaning birth is near.

cry-it-out: A technique in which a baby is left to cry and fall asleep on her own.

cystic fibrosis: An inherited chronic disease affecting the lungs and digestive system.

day care: A facility where children under 5 years old are cared for, with programs to assist their learning and development. Day care centers are staffed by qualified early childhood teachers and aides.

demand feeding: Feeding a baby when she shows hunger cues such as turning her head to search for a nipple, crying, or sucking her fists.

developmental delay: Professionals say that a child has a developmental delay, rather than labeling the child intellectually disabled, when a child's development lags behind average statistics on developmental milestones.

diaper cream: A cream you apply to a child's bottom and genitals to prevent diaper rash.

diaper rash: A skin condition caused by the ammonia in urine and stool on your baby's bottom and genitals. Diaper rash is usually red, flat, and quite sore.

dilation: A term used to describe the widening of the cervix ready for the baby to leave the uterus and enter the birth canal.

discipline: A term used to describe the way you show your children clear boundaries, rules, and consequences. It doesn't mean punishing your child.

dizygotic twins: Twins from two different eggs, also known as *fraternal twins*. These twins do not share identical genetic material as identical twins do. See also **monozygotic twins.**

Doppler: An instrument that allows you to hear the baby's heart beating in the womb.

doula: A paid attendant, usually a woman, who helps support and coach a woman through labor and childbirth. Doulas are also called *childbirth assistants*. They're not common in the United States yet, but more women are interested in having a doula, as moms and other female relatives who would provide support often live far away.

Down Syndrome: A genetic disorder caused by an extra bit of chromosome being replicated in cell division very early on after conception. Children with Down Syndrome have varying degrees of mental and sometimes physical disability.

due date: The date your baby should arrive, though this is not for certain, as only 5 percent of babies arrive on their due date (get used to the idea that you can't plan everything by a watch or calendar when you're a dad). The due date is technically called an EDC, or *expected date of confinement.*

ear infection: An infection of the ear, in which your child will be fussy and tug at or rub his ears. A trip to your pediatrician to check your child's ears thoroughly and prescribe antibiotics is in order.

eczema: Also known as *dermatitis*. The skin is sensitive to certain materials and can become itchy and blotchy.

elimination communication: Rather than using diapers to catch urine and stool, parents watch their baby for signs they need to go to the toilet. The baby is then held over a potty.

embryo: What your unborn baby is called from the time it implants into the uterine wall to about 8–12 weeks into the pregnancy.

engaging: When an unborn baby is getting in position for birth.

epidural: A pain-relief method that involves a needle going into the spinal column with local anaesthetic. Epidurals are used in cesareans so that mom can stay awake and reasonably pain free while the baby is being born. See also **cesarean section.**

episiotomy: Cutting the perineum to make the vaginal opening bigger during labor.

estrogen: Though estrogen courses through the bodies of both men and women, it's found in much higher levels in women. Estrogen is known as the female sex hormone in the same way that testosterone is the male sex hormone. It's responsible for the growth of breasts and contributes to the menstrual cycle in women.

extrusion reflex: A reflex in which a young baby pushes an object out of his mouth with his tongue. One of the signs that your baby's ready to eat solids is when he stops automatically pushing things like spoons out of his mouth.

fallopian tubes: The tubes that connect the ovary with the uterus. An egg is often fertilized in one of the fallopian tubes and travels down the uterus to become an embryo.

fertilization: When sperm meets egg, and the beginnings of a new child are formed.

fetal alcohol syndrome: Condition caused by a woman drinking alcohol heavily in pregnancy. Fetal alcohol syndrome manifests itself as a number of intellectual and behavioral problems in the child.

fetal monitor: A device that monitors fetal heartbeat and movement, and contractions of the uterus to determine the unborn baby's well-being. Fetal monitors are used in prenatal checkups and in the early stages of labor.

fetus: What your unborn baby is called from the time it stops being an embryo, about 8–12 weeks into the pregnancy, until birth.

finger food: When your baby is about eight to nine months old, she becomes interested in small snacks like pieces of toast and crackers that she can eat with her fingers.

folic acid/folate: A vitamin that helps prevent neural tube defects such as spina bifida.

forceps: An instrument like a pair of tongs designed to help with the baby's birth, easing him out of the birth canal if mom needs help while pushing.

formula: A substance, primarily of milk powder, that is given to babies.

fundal height: Measurement of how far the uterus has progressed into the abdomen as your baby grows.

gas (baby): Gas is the name given to air trapped in the stomach. When your baby has gas, you need to get that air out by burping him by rubbing or patting his back.

gas (drug): A mix of nitrous oxide and oxygen that can be inhaled during labor for pain relief. Gas is making a comeback in the United States for pain relief.

gastroenteritis: Infection of the gastrointestinal tract that can be caused by bacteria from infected water, poor hygiene, or bad food.

gestation: Another word for the time your baby spends in the womb. You'll hear your healthcare provider say things like "30 weeks gestation," which means 30 weeks in the womb.

gestational diabetes: A form of diabetes that can be contracted during pregnancy. Your midwife, obstetrician, or family doctor will be on the lookout for it with tests throughout the pregnancy.

gripe water: A fluid given to babies who have trouble bringing up gas. Depending on the brand, it often has fennel, dill, and sodium bicarbonate in it.

group B strep: A life-threatening bacterial infection in newborn babies.

HCG: Also known as *human chorionic gonadotropin,* a hormone made by the embryo to ensure its survival. Most pregnancy tests look for the presence of HCG.

home birth: Your partner labors and gives birth at home rather than in a delivery suite at a hospital.

hospice: A palliative care facility, where people who are in the final stages of a terminal illness are cared for.

hydrocephalus: Also known as "water on the brain," hydrocephalus is a condition in which fluid collects in the brain. It can cause intellectual disability and death.

hyperemesis gravidarum: Extreme morning sickness, with continual nausea and vomiting, weight loss, and dehydration.

hypnobirthing: Using hypnotherapy to control pain during labor.

in utero: Latin for "in the womb."

in vitro fertilization (IVF): A technique in which a harvested egg is fertilized by sperm outside the womb.

induction: The process of artificially starting labor. Substances that mimic the body's natural actions are given to a pregnant woman to kick-start labor.

indulgent parenting: See *permissive parenting.*

infant acne: A newborn baby's acne, caused by pregnancy hormones that are still present in the baby's body.

in-home day care: A paid caregiver looking after your child at her home.

intracytoplasmic sperm injection: A process in which a harvested egg is injected with sperm to ensure fertilization outside the womb.

intrauterine insemination(IUI): Using collected sperm to fertilize a woman's egg inside the uterus.

kindergarten: The first year of "formal" education in most areas of the United States.

lactation consultant: A caregiver specially trained in breastfeeding, who can give one-on-one advice and care in getting breastfeeding up and running. She can also provide support when breastfeeding's not going so well.

last menstrual period (LMP): The first day of your partner's period before getting pregnant is the date that the length of the pregnancy is calculated by. So even though you may have conceived your baby on the 15th day after your partner's period, your baby is already considered two weeks along or at two weeks gestation.

latent phase: The first phase of the first stage of labor, when the cervix is starting to dilate. Contractions shouldn't be too painful and can be managed with natural techniques such as heat packs and moving around.

linea nigra: A darkish line appearing on a pregnant woman's belly as her pregnancy progresses. It's caused by melanin marking where the abdominal muscles are parting to make way for baby. It fades a few weeks after birth.

listeria: Bacteria that live in some foods, such as soft cheese, cold meats, and raw seafood. The illness listeria infection causes, *listeriosis,* is dangerous to an unborn child and can cause miscarriage or stillbirth.

meconium: Thick, tar-like stool your baby produces in the first few days of life.

meningitis: An illness that can cause death. Symptoms include a severe headache, stiff neck, and fever.

midwife: A health professional, usually a woman, who specializes in pregnancy, labor, birth, and newborn care.

miscarriage: When an unborn child dies before 20 weeks gestation.

monozygotic twins: Twins who are formed when one fertilized egg splits. These twins are identical. See also *dizygotic twins.*

morning sickness: A side effect of pregnancy, usually in the first trimester, in which your partner feels nauseated and hypersensitive to foods and smells.

moro reflex: A reflex in which newborn babies seem to suddenly flinch and move the head and arms in a characteristic pattern. It normally disappears around three to four months of age.

Moses basket: A basket that newborn babies can sleep in for the first few months of life.

multiple birth: A set of children born at one time, such as twins, triplets, or more.

muscular dystrophy: A genetic disorder in which muscle strength and function deteriorate over time. Most commonly seen in male babies and young boys; some forms aren't diagnosed until early adulthood.

nanny: A person trained in baby and child care hired to look after children.

neglectful parenting: A parenting style in which children are ignored, abused, or left to fend for themselves.

neural tube defect: The neural tube is an embryo's developing central nervous system and it closes 15 to 28 days after conception. If the neural tube doesn't close, it can cause a birth defect such as spina bifida, where the spinal cord is not fully formed or not enclosed by the vertebrae.

nuchal fold test: An ultrasound scan done at about 12 weeks to scan for birth defects like spina bifida by checking how the vertebrae are developing around the spinal cord.

obstetrician: A medical doctor who specializes in pregnancy and childbirth.

obstetrics: The branch of medicine having to do with reproduction.

occupational therapist: A specialist in helping people regain skills and mobility.

ovaries: A part of female anatomy where eggs are formed.

overdue: Any date past the baby's due date. Even though only about 5 percent of babies are born on their due date, many moms-to-be start to get a little bit cranky the longer their pregnancy goes on past this date.

overtired: When your baby can't get to sleep and is too tired, she'll become overtired and be more difficult to settle.

ovulation: When an egg is released from an ovary, ready for fertilization from a sperm.

oxytocin: The hormone that causes your partner's uterus to contract and is responsible for the milk let-down reflex when she's breastfeeding.

palliative care: Care of a person in the final stages of a terminal illness.

pediatrician: A doctor specializing in pediatrics, or care of children.

permissive parenting: Also called *indulgent parenting.* Parents let their children do anything, and children have no clear boundaries, rules, or understanding of consequences.

physical disability: A condition, disease, or injury that prevents someone from undertaking normal day-to-day activities, such as dressing himself, eating, or walking.

placenta: The lifeline between your baby and her mom, a dinner-plate-sized glob of blood and tissue that is attached to the uterine wall and absorbs nutrients and toxins from the mother. The placenta's connected to the baby by the umbilical cord and is "born" shortly after your baby.

placenta previa: When the placenta covers or is close to the cervix. It can cause bleeding, and your baby will have to be delivered by cesarean.

playgroup: Parent- and family-run activities for children, usually held at someone's home.

pneumonia: An infection of the lungs.

postpartum: The period after your baby is born (usually a year). Also known as *postnatal.*

postpartum depression (PPD): A kind of mental illness after the birth of a child, usually in the early months. People with PPD feel hopeless and detached from their baby.

potty: A small plastic seat and bowl for teaching a baby or young child about going to the toilet.

preeclampsia: A very serious condition that can occur during pregnancy, preeclampsia can cause stroke, organ failure, and seizures in the pregnant woman or cause the placenta to come away from the uterine wall. Symptoms include high blood pressure and protein in urine, so usually your midwife, obstetrician, or general practitioner will test these at each check-up.

premature: A baby born before 37 weeks.

preschooler: A child who is 3 to 4 years old.

primigravida: A Latin term for a woman who is pregnant for the first time.

progesterone: Progesterone is a pregnancy hormone that helps prepare tissue on the uterine wall for its special guest star, the egg, to implant. Throughout the pregnancy, progesterone helps get breasts ready for milk production and is probably responsible for your partner's mood swings.

prolactin: The hormone that stimulates milk-making cells in the breast to produce milk.

prostaglandin: A substance that helps to make the cervix soft so that it can dilate and efface (or shorten) during labor.

psychologist: A health professional specializing in mental health.

pull-ups: Diapers that pull up and down like underpants.

reflux: A condition in which a young baby can't keep food in her stomach and brings up painful stomach acid in the throat.

ripening the cervix: When the cervix becomes soft and ready to dilate. Prostaglandins do this job.

round ligament pain: Pain endured by pregnant women as the pelvis widens.

rubella: Also known as *German measles.* If a pregnant woman contracts rubella, it can cause birth defects in her unborn child.

SAHD: Stay-at-home dad.

schema: Repetitive patterns or shapes that characterize children's play.

separation anxiety: Distress at being away from a parent or main caregiver.

show: During pregnancy, the "show" has plugged up the cervix, keeping the uterus free from infection. The show comes out and makes an appearance in the days or hours leading up to your child's birth.

SIDS: Sudden infant death syndrome. When a baby dies in his sleep for unknown reasons. Also known as *crib death.*

sleepsuit: An all-in-one outfit, usually with long sleeves and legs. Sometimes called a *playsuit* or a *footie.*

sling: A piece of material or simple carrier that allows a baby or toddler to be carried around on a caregiver's body.

solids: First foods that babies eat after breast milk or formula. Solids are usually introduced at about six months of age.

special needs: A term describing children who have a physical or intellectual disability.

spina bifida: A congenital abnormality caused by the vertebrae not closing around the spinal cord while in the womb.

spinal block: The term for spinal anesthesia, most often used for a cesarean section.

spit-up: When a baby has a milk feeding, he may spit up, or vomit, a small amount.

stillbirth: When a child dies in utero after 20 weeks gestation or dies in childbirth.

strep throat: A throat infection accompanied by a high temperature.

stroller: A type of buggy that can be folded easily widthways and can be carried by the handle with one hand. The child faces outward in most strollers. Integrated systems allow infant seats to be attached to stroller frames, allowing the baby to face toward you.

SUDI: Sudden unexplained death of infants, which can have a known cause, like smothering, or be unexplained, such as in the case of sudden infant death syndrome (SIDS). Also known as *crib death.*

swaddle: A term to describe wrapping a baby in a light cloth for sleeping, as well as the name of the cloth used to wrap the baby.

synapses: Connections in the brain.

syntocinon: A synthetic version of oxytocin, a naturally occurring substance that triggers breast milk let-down and contractions.

teething: The process of baby teeth coming up through the gums.

thrush: A fungal infection that babies can get on their bottoms and in their mouths.

toddler: A child who walks, or toddles, up until about age 3.

toilet training: The process of teaching your child to use the toilet. Also known as *potty training*.

tonsillitis: An infection of the tonsils, which are inside the throat. Can be very painful.

toxoplasmosis: An infection caused by a bacteria that lives in the intestines of animals, particularly cats. Humans can also be infected by eating very rare meat. Pregnant women are particularly vulnerable to toxoplasmosis, so take over cat litter box duty and make that steak medium.

transition: A phase of labor between the cervix dilating (first stage) and pushing the baby out of the birth canal (second stage).

tummy time: Having a baby spend time on her tummy to develop head, neck, and back muscles, as well as stimulate her eyes and brain.

ultrasound scan: A handheld scanner is run over your partner's belly to see inside. A picture appears on a TV screen nearby showing a grainy black-and-white image of your baby in the womb. Scans are used in the nuchal fold test to check for the possibility of birth defects, the development of your baby's body at 20 weeks, or the presence of twins, and if you like, you can find out what the baby's sex is before he's born.

umbilical cord: The cord which connects the unborn child to the mother.

uterine wall: The wall of the uterus, in which the fertilized egg nestles.

uterus: The organ in which an unborn child grows.

vacuum: An instrument with a suction cup to help baby be born.

varicocele: Varicose veins in the scrotum which may lead to male infertility.

vernix: A waxy coating that protects baby's skin in the womb.

vitamin K: A substance needed for the body's production of blood-clotting agents. Some babies are at risk of a deficiency and can be given a dose at birth.

water birth: When your baby is born in a birthing pool or water.

whooping cough: Also known as *pertussis,* this is a serious and distressing respiratory tract illness in babies and young children.

word spurt: A stage in toddler development where language skills really take off and seem to progress rapidly.

Index

A

accidents, 333

accreditation programs, 181

acetaminophen, 81, 214

acne, infant, 144

active movement, 268–269, 417

active phase, of labor, 91, 97, 417

activities
  to avoid during first trimester, 46
  during first three months, 148–149
  juggling, 257–258

acupressure, 95

acupuncture, 95, 302

acute illness, 417

additives, food, 284

add-ons, for car seats, 71

ADHD (Attention Deficit/Hyperactivity Disorder), 418

administering medicine, 145–146

adopting, 39

advice, getting, 379–381

afterbirth. See placenta

air travel, for vacations, 201–202

alcohol, during pregnancy, 334, 392

allergens, 417. See also anaphylaxis

allergies
  to cow's milk protein, 143
  defined, 417
  managing, 288–289

almond oil, 80

alphabet, 279

alternative education philosophies, 307–309

alternative medicines/remedies, 302–303

alternative schools, 306

American Academy of Allergy, Asthma and Immunology (website), 343, 414

American Academy of Child and Adolescent Psychiatry, 412

American Academy of Husband-Coached Childbirth, 415

American Academy of Pediatrics (website), 25, 339, 411

American Association of Poison Control Centers, 414

American Cancer Society (website), 334, 343, 412

American College of Obstetricians and Gynecologists, 415

American Council of the Blind, 412

American Diabetes Association (website), 343, 412

American Foundation for the Blind (website), 352

American Lung Association (website), 334

American Society for Deaf Children, 412

American Sudden Infant Death Syndrome Institute (website), 339

amniocentesis, 417. See also Down Syndrome

amniotic fluid, 47, 52, 59, 60, 417

amniotic membrane (amnion), 47, 52, 59, 60

amniotic sac, 417

anaphylaxis, 288, 418. See also allergens

anatomical problems, contributing to conception problems, 32

anger management, 333

antibacterial cream, 80

Apgar score, 104, 418

Apgar test, 104

appointments, attending, 393

eggs, 282

eight-cell stage, 29

elective cesarean, 82

elimination communication (EC), 78, 120, 421

embryo, 28, 421

emergency cesarean, 101–102

emergency phone numbers, 342

empathy, 230

endometrium, 28

endorphins, 98

endurance, as a habit of highly successful dads, 21–22

engaging, 56, 421

entertaining, supplies for, 72–73

epidural, 54, 421. *See also* cesarean section

EpiPen, 289

episiotomy, 101, 135, 421

essential oils, 302

estrogen, 422

excitement, 394–395

exercise
  about, 291–292
  meditation, 293–294
  for postpartum depression (PPD), 159
  relationship with getting pregnant, 30
  workout routines, 292–293
  yoga, 293–294

exhaustion, during first trimester, 45

experience, 12

expiration dates, on car seats, 71

extracurricular activities, 315–318

extrusion reflex, 422

eyes, 52, 121–122, 146

F

face, cleaning, 121–122

factory visit, 274

fallopian tubes, 28, 29, 422

family
  as caregivers, 176
  changes in your, 14
  connecting with, 133–134
  help from, 25–26
  learning as a, 279–280
  for postpartum depression (PPD), 159

Family and Medical Leave Act (FMLA) (website), 304

family expansion
  about, 251–255
  health, 256–257
  safety, 256–257
  siblings, 258–261

family healthcare providers, 36

fast map, 222

fatherhood
  about, 7–8
  help, 23–26
  myths about, 8–15
  new-generation, 17–20
  planning, 15–17
  resources for, 413
  seven habits of highly successful dads, 21–23

fats, 282, 286

febrile seizures, 216

feeding. *See also* bottle feeding; breastfeeding
  demand, 127
  during months 3–6, 168
  during months 12–24, 211–213
  newborns, 123–127
  supplies for, 72–73

female reproductive system, 28–29

fertility, 31

fertilization, 28–29, 422

fetal alcohol syndrome, 422

fetal heartbeat monitor, 50, 422

fetus, 422

fever, 144, 215

help *(continued)*
  as primary caregiver, 383–384
  with settling baby, 129
hemorrhoids, during third trimester, 57
highchair, 72, 187
histamines, 288
hitting, during months 12–24, 228–229, 230–231
holding newborns while bathing, 121
home, going, 106–107
home birth, 55, 337, 423
home birth list, 88
home birthing equipment, assembling, 84
home safety, 339–340
homeopathy, 302
homework, 313–314
honey, 186
hospice, 423
hospital bags, 84–87, 88
hospital birth, 55, 83
human chorionic gonadotropin (HCG), 35, 423
hybrid diapers, 79
hydrocephalus, 423
hyperemesis gravidarum, 423
hypnobirthing, 423

I

ibuprofen, 81, 214
icons, explained, 2–3
ICSI (intracytoplasmic sperm injection), 33, 424
"ignorance is bliss" attitude, 252
illness
  coping with, 340–343
  resources for, 412–413
"I'm bored" blues, 271–272
immunization records, 174

immunizations, 213, 296, 301
implantation, 29
in utero, 423
in vitro fertilization (IVF), 33, 34, 423
indoor play, 274
induction, 423
indulgent parenting. *See* permissive parenting
infant acne, 144, 424
infant car seat, 70–71, 72
infertility
  about, 31, 32
  alternative treatments, 33–34
  factors contributing to, 32–33
information, sources of, 24–25
in-home day care, 182, 424
injury, coping with, 340–343
inner child, 268
insect repellent, 80
insomnia, during third trimester, 57
insurance, 173
intellectual disabilities, 353–354
interests, stimulating, 243–244
The International Childbirth Education Association, 415
Internet research, 25
intracytoplasmic sperm injection (ICSI), 33, 424
intrauterine insemination (IUI), 33, 424
iron supplements, 51, 186
IUI (intrauterine insemination), 33, 424
IVF (in vitro fertilization), 33, 34, 423

J

jackets, 64
jaundice, 140
jealousy, coping with, 259–260
juice boxes, 212, 283
jumping, 269

K

kicks, feeling, 49–50

kindergarten, 424

kitchen, baby-proofing, 150–151

Kitzinger, Sheila (natural birth advocate), 98

L

labor
  about, 90–92
  apps for, 93
  process of, 96–102
  your role in, 92–94

lactation consultant, 424

lactose intolerance, 213

Lamaze International, 415

languages
  about, 153
  ages and stages of, 237
  learning, 316

Lanolin nipple cream, 86

last menstrual period (LMP), 424

latent phase, of labor, 91, 97, 424

laundry, baby-proofing, 151

lawyer, 367, 380–381

leading by example, 285–286

learning languages, 316

leg cramps, during second trimester, 51

legal aid, 367

legs, cleaning, 121

legumes, 282, 283

lifelong learning, for preschoolers, 277–280

lifestyle
  changes in your, 14
  changing due to disabilities, 361–362
  contributing to conception problems, 32
  trading in your, 13–15

ligaments, softening, 51

linea nigra, 424

listeria, 43–44, 424

listeriosis, 335

liver, 186

living areas, baby-proofing, 150

LMP (last menstrual period), 424

local farms, 272

lockable medicine box, 75

loss of baby, 331–332, 414

lying, to children, 369

M

managing
  allergies, 288–289
  disabilities, 355–356
  with the loss of a child, 347–348
  work-life balance, 135

mapping preschooler years, 266

massage
  about, 302
  baby, 147–148
  during months 3–6, 168
  to settle baby, 131

maternity bras, 86

maternity pads, 86

mature follicle, 29

"Me" time, for the pregnant woman, 393

measuring baby, 105

meats, 282, 283

meconium, 106, 119, 424

mediator, 367

medical vocabulary, 44, 50–51, 56

medication
  administering, 145–146
  alternative, 302–303
  relationship with getting pregnant, 30

meditation, 293–294

memories, recording, 205

memorizing, 237

meningitis, 298–299, 424

Men's Divorce Forum, 413

R

S

of bronchiolitis, 295
of chickenpox, 295
of common cold, 296
of conjunctivitis, 297
of ear infections, 297
of gastroenteritis, 298
of meningitis, 299
of pneumonia, 299
of tonsillitis, 300
of whooping cough, 300
synapses, 428
syntocinon, 428

T

tag, playing, 404
talents, bringing out, 274–275
talking
    during months 0–3, 149
    during months 6–12, 193–194
    during months 12–24, 221–222
    during months 24–36, 236, 244–245
tantrums, during months 12–24, 228–230
taste problems
    during first three months, 154–155
    during third trimester, 58
taxes, 174
teachers, father as first, 277
team sports, during months 12–24, 225
teamwork, 276
tear, 135
Technical Stuff icon, 3
teenage babysitters, 178
teething
    about, 68, 145
    defined, 428
    diaper rash and, 145
    during months 6–12, 187–188, 203–204
teething relief, 81

temperature
    of bathwater, 121
    of formula, 149
    of room, 121
tenderness, of breasts, 46
therapy, 370
thermometer, 81
third stage, of labor, 91
third trimester
    about, 53
    birth choices, 54–55
    common side effects, 57–58
    medical vocabulary, 56
    preparing for delivery, 58–60
"this too will pass" mantra, 12
thrush, 428
time
    learning about, 279
    for yourself, 132
timing, 15–17
Tip icon, 2
tiredness, from school, 312
toddlers
    about, 210–216
    defined, 429
    development of, 218–221
    engaging with, 403–407
toilet training, 223–225, 429
toiletries, 86
tonsillitis, 299–300, 429
touch, during first three months, 155
towels, 84, 119
toxins, 69
toxoplasmosis, 335, 429
toy box, 75
toys
    age-appropriate, 150
    during months 3–6, 168–169
    during months 6–12, 197–198
    shopping for, 67–69

transition phase, of labor, 91, 429

transport, 88

treatment

  of bronchiolitis, 295

  of chickenpox, 295

  of common cold, 296

  of conjunctivitis, 297

  of ear infections, 297

  of gastroenteritis, 298

  of meningitis, 299

  of pneumonia, 299

  of tonsillitis, 300

  of whooping cough, 300–301

trimester. *See* first trimester; second trimester; third trimester

trimming nails, 146

triplets, 48

trips, 272, 274

tummy time, 131, 148, 165, 400, 429

tummy tub, 72

TV, 247–248

twins, 48

two-cell stage, 29

U

ultrasound, 49, 50, 429

umbilical cord, 47, 52, 59, 60, 122, 429

underwear, 86

United Cerebral Palsy (website), 352, 413

urine sample, 50–51

U.S. Department of Education (website), 315, 358, 413

U.S. Department of Health and Human Services (website), 143

uterine wall, 429

uterus, 28, 29, 47, 52, 59, 60, 90, 429

V

vacations, 14, 199–202, 311

vacuum, 429

vacuum extraction, 101

vagina, 29, 47, 52, 59, 60

varicocele, 429

varicose veins, during third trimester, 57

vegetables, 43, 282, 283

vegetarian, 289–290

vernix, 53, 429

videos, 247–248

violence-free home, providing a, 332–333

visitors, dealing with, 134

vitamin A, 186

vitamin C, 290

vitamin K, 429

voice, listening to your, 53

W

Waldorf/Rudolf Steiner, 308–309, 411

walking

  about, 268, 269

  to bring on labor, 95

  during months 6–12, 191–193

  with newborns, 402

  to settle baby, 131

warm bath, 130

warmers, 80, 119

Warning icon, 2

water birth, 429

water breaks, 92

water games, 406

waterproof mats, 84

WebMD Postpartum Depression Health Center, 415

websites

  allergies, 289

  American Academy of Allergy, Asthma and Immunology, 343, 414

  American Academy of Child and Adolescent Psychiatry, 412

  American Academy of Husband-Coached Childbirth, 415

About the Authors

Sharon Perkins, RN, has been a registered nurse, mostly in maternal-child health, for 30 years, a mother to five children for much longer, and a grandmother of three for the 14 best years of her life. Sharon has been proud to be a *For Dummies* writer for almost the same length of time, writing many *For Dummies* books, including *Dad's Guide to Pregnancy For Dummies, Breastfeeding For Dummies,* and *Infertility For Dummies.*

Stefan Korn is a New Zealand–based Internet entrepreneur. He is passionate about e-commerce and the web, and in general loves getting involved in new businesses. His wife, Raquel, gave birth to their son, Noah, in May 2007, and the experience of becoming a father, as well as the challenges of looking after Noah, prompted him to join DIYFather.com. Stefan has a PhD in artificial intelligence and an MBA in international business. Before becoming an entrepreneur, Stefan held senior management roles for large international corporations in the IT, telecommunication, and hospitality sectors. In addition to DIYFather, Stefan runs an investment company for online startups, WebFund. Stefan is also actively engaged in community projects and enjoys tutoring for Wellington Community Education.

Scott Lancaster is the founder of DIYFather.com. He is married to Renee, who gave birth to their daughter, Pyper, in July 2007. After discovering what little parenting information was available for fathers, Scott approached the other two directors, who helped him build DIYFather. Scott looked after Pyper full-time for the first two years of her life and experienced being a stay-at-home dad (SAHD). Scott has an applied science degree with a major in agriculture and comes from a farming background.

Eric Mooij is married to Andrea, who welcomed baby Ava into the world in April 2008. Eric is also father to Nastassja, Christian, and Amber. Although he is not living with his three older children, Eric has regular contact with them and supports them in every way possible. Eric is keen to make a stand for separated families. Coming from a broken family himself and having relived this experience with his first three children, he works hard to be a positive role model. Outside of DIYFather.com, Eric works in IT and project management.

Dedication

Sharon: This book is dedicated to all dads, everywhere, including my son Matt and son-in law Matt, two of the best dads I know. And of course, my own dad, who was a product of his times and wouldn't have changed a diaper if his life depended on it.

Author's Acknowledgments

Sharon: Lots of people help create a book, whether they know it or not. Obviously, editors like senior acquisitions editor Tracy Boggier, project manager Michelle Hacker, development editor Georgette Beatty, copy editor Christy Pingleton, technical reviewer Anne McCartney, art coordinator Alicia South, and other behind-the-scenes people at Wiley know the part they played.

But every dad I know has contributed by planting ideas in my head about what a dad can and should be. Just watching dads at the grocery store, in church, or at the park has allowed me to observe great dads in action and steal their ideas for ways dads can spend time with their kids.

Last but not least, I thank Jackie Thompson, who got me into this whole Dummies thing to begin with.

Publisher's Acknowledgments

Senior Acquisitions Editor:
Tracy Boggier

Project Manager: Michelle Hacker

Development Editor:
Georgette Beatty

Copy Editor: Christine Pingleton

Technical Editor: Anne McCartney

Art Coordinator: Alicia B. South

Production Editor:
Selvakumaran Rajendiran

Illustrator: Kathryn Born, MA

Cover Image:
©monkeybusinessimages/
iStockphoto.

Apple & Mac

iPad For Dummies, 6th Edition
978-1-118-72306-7

iPhone For Dummies, 7th Edition
978-1-118-69083-3

Macs All-in-One For Dummies,
4th Edition
978-1-118-82210-4

OS X Mavericks For Dummies
978-1-118-69188-5

Blogging & Social Media

Facebook For Dummies,
5th Edition
978-1-118-63312-0

Social Media Engagement
For Dummies
978-1-118-53019-1

WordPress For Dummies,
6th Edition
978-1-118-79161-5

Business

Stock Investing For Dummies,
4th Edition
978-1-118-37678-2

Investing For Dummies,
6th Edition
978-0-470-90545-6

Personal Finance For Dummies,
7th Edition
978-1-118-11785-9

QuickBooks 2014 For Dummies
978-1-118-72005-9

Small Business Marketing Kit
For Dummies, 3rd Edition
978-1-118-31183-7

Careers

Job Interviews For Dummies,
4th Edition
978-1-118-11290-8

Job Searching with Social Media
For Dummies, 2nd Edition
978-1-118-67856-5

Personal Branding For Dummies
978-1-118-11792-7

Resumes For Dummies,
6th Edition
978-0-470-87361-8

Starting an Etsy Business
For Dummies, 2nd Edition
978-1-118-59024-9

Diet & Nutrition

Belly Fat Diet For Dummies
978-1-118-34585-6

Mediterranean Diet For Dummies
978-1-118-71525-3

Nutrition For Dummies,
5th Edition
978-0-470-93231-5

Digital Photography

Digital SLR Photography
All-in-One For Dummies,
2nd Edition
978-1-118-59082-9

Digital SLR Video & Filmmaking
For Dummies
978-1-118-36598-4

Photoshop Elements 12
For Dummies
978-1-118-72714-0

Gardening

Herb Gardening For Dummies,
2nd Edition
978-0-470-61778-6

Gardening with Free-Range
Chickens For Dummies
978-1-118-54754-0

Health

Boosting Your Immunity
For Dummies
978-1-118-40200-9

Diabetes For Dummies,
4th Edition
978-1-118-29447-5

Living Paleo For Dummies
978-1-118-29405-5

Big Data

Big Data For Dummies
978-1-118-50422-2

Data Visualization For Dummies
978-1-118-50289-1

Hadoop For Dummies
978-1-118-60755-8

Language & Foreign Language

500 Spanish Verbs For Dummies
978-1-118-02382-2

English Grammar For Dummies,
2nd Edition
978-0-470-54664-2

French All-in-One For Dummies
978-1-118-22815-9

German Essentials For Dummies
978-1-118-18422-6

Italian For Dummies, 2nd Edition
978-1-118-00465-4

 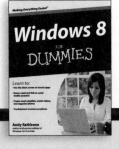  

e Available in print and e-book formats.

Available wherever books are sold.

For more information or to order direct visit www.dummies.com

Math & Science

Algebra I For Dummies,
2nd Edition
978-0-470-55964-2

Anatomy and Physiology
For Dummies, 2nd Edition
978-0-470-92326-9

Astronomy For Dummies,
3rd Edition
978-1-118-37697-3

Biology For Dummies,
2nd Edition
978-0-470-59875-7

Chemistry For Dummies,
2nd Edition
978-1-118-00730-3

1001 Algebra II Practice
Problems For Dummies
978-1-118-44662-1

Microsoft Office

Excel 2013 For Dummies
978-1-118-51012-4

Office 2013 All-in-One
For Dummies
978-1-118-51636-2

PowerPoint 2013 For Dummies
978-1-118-50253-2

Word 2013 For Dummies
978-1-118-49123-2

Music

Blues Harmonica For Dummies
978-1-118-25269-7

Guitar For Dummies, 3rd Edition
978-1-118-11554-1

iPod & iTunes For Dummies,
10th Edition
978-1-118-50864-0

Programming

Beginning Programming with C
For Dummies
978-1-118-73763-7

Excel VBA Programming
For Dummies, 3rd Edition
978-1-118-49037-2

Java For Dummies, 6th Edition
978-1-118-40780-6

Religion & Inspiration

The Bible For Dummies
978-0-7645-5296-0

Buddhism For Dummies,
2nd Edition
978-1-118-02379-2

Catholicism For Dummies,
2nd Edition
978-1-118-07778-8

Self-Help & Relationships

Beating Sugar Addiction
For Dummies
978-1-118-54645-1

Meditation For Dummies,
3rd Edition
978-1-118-29144-3

Seniors

Laptops For Seniors
For Dummies, 3rd Edition
978-1-118-71105-7

Computers For Seniors
For Dummies, 3rd Edition
978-1-118-11553-4

iPad For Seniors For Dummies,
6th Edition
978-1-118-72826-0

Social Security For Dummies
978-1-118-20573-0

Smartphones & Tablets

Android Phones For Dummies,
2nd Edition
978-1-118-72030-1

Nexus Tablets For Dummies
978-1-118-77243-0

Samsung Galaxy S 4
For Dummies
978-1-118-64222-1

Samsung Galaxy Tabs
For Dummies
978-1-118-77294-2

Test Prep

ACT For Dummies, 5th Edition
978-1-118-01259-8

ASVAB For Dummies, 3rd Edition
978-0-470-63760-9

GRE For Dummies, 7th Edition
978-0-470-88921-3

Officer Candidate Tests
For Dummies
978-0-470-59876-4

Physician's Assistant Exam
For Dummies
978-1-118-11556-5

Series 7 Exam For Dummies
978-0-470-09932-2

Windows 8

Windows 8.1 All-in-One
For Dummies
978-1-118-82087-2

Windows 8.1 For Dummies
978-1-118-82121-3

Windows 8.1 For Dummies, Book
+ DVD Bundle
978-1-118-82107-7

Available in print and e-book formats.

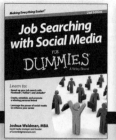

Available wherever books are sold.

For more information or to order direct visit www.dummies.com

For Dummies is the global leader in the reference category and one of the most trusted and highly regarded brands in the world. No longer just focused on books, customers now have access to the For Dummies content they need in the format they want. Let us help you develop a solution that will fit your brand and help you connect with your customers.

Advertising & Sponsorships

Connect with an engaged audience on a powerful multimedia site, and position your message alongside expert how-to content.

Targeted ads · Video · Email marketing · Microsites · Sweepstakes sponsorship

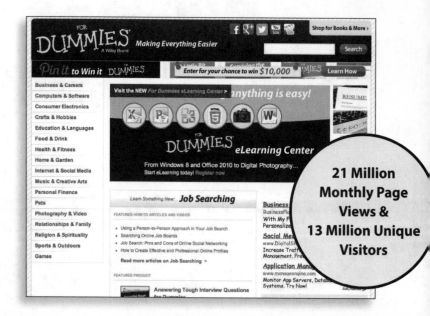

Custom Publishing

Reach a global audience in any language by creating a solution that will differentiate you from competitors, amplify your message, and encourage customers to make a buying decision.

Apps • Books • eBooks • Video • Audio • Webinars

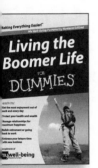   

Brand Licensing & Content

Leverage the strength of the world's most popular reference brand to reach new audiences and channels of distribution.

For more information, visit www.Dummies.com/biz

A Wiley Brand